VIRGINIA CIDER

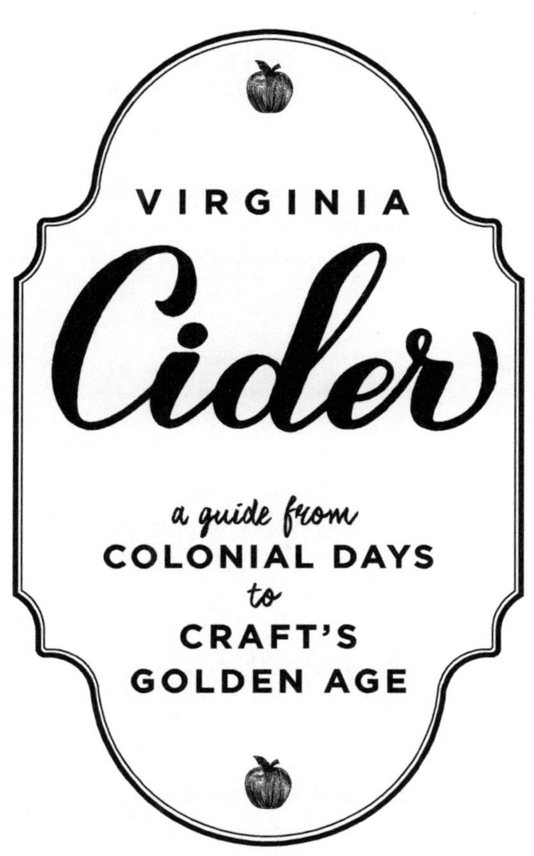

GREGORY J. HANSARD

RIVANNA BOOKS
University of Virginia Press
Charlottesville and London

The University of Virginia Press is situated on the traditional lands of the Monacan Nation, and the Commonwealth of Virginia was and is home to many other Indigenous people. We pay our respect to all of them, past and present. We also honor the enslaved African and African American people who built the University of Virginia, and we recognize their descendants. We commit to fostering voices from these communities through our publications and to deepening our collective understanding of their histories and contributions.

Rivanna Books
An imprint of the University of Virginia Press

Printed in the United States of America on acid-free paper

First published 2024

1 3 5 7 9 8 6 4 2

Library of Congress Cataloging-in-Publication Data

Names: Hansard, Gregory J., author.
Title: Virginia cider : a guide from colonial days to craft's golden age / Gregory J. Hansard.
Description: Charlottesville : Rivanna Books, University of Virginia Press, 2024. | Includes bibliographical references and index.
Identifiers: LCCN 2024002736 (print) | LCCN 2024002737 (ebook) | ISBN 9780813951966 (paperback ; acid-free) | ISBN 9780813951973 (ebook)
Subjects: LCSH: Cider industry—Virginia—History. | Cider industry—Virginia—Guidebooks.
Classification: LCC HD9398.U63 H36 2024 (print) | LCC HD9398.U63 (ebook) | DDC 338.4/766363—dc23/eng/20240412
LC record available at https://lccn.loc.gov/2024002736
LC ebook record available at https://lccn.loc.gov/2024002737

Cover art: Nes/istock.com
Cover design: Cecilia Sorochin

To the many hands that have grown the fruit
and produced this historic beverage
in the Old Dominion

Contents

Preface

From 2005 to 2017, I worked at the Virginia Historical Society, now the Virginia Museum of History and Culture (VMHC), located in Richmond, Virginia. The museum's collections consist of millions of manuscripts, rare books, and miscellaneous objects related to Virginia's history. I was very fortunate to be immersed in and surrounded by these monumental artifacts during my career at the museum, but it was some of the lesser-known items that allowed me to really experience history—and even taste history!

One of my favorite projects was "History on Tap," where staff members scoured the manuscript and rare book collections to find interesting recipes related to alcohol. When we were lucky enough to find one, we partnered with a local brewery, meadery, or cidery to recreate the recipe. The final part of the program included a special tasting of the historic beverage and a panel discussion with both alcohol and history experts. Instead of a scholar researching a manuscript to cite in a book, a cider maker used an eighteenth-century recipe to recreate the beverage.

The program was very well received, and most of the tastings sold out. My favorite beverage collaboration was with Blue Bee Cider. In December 2014, Courtney Mailey, owner of the Richmond cidery, and VMHC staff selected a recipe from *The Compleat Housewife* by Eliza Smith. Published in England in 1727, it later became the first cookbook published in the thirteen colonies when it was printed in Williamsburg in 1742. This rare gem contains recipes for preparing and preserving food, medicine, housekeeping advice, and alcohol production.

The cider recipe appealed to Courtney not only because

of the historic connotations, but also because it called for raisins. Courtney had never worked with raisins, so she was excited to ferment the apple juice and three pounds of raisins in a fifty-gallon barrel.

Cider Recipe from *The Compleat Housewife*

> To make Cyder.
>
> Pull your Fruit before 'tis too ripe, and let it lie but one or two days to have one good Seat your apples must be Pippins, Pearmain, or Harvey, (if you mix Winter and Summer Fruit together 'tis never good) grin your Apples and press it, and when your Fruit is all pressed, put it immediately into a Hogshead where it may have some room to work; but no Vent, but a little hole near the Hoops, but close bung'd; put 3 or 4 pound of Raisins into a Hogshead, and two pound of Sugar, it will make it work better; often racking it off is the best way to fine it, and always rack it into a final Vent-hole; if it should work after racking, put into your Vessel some Raisins for it to feed on, and bottle it in March.[1]

A special tasting and discussion was held at Blue Bee Cider on April 21, 2015. Dr. Sarah Hand Meacham, author of *Every Home a Distillery: Alcohol, Gender, and Technology in the Colonial Chesapeake,* discussed how cider was colonial America's beverage of choice and noted that the main producers of alcohol during this time were women and enslaved workers. The next part of the program was the tasting of the Compleat Cyder, the name, of course, a play on the book's title and the Old English spelling for cider. As a self-proclaimed connoisseur of alcoholic beverages, I suspected that such an old recipe was not going to impress our modern palate. But I was astonished—the cider was fantastic! The still (not sparkling) golden liquid was dry, complex, and tasted like history, in a good way.

After experiencing the Compleat Cyder "History on Tap" program, I knew that there was a story to be told about Virginia's rich cider history and the accounts of the diverse cideries in the Commonwealth. This book is a journey through the Old Dominion's beverage landscape as cider establishes (and reestablishes!) itself as a staple product throughout the state. The first half of the book takes the reader on a voyage to see how cider and apples became a major part of American society. The book focuses on different historical figures (from plantation owners to the enslaved individuals who grew the apples and produced the cider), the different regions, and stories that have created a rich apple and cider base. The second half of the book begins with an educational tool that helps the reader gain a better understanding of cider apples, cider styles, and production methods. The book finishes with a tour of fifty cider producers in the state and detailed descriptions of thirty-three cideries containing an overview of the establishment, their mission, and their cider style as well as a special section called **Try this** where I give recommendations on what I believe are "must tries" from the various cideries. As I think back to the Compleat Cyder tasting of that centuries-old recreated recipe, I continue to ask myself, how could something this old taste *this* good? But it's all about apples, and that's what cider is all about, so we should start there.

I would like to thank several people who were instrumental in helping produce this book. First, I am forever in debt to acquisitions editor Boyd Zenner who saw something special in the project and gave me an opportunity to publish with the University of Virginia Press. As an alumnus of the great university, it had always been a dream of mine to publish with UVA Press. Unfortunately, Boyd passed away tragically in 2022, and I was not able to share the finished product with her, but I know that she would be proud of the result and share a glass of cider with me to celebrate if she was here. My dear friend and editor Nelson Lankford answered the call once again when I asked him to read through my manuscript. His dedication and encouragement during both of my book projects helped to move my narratives forward. I also had a tremendous amount of help from other staff at the University of Virginia Press. Mark Mones helped guide me throughout the process. My copyeditor J. Andrew Edwards provided very thoughtful comments and edits that helped prepare the manuscript for publication. Their organization and project management helped keep this publication on track. I am very thankful for Mark Muse of Muse Orchard and Widow's Watch Cider for his suggestions and edits to my chapters on apples, the cider process, and the glossary. His expertise as a cider maker and orchardist helped wade through some of the difficulties of these sections. He and his wife Gloria are wonderful evangelists for Virginia cider and have been a shining light throughout the process. Diane Flynt, author of *Wild, Tamed, Lost, Revived: The Surprising Story of Apples in the South,* was one of the first people that I interviewed for the project. She has paved the way for many cider makers and growers throughout the south. I am very grateful for her support and review of some pieces of the section on cider's downfall and reemergence (chapter 3). This book also would not be possible without my friend, fellow alcohol aficionado, and author of *Virginia Beer: A Guide from Colonial Days to Craft's Golden Age,* Lee Graves. His careful research of the history of beer in Virginia and his story of the craft brewing scene in the Old Dominion helped inspire me that there was a similar story to be told about cider. I am also thankful for my friend and historian Sarah Meacham's research on women and alcohol production in colonial Virginia. Her book, *Every Home a Distillery* was instrumental in my understanding of alcohol production in the seventeenth- and eighteenth-century Chesapeake region. Others who helped with this project were Marianne Martin at the Colonial Williamsburg Foundation, Leah Stricker at Preservation Virginia, Anne Causey at Albert & Shirley Small Special Collections Library, University of Virginia, L. Paige Newman, John McClure, Matthew Guillen, and Graham Dozier at the Virginia Museum of History and Culture, Rebecca Schneider at the Library of Virginia, Rebeca Parrott at Brightpoint Community College, Anna Berkes at the Thomas Jefferson Foundation, David Sewell at the University of Virginia Press, The Honorable Susan Walker, Peter Hatch and Lisa A. Francavilla at Monticello, Samantha Snyder at Mount Vernon Ladies' Association, Marc Brodsky at Newman Library, Virginia Tech, and Ryan Dostal and Samantha Dorsey at Gunston Hall. Above all, I'd like to thank my wife, Erin, and our son, Grant, for their unwavering love and support.

A Note on Terminology: Cider versus Hard Cider

As a kid, I always thought that cider meant that dark murky (nonalcoholic) but still tasty stuff that my mom brought home from the grocery store around Halloween. For the rest of the world cider means the alcoholic fermented juice of apples. Only in America have we created confusion about a distinction between cider and hard cider. If you request a glass of cider in any other part of the globe, you will be given an alcoholic version of what I enjoyed so much as a kid. The issue with the word "cider" in America has a lot to do with the temperance movement of the nineteenth and early twentieth centuries (and Prohibition) when alcoholic beverages were labeled as the devil's elixir. Many Americans started to embrace "sweet cider" or fresh pressed apple juice that was not fermented. This came to be known simply as "cider" in the United States, and the fermented devil's juice (or heavenly nectar depending on how you look at it) took on the name of "hard cider" to signify that it contained alcohol.[2] I'm not a big fan of the term "hard cider," as the adjective "hard" can obscure the sophisticated and complex components of cider, as well as lower the perceived value of the beverage, so throughout this book, I will be referring to alcoholic cider as simply "cider."

VIRGINIA CIDER

Virginia's Cideries

See appendix B (pages 191–96 for full listings, including addresses and websites)

Shenandoah Valley

FREDERICK COUNTY/ WINCHESTER

1 Winchester Ciderworks
2 Old Town Cidery (Glaize Apples)

SHENANDOAH COUNTY

3 Widow's Watch Cider (Muse Orchard)
4 The Winery at Kindred Pointe

ROCKINGHAM COUNTY/ HARRISONBURG

5 Old Hill Cider (Showalter's Orchard)
6 Sage Bird Ciderworks

AUGUSTA COUNTY

7 Stable Craft Brewing
8 Ciders from Mars

Blue Ridge and Appalachia

HIGHLAND COUNTY

9 Big Fish Cider Co.

BATH COUNTY

10 Troddenvale at Oakley Farm

ROCKBRIDGE COUNTY

11 Halcyon Days Cider Co.

BEDFORD COUNTY

12 Apocalypse Cidery & Winery

FLOYD COUNTY

13 Chateau Morrisette

WASHINGTON COUNTY

14 Tumbling Creek Cider Company

Charlottesville Area

GREENE COUNTY

15 Moss Vineyards

ALBEMARLE COUNTY/ CHARLOTTESVILLE

16 Castle Hill Cider
17 Patois Cider
18 Rockfish Brewing Company
19 Bold Rock Hard Cider Carter Mountain Orchard
20 Potter's Craft Cider
21 Albemarle CiderWorks
22 Henley's Orchard Estate Cidery
23 Bold Rock Hard Cider Chiles Peach Orchard

NELSON COUNTY

24 Bold Rock Hard Cider Nelson County
25 Blue Toad Hard Cider
26 Bryant's Cidery and Brewery (The Farm)

Richmond Area

LOUISA COUNTY

27 Coyote Hole Craft Beverages

GOOCHLAND COUNTY

28 Courthouse Creek Cider

RICHMOND

29 West Creek Cider (Hardywood Park Craft Brewery)
30 Blue Bee Cider
31 Buskey Cider (Scott's Addition)
32 Garden Grove Brewing and Urban Winery
33 Bryant's Cidery & Brewery (RVA Tasting Room)

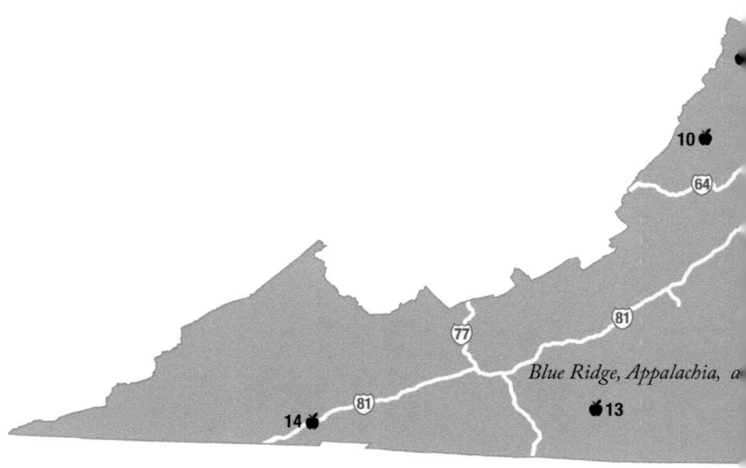

Chesapeake and Eastern Shore

VIRGINIA BEACH

34 Back Bay Brew House (Farmhouse)
35 Back Bay Brew House (Beach House)

HAMPTON

36 Sly Clyde Ciderworks

NORTHAMPTON COUNTY

37 Buskey Cider on the Bay (Outpost)

GLOUCESTER COUNTY

38 Zoll Vineyards

NORTHUMBERLAND COUNTY

39 Ditchley Cider Works

WESTMORELAND COUNTY

40 Monroe Bay Winery

Northern Virginia

ALEXANDRIA

41 Lost Boy Cider

FREDERICKSBURG

42 Wild Hare Cider (Pub & Courtyard)

SPOTSYLVANIA COUNTY

43 Cider Lab

ORANGE COUNTY

44 Son of a Bear Ciders (Teaghlaigh Vineyard)

CULPEPER COUNTY

45 Mountain Run Winery
46 Old Trade Brewery & Cidery

FAUQUIER COUNTY

47 Cider Lab
48 Wild Hare Cider (Grainery)
49 Cobbler Mountain Cider
50 Valley View Farm

LOUDOUN COUNTY

51 Mt. Defiance Cidery and Distillery (Cider Barn)
52 Crooked Run Fermentation (Sterling)
53 Henway Hard Cider
54 Crooked Run Fermentation (Leesburg)
55 Wild Hare Cider (Cabin)
56 Fabbioli Cellars
57 Loudoun Cider House
58 Corcoran Vineyards and Cidery
59 Notaviva Farm Brewery and Winery

CLARK COUNTY

60 Wild Hare Cider (Tasting Room)

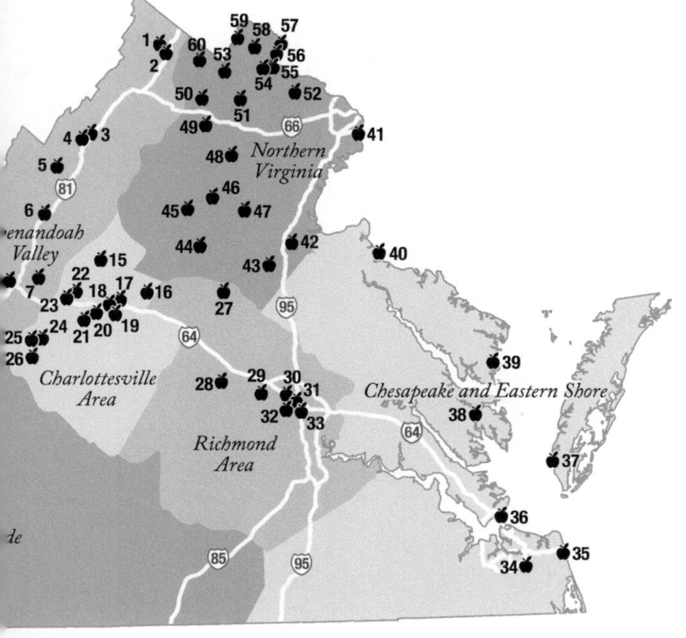

CHAPTER 1

Cider's Beginnings and Spread to North America

History of the Apple

As we begin our journey into the wonderful world of cider, we must start with apples, because cider in its simplest form is the fermented juice of apples. Historians date the presence of this so-called forbidden fruit to more than ten thousand years ago, and it is likely that some form of cider was being produced then. The nutritious beverage was probably formed when wild apples were accidently crushed in a basket or vessel or a hollowed-out tree. The resulting liquid fermented with natural yeast from the air and surrounding environment. A thirsty traveler possibly came across the pool of murky substance, scooped up a handful and enjoyed the first taste of this beautiful beverage. There's no evidence that this is how it was first created, but it's a plausible explanation, and cider and apples would certainly play a major role in the world's history—especially America's history.[1]

Americans tend to think of the apple as, well, "American," but the domestic apple is not native to the Americas, and the journey of *Malus domestica* (or the apple that the majority of us consume today) to the United States is a long story. The origin of this delectable fruit begins in Central Asia, in the valleys of southeastern Kazakhstan, more than ten thousand years ago. Travelers on the Silk Road ate a small wild apple called *Malus sieversii,* which still grows in the Tian Shan mountains. Seeds spread along the side of the road, new apple trees formed, and then bears, deer, birds, and other animals ate the fruit and began spreading new varieties across the countryside. Eventually after several hundreds of years of repeating this process and creating new trees, the *Malus domestica/pumila*—the domesticated apple tree—was created.[2]

Not so different from those weary travelers on the Silk Road, I like to toss my post-walk finished apple snack into the woods in hopes of one day having my own Fuji apple tree. Unfortunately, this is not how to recreate specific apple trees. (If this was the case, then I would have a large suburban Fuji orchard by the side of my house.) It's important to understand that the pip (or apple seed) is made up of two parents: the apple tree (or host with the roots grown from the seed) and another tree that pollinates the blossom.[3] In order to duplicate a specific apple, you need to graft, which is to attach a piece of scion wood (or a spur of wood from the tree that you would like to replicate) to another planted rootstock, which will enable the two to bond. When you graft, you are tricking the trees into merging together and producing fruit from the scion wood (or top part). You can see a nodule on most apple trees where the two trees have fused to one another.[4] Today, *Malus domestica* has more than 7,500 cultivars and a production of 83.1 million globally, and these species vary from the highly commercial Fuji apple to the celebrated cider apple Harrison.[5]

The apple has had many roles throughout history including consumption, drying, and medicinal, but one of the most important uses for this fruit was cider. This alcoholic beverage has provided much-needed nutrients to humans for centuries. The chemical process of fermentation created a safe liquid (when consumed in moderation) required for sustenance. Some of the first written references to cider production come from Greek and Roman sources. Around 55 BC Roman soldiers, during their conquests of Britain, discovered that Celts produced an alcoholic beverage from the juice of crab apples.[6] Also in the first century BC, the Greek historian Diodorus Siculus (or Diodorus of Sicily) wrote his observations of the Britons and noted that they produced an intoxicating beverage by fermenting honey and apples.[7] (This is also known as a "Cyser.") The Roman philosopher and writer Pliny the Elder noted in his book *The Natural History* (77–79 AD) that "wine is made, too, of the pods of the Syrian carob, of pears, and of all kinds of apples."[8] Over the next several hundred years, knowledge of orchard practices like grafting and pruning became more well-known and as orchard management improved so did the popularity of cider throughout Europe. By the 1500s, cider was a staple beverage in England and several other parts of Europe.[9]

This increase in cider popularity corresponded with England's golden age of exploration and colonization. By the turn of the seventeenth century, England embarked on a period of global discovery (and conquest) and would eventually establish the thirteen colonies in North America. Among other developments the merits of which continue to be debated, this time would be marked by land acquisition, technological advancements, and the spread of new ideas. In England, new methods and research produced a better understanding of fermentation and this led to better tasting alcohol.[10] As the quality and interest in cider increased, the beverage competed with English ale as the nation's top drink. European explorers ventured to unknown lands, and they brought with them alcohol and knowledge of cider production and orchard management.[11]

Apples and Cider Make It to Jamestown

The Old Dominion plays a major role in the story of cider in America with the first permanent English settlement at Jamestown. In 1607, more than one hundred men and boys arrived in the Chesapeake Bay and moved forty miles inland along the James River. These settlers set up a fort at Jamestown but struggled during the first few years due to poor conditions and relationships with local Native Americans. They saw some improvements after receiving supply shipments and creating a profitable crop of tobacco.

Other crops, like apples, were eventually grown at Jamestown, but it would take time to establish orchards; most of the early trees in colonial Virginia were seedlings and took at least five years to bear fruit. With seedlings you were not exactly sure what you would get (if the product wasn't adequate for fresh eating, then it could be used for cider). One problem with many of the European tree varieties grown in the Americas was that they were susceptible to the tropical heat. Planters adapted by using grafting and management practices that would allow for new apples best suited for this warm climate.[12] Grafts of apple trees were sent to Virginia in September 1620, and beehives were also exported in 1621.[13] The importation of honeybees as pollinators would have an impact on the establishment of not just one or two apple trees, but entire orchards.[14] Littletown plantation owner George Menefie began an orchard as early as 1623 on his 1200-acre Williamsburg farm, and according to John Smith, by 1629 numerous apple trees were bearing fruit throughout the Tidewater region.[15] English ships also brought provisions that included cider. In 1619, the *Margaret* arrived a few miles west of Jamestown and colonists founded the short-lived Berkeley Hundred settlement. Their ship contained all the essentials, including a large supply of beer and cider for the voyage.[16] Other English supply ships also brought alcohol to Virginia, but the settlers still hadn't established a steady production of cider due to the lack of established orchards.

The crown made Virginia a royal colony in 1624, and the government became vested in apple growth throughout the settlement for economic purposes. In 1639, the colonial General Assembly ordered anyone who obtained a patent of one hundred acres of land to establish an orchard.[17] Three years later in 1642, King Charles I gave orders that all colonists in Virginia fence in every five hundred acres of orchards or gardens. This would be to ensure that the fruit trees were protected against animals.[18] Orchards began to pop up throughout the Chesapeake landscape, and by the turn of the century Virginia apples became well known not only in the Americas but also throughout Europe. In 1701, while on a visit of North America, Francis Michel of Bern, Switzerland claimed that the "apple trees [in Virginia] are exceedingly fruitful. I was at many places where I could not estimate the large quantities where they were rotting on the ground. They are the nicest apples I have ever seen."[19]

Virginians were also concerned with taking care of their new orchards, and cattle (and other animals) posed a hazard for their crops. Livestock stripped the bark of apple trees. The writer and planter Robert Beverley remarked in 1714 that "Many that have good orchards expose the trees to be torn and barked by the cat[t]le."[20] The Virginia Assembly implemented laws to protect orchards against livestock. Owners could be fined, or the animal could be put to death for violating the law.[21] Joseph Ball (George Washington's half-uncle) of the Epping Forest plantation moved to England by 1743, but he still managed his property in Lancaster County from abroad. He instructed his nephew in 1743 to construct "a strong crotchy fence around the trees to keep cattle, and horses, from tearing and barking and killing the orchard trees."[22] Another plantation owner, Landon Carter, complained that some of his orchards had been destroyed by pigs who had gotten out of their enclosure in June 1771, "The home orchard much injured by the sows and pigs."[23] Some landowners like William Byrd II had specific methods for caring and maintaining fruit trees. He wrote in his commonplace book that

"When a fruit tree is cankerd rub off the canker and then apply tar and grease to it and twill recover itself again."[24] Different locales in Virginia ensured orchard growth through legislation. In 1748, Lord Fairfax, the proprietor of the northern part of Virginia, stated in a deed that all people within his region were required to plant at least a hundred apple trees on each land grant.[25] One of the main reasons for establishing and maintaining orchards in America was to make cider, and the beverage provided a good alternative to the potentially unstable water of the Tidewater region.

Europeans had already substituted alcohol for the polluted water in their cities, so this was an easy example for them to follow in their new home in the Americas. Though North America had plenty of fresh, unspoiled water, early settlers became sickened and sometimes died from polluted sources like swamps and other stagnate creeks and streams. At Jamestown, they dug wells that were covered in mosquito larvae, excrement, and other unsavory things that made them sick.[26] Diseases ranged from typhoid fever and dysentery to salt poisoning. An account from one of the original settlers, George Percy, sheds light on some of the dangers of the Chesapeake area, as he explained how the water was "at a flood verily salt, at a low tide full of slime and filth, which was the destruction of many of our men."[27] Even when the water was safe to drink, the liquid needed to rest in a bucket so that the mud settled at the bottom before they could scoop out some to drink. Poor water conditions continued to be a problem into the eighteenth century. Ebenezer Hazard, who served as the surveyor general of the Continental Post Office, traveled through Virginia in 1777 and cautioned that the water "is very bad . . . which, with the Heat of the Weather is sufficient to keep a Man in continual Fever."[28] A somewhat comical report in the Virginia Almanack in 1766 said "Now we advise that you would not/Drink water when you're very hot;/ For doing so, the blood congeals,/ And throws the grease into your heels."[29] These accounts clearly showed the dangers of contaminated water and justified why fermented beverages were a better option in most cases.

A safer alternative was not the only reason colonists consumed cider. Alcohol consumption was part of European customs, and English settlers carried on the tradition of partaking in the pleasures of fermented beverages in the New World. They drank for nearly every occasion: weddings, court days, births and deaths, elections, church services, and militia musters. Women sipped cider at sewing circles, and it was a regular part of every meal, even breakfast.[30] The English novelist Edward Kimber, who visited America in the mid-eighteenth century, noted that breakfast many times contained "the cold Remains of the former Day, hash'd or fricasseed; Coffee, Tea, Chocolate, Venison-Pasty, Punch, and Beer, or Cyder."[31] Women and men enjoyed cider throughout the day while children enjoyed a lower alcohol version of cider called ciderkin. Ciderkin was made by re-pressing the apples, and the resulting juice fermented to a much lighter beverage. (This is a similar process to how small beer was made, by re-mashing the spent grains.) Some enslaved workers were given cider as a reward, while laborers' contracts usually contained a reasonable amount of alcohol. Other beverages like tea, coffee, and milk were not typically consumed in England or Colonial America until the mid- to late eighteenth century. Tea and coffee were expensive to import, and milk was costly, due to the care of livestock. Fruit juices were also not normally consumed due to a lack of knowledge of pasteurization.[32]

Cider was a part of holiday festivities, celebrations, and other events, especially during the Christmas season. The Virginia planter William Byrd II of Westover spent the evening of December 24, 1711, sitting by the fire eating

THE ENGLISH HOUSEWIFE COMES TO JAMESTOWN

Many families had recipes that were passed down through generations, but there were also published cookbooks that provided information on cider production and recipes.

The English Housewife was published in London in 1615 by Gervase Markham and includes food, medicinal, and drink recipes. The book arrived on a supply ship to Jamestown in 1620 and would provide settlers with information on the four main beverages produced in England: beer, ale, perry, and cider.

Another section of the book entitled "Of making perry or cider" includes important information on harvesting and fermenting fruits:

> After your pears or apples are well picked from the stalks, rottenness, and all manner of other filth, you shall put them in the press mill which is made with a millstone running round in a circle, under which you shall crush

"some toast and cider and roast apples" at Queen's Creek plantation in York County, near Williamsburg.[33] According to a December account from the *Virginia Almanack* in 1772, "This Month much Meat will be roasted in rich Mens Kitchens, the Cooks sweating in making of minced Pies and other Christmas Cheer, and whole Rivers of Punch, Toddy, Wine, beer, and Cider consumed with drinking."[34] But cider didn't only flow during the Christmas holidays;

your pears or apples, and then, straining them through a bag of haircloth, tun up the same, after it hath been a little settled, into hogsheads, barrels, and other close vessels. Now after you have pressed all, you shall save that which is within the haircloth bag, and, putting it into several vessels, put a pretty quantity of water thereunto, and after it hath stood a day or two, and hath been well stirred together, press it over also again, for this will make a small perry or cider, and must be spent first. Now of your best cider, that which you make of your summer or sweet fruit, you shall call summer or sweet cider or perry, and that you shall spend first also; and that which you make of the winter and hard fruit you shall call winter and sour cider, or perry; and that you shall spend last, for it will endure the longest.

Sources: Correspondence with Merry Outlaw and Leah Stricker, Historic Jamestowne, and Gervase Markham, *The English Housewife,* ed. Michael R. Best (Montreal: McGill-Queen's University Press, 1986), 204–9.

Independence Day was also a celebration where the fermented beverage was enjoyed. Future president James Madison attended a Fourth of July celebration in 1798 where cider was served and used to toast to the celebration. "After a temperate but cheerful repast the following toasts were drunk in the best American Cyder," recalled Madison.[35] The elixir was also commonly consumed as part of outdoor celebrations. When colonial surveyors claimed new land for Governor Spotswood in 1716, they noted that we "loaded all our arms and we drunk to the Kings' health. . . . We drunk the Governor's health and fired another volley. We had several sorts of liquors, namely Virginia red and white wine, Irish usquebaugh, brandy, shrub, two sorts of rum, champagne, canary, cherry punch, cider."[36]

Most people in Colonial America believed that alcohol had great medical benefits. Cookbook writers placed alcohol recipes in their books, and medical professionals prescribed and sold alcohol to patients. Many believed that regular cider consumption was healthy, kept the body strong, and increased longevity. In 1805, John Adams, former president and cider afficionado, wrote to his friend Benjamin Waterhouse, a physician and cofounder of Harvard Medical School, discussing some advice he received on cider's health benefits from a Virginia doctor. Adams, who was known to drink a tankard of cider at breakfast every morning, explained that a veteran physician from Virginia told him that in his thirty years of practice he had learned "that those who drank Cyder, for their ordinary Beveredge were the most healthy and the longest Livers."[37] Alcohol (and cider) were viewed to provide certain nutrients and assist with specific medical conditions such as constipation, rheumatism, and the common cold.[38]

Despite the praise for cider from some medical professionals, there were skeptics who questioned the benefits of alcohol. The man most responsible for changing American medical opinion about alcohol was Benjamin Rush. In 1784, Rush, a Philadelphia physician, published a pamphlet titled *An Inquiry into the Effects of Ardent Spirits upon the Human Body and Mind*. This work blamed heavy alcohol abuse for medical problems such as vomiting, tremors, psychotic disorders, and liver problems. He recommended alcohol use be limited to cider, beer, and wine in

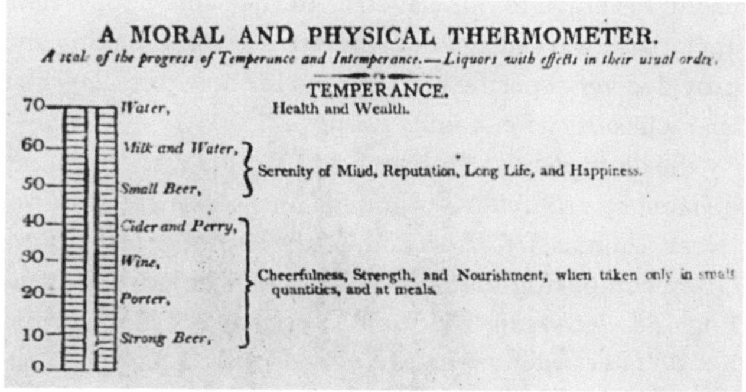

Benjamin Rush, "A Moral and Physical Thermometer: A scale of the progress of Temperance and Intemperance," with cider and perry listed under Temperance (with the associated benefits of "Cheerfulness, Strength, and Nourishment, when taken only in small quantities, and at meals"), from *An Inquiry into the Effects of Ardent Spirits Upon the Human Body and Mind,* 1819. (Courtesy National Library of Medicine)

modest amounts, compared to hard spirits that contained more alcohol. Dr. Rush even created a visual aid to help this crusade for moderation.[39] Although a supporter of the temperance movement, he viewed cider as harmless. Cider was an "excellent liquor" according to Rush, that contained "a small quantity of spirit, but so diluted and blunted by being combined with a large quantity of saccharine matter, and water, as to be perfectly inoffensive and wholesome." Cider promoted "cheerfulness, strength, nourishment, when taken only at meals, and in moderate quantities," proclaimed Rush.[40] John Taylor, one of the leading agricultural writers of the nineteenth century and a friend of Thomas Jefferson, reiterated Rush's support of cider over liquor when he wrote, "Good cyder would be a national saving of wealth, by expelling foreign liquors; and of life, by expelling the use of ardent spirits. The cyder counties of England are said to exhibit the healthiest population of the kingdom. Even hard cyder would be a useful beverage to our slaves."[41] In the same publication, Taylor also warned against ignorance in cider making and provided very specific instructions for how to make cider that will suffice for "family purpose."[42]

The discussion of the benefits of alcohol was commonly debated by prominent Virginians. In a series of letters between Thomas Jefferson and Connecticut physician Vine Utley comparing drinking habits in Virginia and New England, Jefferson told the doctor that "I cannot drink, nor do I use ardent spirits in any form. Malt liquors & cyder are my table drinks."[43] Utley responded and said that Jefferson's routine may be mild compared to other Virginians, but excessive and destructive compared to New Englanders:

> The manner of living here is very destructive to health and long life, particularly the wealthy. At breakfast they take bitters mixed with ardent spirits, to brace the exhausted Stomach. Then eat animal food, butter, cheese, drink coffee and Cider. At dinner they drink rum or brandy sling, and eat plentifully of animal food, swimming in butter, or hogs lard, strong condiments, some take distilled Spirits with their food, Cider Strong beer &c. &c.
>
> After noon, Rum, Gin, brandy, Cider, and beer
>
> At supper comes Animal food again or fish or both, with butter lard, pepper, mustard, Cider tea, &c. The evening is spent in smoaking tobacco.—
>
> Rum, brandy, Gin, and Cider, together with malt liquor, are used by the people here with dreadful prodigality, which bring on a dark train of evils, such as Gout, Rheumatisms, Dropsies Apoplexis, consumptions, and premature old age, or death.[44]

Despite some of the arguments against alcohol and cider consumption, cider became a regular part of both small and large planter households, and the main producers of alcohol in the Chesapeake were women and enslaved laborers.

Orchards and Cider in Large and Small Homesteads

Another social custom carried over from England to Virginia was that women were the main manufacturers of cider in small homesteads. Traditional female gender roles such as domestic chores and alcohol production were transferred to the colonies.[45] Starting in the seventeenth century, Virginia women were the main cider makers in small planter households in the Chesapeake region. These were homes between one and two hundred acres, typically consisted of around six people (an immediate family and several servants or slaves), and consumed around ninety gallons of cider annually.[46] Women's ability to produce cider kept these families going by providing much needed nutrients. Male family members and servants were sometimes involved in the production process by mashing the fruit and pressing the pulp to extract the juice. After the juice was collected, the liquid would then sit for at least twenty-four hours during fermentation. Once primary fermentation was complete, the cider was transferred into another vessel and put into casks or bottles.[47] Many of these families lacked the technology to preserve the finished product, so when they ran out, they had to look to alcohol from the surplus of larger planters.[48]A large planter household had around thirty people (at least twenty slaves, an overseer, a couple of servants and day laborers, two adults, and children) and produced around 450 gallons of cider annually, which met the needs of the household and provided an economic outlet to sell excess inventory to taverns or other patrons.[49] By the mid-seventeenth century, almost every plantation in the Chesapeake possessed apple and pear orchards.[50] Writer Thomas Glover described this phenomenon in his 1676 essay, *An Account of Virginia,* in which he wrote that some Virginia planters "have twelve hundred trees and upward, bearing all sorts of English apples . . . of which they make great store of cider."[51] As early as 1642, large landowner and governor of Virginia Sir William Berkeley had a thriving orchard of more than 1,500 trees at his Green Spring plantation near Jamestown, where he made cider.[52] By the turn of the century, politician and plantation owner William Fitzhugh had one of the largest orchards in the English colonies in Westmoreland County that included at least 2,500 apple trees. His orchard was full of English varieties that could produce nearly 10,000 gallons of cider a year.[53] Another Virginian politician—William Byrd II (member of the governor's Council from 1709 to 1744)—produced such an immense amount of cider at his Westover plantation in Charles City County that he regularly sold the surplus to taverns in Williamsburg, including Susanna Allen's.[54] A man of letters, he kept a detailed diary and correspondence that included information about his fruit plantings at his plantation and published *William Byrd's Natural History of Virginia: or, The Newly Discovered Eden* in 1737, which listed descriptions of the natural surroundings of Virginia including thirteen European varieties of apples.[55]

Larger planters had access to better technology: more advanced presses, barrels, grafting capabilities, cellars, bottles, and so on. They produced a larger amount of cider that could be kept for longer periods of time. Planters also shared scion cuttings with one another, so that they could experiment and see which varietals grew best in the Virginia climate and graft them according to their specific needs.[56] Planter Robert Beverley of James City County focused on improving cider, brandy, and winemaking practices. His work *The History and Present State of Virginia, In Four Parts* (1705) even included a section where he laid out his strategies and instructions for orchard management.[57] Beverley was interested in the latest technological advancements in alcohol production, like the industrial cider press. In 1738, he requested that his merchant send him an "ingenio or cyder mill to turn by hand with lignum vitae roll[e]rs brass pegs & a screw press."[58] Large planters also had access to coopers (barrel makers) and cellars, which were very important for safeguarding the finished product. A cooper was knowledgeable about the best type of wood to use for storage and could make a couple of barrels a day. Even with access to cooperage and cellars, some argued that Virginia cider was still not aged long enough. In 1724, author and chaplain to the House of Burgesses Hugh Jones compared the reputable English Herefordshire cider apples to Virginia cider apples, concluding that the main difference between the two was storage. Jones explained that Virginia apples "makes, with good Management, an excellent *Cyder,* not much inferior to that of Herefordshire, when kept to a good Age; which is rarely done."[59] William Grove of England made similar remarks about Virginians' failure to store cider long enough. On a trip to Virginia in 1732, he wrote that Virginians "made good cider but will not keep [it] but drink it by the pailfills never worked [aged]."[60] Despite these criticisms of storage, some Virginia planters attempted to improve practices by using sawdust or sand to keep cider bottles cool during the hot summertime. Virginia statesman, author, and plantation owner Landon Carter devised an intricate method for storing bottled cider in the mid-eighteenth century. Once the cider "fines in cask" Carter explained, "I shall bottle, tie down the corks, and wax them; and lay the bottles leaning buried 4 inches in dry sand according to *Miller's Dictionary* and hope to get a pleasant liquor."[61] Most of the orchard maintenance and cider production on large plantations in the south was performed by enslaved people. Robert "King" Carter of Lancaster County had more than 295,000 acres of land and hundreds of slaves who produced more than "twenty butts of cider" or almost 3,000 gallons during fall harvest in the late seventeenth century.[62] Southern planters made their profits on the backs of African slave labor for cash crops, and this was also true for alcohol production. Prominent Virginia planters had numerous slaves and exploited them for their benefit. The specific records on enslaved individuals on Virginia plantations and their activities is limited, but what we do know is that anytime planters referred to work completed on the plantation, the workers were enslaved people or servants.

Cider Tax Protest and the Coming of a Revolution

As cider began to transform Virginia's society and economy throughout the seventeenth and eighteenth centuries, a storm was growing over American colonists' rights to their own self-sustaining government, and cider would play a part in this political revolution. By the mid-eighteenth century, many Virginians (and other colonists) wanted full English rights including direct representation from their elected colonial councils like the House of Burgesses, not parliament.[63] The American Revenue Act (or Sugar Act) of 1764 and Stamp Act that passed the following year created major dissent from colonists and are often cited as among the earliest causes for revolution. (The American Revenue Act placed duties on items that had to be imported, and the Stamp Act required colonists to purchase revenue stamps to place on all printed matter. After fierce opposition, the Stamp Act was repealed in 1766.) Virginians protested England's tyranny by avoiding British products. They signed non-importation agreements banning merchants from buying enumerated British goods. English cider was listed as one of the items on several of the documents. One Virginia Nonimportation

Resolution stated that "the Subscribers will not hereafter, directly or indirectly, import or cause to be imported from *Great-Britain,* or any Part of *Europe* . . . Spirits, Wine, Cyder, Perry, Beer, Ale, Malt, Barley." The document was signed by the House of Burgesses on May 18, 1769, which included the signatures of several prominent Virginians, including George Mason, George Washington, and Thomas Jefferson.[64]

As a result of the non-importation agreements and growing hostility between the mother country and her subjects, more Americans focused on producing items at home. Whiskey and cider became increasingly popular because these items could be made with corn and apples, which were readily available in the colonies.[65] These beverages were promoted as patriotic products made with American raw materials, unlike imported British ale. Rum also suffered a similar fate as English beer, as cheap molasses (used for distilling) from the Caribbean Islands became difficult to acquire due to stricter trade policies.[66] As cider was elevated to patriotic status, it is no wonder that it would be a popular beverage for American soldiers during the Revolutionary War.

Cider's Role in the Revolutionary War

These protests for English rights eventually led to the American Revolution, its first shots fired at Lexington and Concord in the spring of 1775. George Washington was appointed Commander-in-Chief of a young inexperienced Continental Army in June 1775, and soon after he took command, it was evident that cider would play a large role in fueling his men for the war effort. As early as August 1775, Washington made clear the importance of alcohol to his troops. In his General Orders on August 8, he requested that his soldiers' rations be "1 quart of spruce beer or cyder per man per day."[67]

Washington was not only concerned about the amount,

but also the quality of the cider that his men received. Later that month, he issued another general order complaining that he will not tolerate "New Cyder" as a ration for his men, as it was not properly produced and aged. Washington knew that this cider would not last as long as well-made cider and could easily spoil. After drinking some of the "New Cyder," General John Sullivan's brigade felt under the weather. Sullivan requested that he and his men be relieved from "ordinary Camp duty," so that they could conserve their energy for mustering. In response to the issues with "New Cyder" the general issued another order banning the improperly fermented beverage from the camp, "as nothing is more pernicious to the health of Soldiers, nor more certainly productive of the bloody-flux; than drinking New Cyder."[68]

If soldiers ran out of cider, or if it wasn't included in their rations, they could buy it from sutlers or tavern keepers, but sometimes army payments were delayed, hindering soldiers' ability to purchase beverages. Brigadier General William Heath wrote to General Washington on March 22, 1776, that his men had not received their pay, so they could not purchase cider.[69] As the war dragged on, Washington was displeased with ongoing supply issues. He wrote to the Continental Congress Committee in July of 1777 complaining about the lack of basic rations, including cider. Washington exclaimed that "no Army was ever worse supplied than ours . . . neither have they been provided with proper drink—Beer or Cyder seldom comes within the verge of the Camp."[70] It wasn't just the lack of cider but also the price that Washington was concerned about. He discussed the high cost of "cyder royal" or cider mixed with brandy/liquor in a general order in 1778, and that "the venders of these Articles have taken advantage and therefore sell them at the most exorbitant rates."[71] At this time, he also developed a keen interest in applejack made by the Laird Family of New Jersey. Robert Laird was one of Washington's soldiers, and the Laird family had an applejack recipe that Washington coveted. They provided rations of this liquor to the Continental Army during the war. Washington loved the drink so much that he requested the recipe; it is notable that he is the only person outside of the immediate family granted that privilege.[72] Despite these difficulties with supplying troops with America's beverage, the United States would defeat the British in 1781 at Yorktown, and the formal surrender would take place two years later with the Peace of Paris.

Cider: An Incentive to Vote

Cider provided key nourishment and a morale boost for Continental soldiers during the Revolutionary War. But it has also served as an incentive to attract voters and reward loyal constituents during elections. Alcohol (and cider specifically) and political campaigns have been intertwined throughout history. George Washington claimed that he lost his 1755 bid for the House of Burgesses election because he failed to provide enough alcohol to voters. He learned his lesson for the next election when he gave his loyal supporters over 140 gallons of alcohol including beer, rum, punch, and cider, and easily won.[73] Washington's victory in 1758 came at a cost of 39 pounds and 6 shillings, but it was worth it, because it kickstarted his political career.[74] Another Virginian failed to adequately compensate his constituents with alcohol during his 1777 House of Delegates election. James Madison ignored the tradition of rewarding voters, and he suffered from this decision when he lost to an inexperienced candidate. He would learn from his mistake and serve a hefty amount of alcohol to secure a delegate seat in the 1780 election.[75]

The most well-known election involving alcohol was the presidential election of 1840, known as the "Log Cabin

Woodcut highlighting Harrison and Tyler's "Log Cabin and Hard Cider Campaign," 1840. (Prints and Photographs Division, Library of Congress)

and Hard Cider Campaign." The Whig party nominated two Virginians for the ticket, William Henry Harrison for president, and John Tyler for vice president. General Harrison was born in Charles City County, Virginia, in 1773 and became a military leader who was credited with winning the Battle of Tippecanoe against the Shawnee in 1811 and served in the War of 1812.[76] In 1836, the former governor of the Indiana Territory and Ohio representative was nominated for the Whig's presidential ticket but was defeated by the Democratic candidate, Martin Van Buren. He ran again in the following election and defeated Van Buren. During the 1840 campaign, John de Ziska, a Democratic supporter, tried to harm Harrison's reputation by labeling him as an old drunkard. All the presidential candidate required, reported Ziska in the *Baltimore Republican,* was a generous allowance of "a barrel of hard cider" and he could "sit the remainder of his days in his log cabin by the side of a 'sea coal' fire, and study moral philosophy." Ziska's objective was to hurt the Whig candidate's reputation, but his attack led to one of the greatest blunders in political history. Once Harrison was labeled a cider drinker, it made him more likeable to the average citizen. The Whigs now painted Harrison as an everyday American, man of the people, who drank the national beverage, and his opponent Van Buren was portrayed as the champagne-sipping candidate for the wealthy. The slogan and campaign pushed Harrison into the White House. Ironically, Harrison was not a regular cider drinker.[77]

CHAPTER 2

Becoming Colonial Virginia's Beverage of Choice

Since the start of Jamestown, apples and cider played pivotal roles in Virginia. By the mid-eighteenth century, specific Virginia apples like Hewe's Crab were starting to be sold at nurseries throughout the state. In Surry County, William Smith's nursery listed in their 1755 catalog "twenty-two apple varieties, seven were Virginia cider cultivars, including Hewes, White, Clarke, Pearmain, and Father Abraham."[1] Planters throughout the Commonwealth grew apples for cider. The alcohol landscape was intertwined with the political, social, and economic history of the Old Dominion. Prominent Virginians like Thomas Jefferson and George Washington developed and improved orchard maintenance and cider quality throughout the eighteenth century, which would elevate cider's popularity.

Benjamin Franklin

Though Benjamin Franklin was not from Virginia, he was a proponent of cider, especially Virginia cider. The Pennsylvania statesman was full of puns and quips that referred to the fermented apple. When discussing the story of Adam and Eve, he said that one of the morals is that "It's indeed bad to eat apples, it's better to turn them all into cyder."[2] Another Franklin cider quote confirmed his belief that cider was the peoples' beverage meant to be enjoyed with company and friends. "He that drinks his cyder alone," exclaimed Franklin, "let him catch his horse alone."[3] Franklin was also passionate about having the best product, and he believed that the highest quality cider came from Virginia. In 1758, he compared the Virginia Crab apple to the best English cider apples in a series of correspondence with his friend and Philadelphia merchant Charles Norris: "I do not find that England anywhere produces Cyder of equal Goodness with what I drank frequently in Virginia made from those Crabs. They are also said to be plentiful Bearers, and seldom fail. I should be glad to see the Industry of our People supplying the Neighbouring Colonies with that Cyder. I think it would even be valued here."[4] His idea that Virginia cider was not only good enough for his palate but also should be distributed to the neighboring colonies, and especially his home area of Pennsylvania, clearly showed the value of Virginia cider.

James Monroe

James Monroe, fifth president of the United States and former governor of Virginia, was also a cider enthusiast. He purchased his Charlottesville plantation Highland, which was adjacent to Thomas Jefferson's Monticello, in 1793. While serving as George Washington's minister to France from 1794 to 1796, he relied on family members and enslaved workers to establish an orchard on his property. In 1794, Monroe wrote from Paris to his uncle Joseph Jones, asking him to select the best place for "orchards, apples, peaches, &c, in concert with Mr Jefferson: & have them planted this winter or next spring. Let the trees be procured where to be had of the best kind not forgetting to include some crab: for cider."[5] There was a significant amount of collaboration between the neighboring planters. They would discuss best practices for orchard management and cider production and share scions from their farms.

James Madison

Another of the Commonwealth's most prominent politicians who regularly enjoyed cider was James Madison. The previous chapter mentioned the electoral lesson that Madison learned from using cider to reward his constituents. Decades later, while president in 1810, he received shipments of Virginia wine and cider from Virginia delegate John Roane of King William County. Roane gave him "a few bottles of wine, made of the native grape of Virginia & also a little cyder, the product of a newly discovered seedling apple."[6] This cider was known as Roane's White Crab, a seedling of a Virginia crab, most likely Hewe's. Unfortunately, Roane's White Crab has since disappeared. As president, Madison received requests from cider makers to protect the value of their product. In 1814, Lekeel Cosmeaux sent a letter to Madison from Boston asking that brandy be taxed so that the price of cider will go down. "Cyder is a Drink for all the people of the U States but at Present so much is distilled into Brandy that the Poor is unabled to buy It," explained Cosmeaux. He argued that in order to protect the value of cider, there needed to be a tax put on brandy.[7] It's unclear if a tax was levied on the spirit due to Cosmeaux's request, but it is evident that throughout America cider makers wished to protect their product.

George Mason

Virginia law maker and plantation owner George Mason was another one of the Old Dominion's greatest cider champions. Mason had orchards at his plantation, Gunston Hall, in Fairfax County and regularly made cider. In 1785, two years after the end of the Revolutionary War, he wrote to George Washington alerting him that he was sending him some of his best "Red Streak Apple" cider. Mason was worried, however, that some of the liquid might not have been as clear as usual "from what Cause I don't know, unless that I ground my apples last Fall rather later than usual." He concluded with a piece of advice, "If you use it out of the barrel, you will find it (as all sweet Cyder is) much more grateful to the Stomack, by having a little Ginger grated upon it."[8] Ginger was often used to assist with digestion. The thorough and detailed report of the cider, its properties, storage, and drinking instructions show that this elixir was important to prominent Virginians like Washington and Mason.

When Mason leased out his land to workers, his contracts ensured that the tenants improve the land. In several cases property enhancements meant growing and tending to orchards. In a land lease document from Mason on December 29, 1752, he agreed to rent out part of his land to Thomas Halbert if he would plant apple trees. The contract was for seven years and according to the document Halbert must plant "an Orchard of two hundred *Winter* Apple Trees, at thirty feet Distance every Way from each other," and he must keep up with maintenance and protection of the trees. The arrangement also stipulated that "if any of them should die or decay . . . shall plant others of the same Kind in the Room of them, so as during the Continuance of this Demise, always to keep up the same Number."[9] The contract showed how invested planters were in the future of their orchards. The lease not only guaranteed the new growth of apples for current cider production but also the continued care of the orchard for future fruit. Cider was clearly a key piece of Virginia society, and it is no wonder that two of the most famous Virginians, Thomas Jefferson and George Washington, would enjoy this historic beverage as well.

Thomas Jefferson

Thomas Jefferson was a planter, slaveholder, inventor, politician, writer, and agriculturalist—and one of the biggest fans of the fermented apple. Jefferson was born at Shadwell, at the foot of the Blue Ridge Mountains, in 1743 to Peter Jefferson and Jane Randolph. Thomas spent his childhood years from 1746 to 1751 in Goochland County at his mother's family's home, Tuckahoe, where he went to school and played with his siblings and cousins. His father, Peter, was a surveyor and held many public offices, including as a representative in the House of Burgesses and an officer in the colonial militia. While acting as one of

PETER HATCH AND THE GARDENS AT MONTICELLO: A LIVING MUSEUM FOR APPLE LOVERS

Jefferson's garden and orchards have been recreated based on his own 1811 plan and other archival and archaeological research. Peter Hatch, Director of Gardens and Grounds Emeritus for the Thomas Jefferson Foundation, was charged with the maintenance, interpretation, and restoration of the 2,400-acre landscape at Monticello from 1977 to 2012. He is also responsible for apple varieties still grown at Monticello like Hewe's Crab, Albemarle Pippin, Esopus Spitzenburg, and Roxbury Russet. These fruit trees, the grounds, and their bounty are part of the Monticello Museum. "The Fruits and Fruit Trees of Monticello are regarded as part of the museum collections," explained Hatch, "efforts are made to doc-

the first magistrates of Albemarle County in 1745, he set the prices at local taverns and ordinaries, which included establishing the rates for cider.[10] Peter was part of a group that mapped out the Rappahannock and North Branch Potomac Rivers in 1746, and while on the journey, they used "syder, rum, whiskey, punch and more" to ease their hardships.[11] Thomas was introduced to beer and cider at Shadwell and Tuckahoe, and the brewers and cider makers were most likely the women of the household such as

ument and care for these plants with the same amount of attention as is given to indoor museum collections." Hatch—who is author of several books including *A Rich Spot of Earth: Thomas Jefferson's Revolutionary Garden at Monticello* and *The Fruits and Fruit Trees of Monticello*—has led tastings of the fruits at Monticello along with other apple experts and museum staff members, thus allowing visitors to get a firsthand experience or taste of Jefferson's historic apples and their legacy.

Sources: Hatch, *Fruits and Fruit Trees*, xvi; email correspondence with Hatch, May 27, 2022.

Jane, and the enslaved workers. Cider was often served to guests visiting the plantations, and one of their regular visitors at Shadwell was a Cherokee chief named Outassetė Ostenaco.[12] Thomas fondly remembered these occasions where the chief dined and drank cider with Peter and others.[13] In 1769, twelve years after his father's death, Jefferson completed an inventory of Shadwell and found over 200 bottles of alcohol "including rum (85 bottles), Madeira (15 bottles), cider (54 bottles), Lisbon wine (4 bottles [+ 52 more?]), small beer, and empty bottles."[14] This clearly indicated that cider was a major part of the Jefferson's livelihood, and this love of alcohol would remain with Thomas throughout his life.

Jefferson started building Monticello in 1769 and lived there from 1770 until his death in 1826. Situated just outside of Charlottesville, his plantation consisted of close to five thousand acres. The third president of the United States owned more than 600 slaves, and at least 400 enslaved individuals lived and worked at Monticello.[15] His

Apple trees at Monticello. (Photograph by Gregory J. Hansard)

enslaved workers and white laborers planted 1,031 fruit trees and grew eighteen different apple varieties in his orchards. Jefferson concentrated on four main types for cider production: Hewe's Crab, Taliaferro, Newtown Pippin, and Esopus Spitzenburg.[16] Alcohol was an integral part of Jefferson's life at Monticello, and his typical table drink was small beer and cider. His dedication to orchard management of his more than 250 apple trees is evident in his farm and garden book, where he kept detailed notations about farming practices and crop production.[17] His correspondence also shows that his passion and love for cider was so resolute that he regularly compared Virginia cider to the finest European wine.

Jefferson was often absent from Albemarle County due to schooling and government positions, but cider was still a part of his life away from home, especially in Williamsburg. He studied in the colonial city throughout the 1760s; first attending the College of William & Mary, and then reading the law with his mentor, George Wythe.[18] Cider was a standard offering at the dining hall of the college, and he and his teacher regularly enjoyed cider together.[19] Wythe even gave Jefferson two silver drinking cups that the pupil would have altered and etched with the initials "G.W. to T.J." Jefferson would use these cups to serve cider at dinners at Monticello. Once he was elected governor, he took up residence again in Williamsburg, but this time at the Governor's Palace from 1779 to 1780. Fortunately for Jefferson, these accommodations had a large cellar for alcoholic beverages, including cider.[20]

Jefferson served as the first secretary of state and the third president of the United States, and his interest in cider continued at these new government posts. While living in Philadelphia and serving in Washington's cabinet, he regularly requested cider from various merchants.[21] Unfortunately for Jefferson, Hewe's Crab was hard to come by, but even when the cider was found and sent to him,

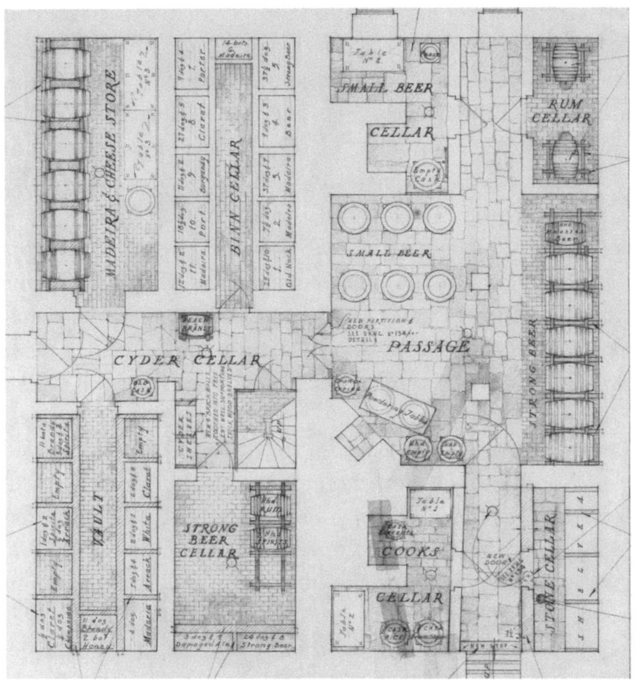

Detail of the plan for Governor's Palace cellars, showing the "Cyder Cellar" at center, Colonial Williamsburg, Perry, Shaw & Hepburn, Architects, 1940. (Special Collections, John D. Rockefeller Library, The Colonial Williamsburg Foundation)

it was not always to his liking.[22] In December of 1791, a Tidewater merchant named Adam Lindsay acquired some Hewe's for Jefferson, but he responded that, "Respecting the Cyder I found none to my entire liking."[23] It wasn't just Philadelphia where Jefferson had difficulty finding good cider, however, as he found a similar situation when he moved into the White House in 1801. Both President Jefferson and his Secretary of State James Madison corresponded regularly with merchants to obtain cider. By the end of the fall of 1801, Jefferson had purchased around a year's supply of Hewe's Crab cider from Norfolk merchant Thomas Newton.[24] In addition to Newton's shipments, Jefferson also acquired cider from other sources while in Washington, DC. In the winter of 1802–3, Jefferson received fifty-two barrels of Newark cyder from John Condit, a Democratic-Republican congressman from New Jersey. Pleased with the Newark Cyder, Jefferson requested more over the next two years.[25]

While serving as president, Jefferson continued adding to his orchards at Monticello. In 1804, he received several apple tree cuttings, including Calville Blanc d'Hiver and Ox Eye Striped (also known as Newtown Spitzenburg) from Colonel John Armstrong's nursery in Ohio and had them grafted at Monticello. Armstrong was aware that Jefferson was an apple connoisseur because Captain Meriwether Lewis (Jefferson's friend) mentioned to the colonel that the president would like to have some of the apple trees. According to Armstrong, "Captain Lewis on his way to the Westward called on me and requested that I would at the proper season furnish you with some cuttings, from my Nursery, which you will receive herewith." Colonel Armstrong described the apple scions he sent to Jefferson and gave instructions for planting the cuttings. He also requested that the president in return send some Hewe's Crab.[26]

Jefferson documented his farming methods in his farm book. Since 1774, he kept copious notes, dedicating an entire section to his orchards and recording how he cultivated apple trees and processed cider. He also discussed ways to maintain the soil, like placing straw near the roots of the tree to help prevent weeds and grass from growing and addressed the need to rake the soil and use manure to assist with growth.[27] Notations like this and a drawing of an apple mill and press show the value of the farm book

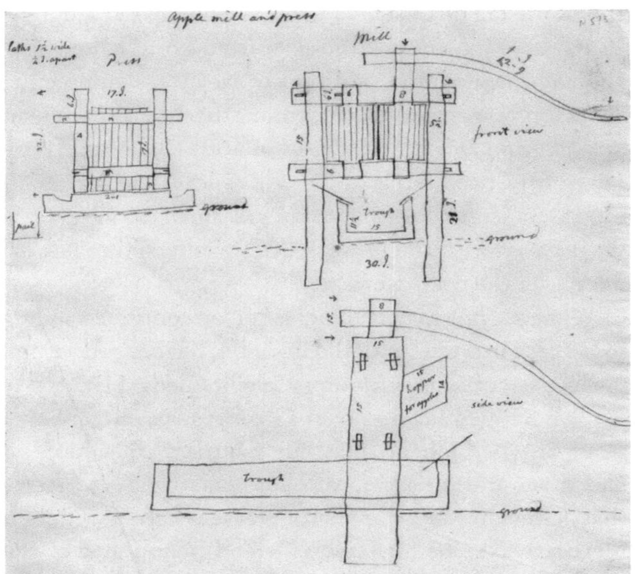

Thomas Jefferson, drawing of an apple mill and press, undated. (Coolidge Collection of Thomas Jefferson Manuscripts, Massachusetts Historical Society, N573)

to understanding his obsession with agriculture and cider making.

Enslaved Laborers and Cider Management at Monticello

In his farm book and correspondence, Jefferson documented his enslaved laborers' duties, which included cider production. Jefferson used enslaved individuals for this important job. He purchased George Granger Sr. and his wife, Ursula, as well as their son, George Jr., from a Cumberland County plantation owner in the early 1770s, and the Granger family (including their other sons Isaac and Bagwell) would serve in key positions at Monticello for the next several decades. The Grangers not only made cider, but also took care of the orchards at Monticello as early as 1784. George was tasked with maintaining the orchards while his master was away in Paris and continued his duties upon Jefferson's return to Virginia. Jefferson was clear that George would be in charge while he was away in Philadelphia serving as secretary of state under Washington; "George still to be reserved to take care of my orchards," Jefferson wrote to his overseer in July 1790.[28] He continued to rely on George for his knowledge of orchard management and cider production, and in November of 1799 Jefferson wrote that "70. bushels of the Robinson & red Hughes (about half of each) have made 120. gallons of cyder. George says that when in a proper state (there was much rot among these) they ought to make 3. galls. to the bushel, as he knows from having often measured both." George Sr., George Jr., and Ursula all succumbed to disease in 1799 and 1800.[29]

Another of Jefferson's enslaved cider makers, Jupiter Evans, was born at Shadwell the same year as Jefferson, and served as Jefferson's personal attendant for ten years, in addition to his roles as overseer of the stables and stonemason.[30] His value to Monticello's cider operation is evident in a letter Jefferson wrote to his son-in-law, Thomas Mann Randolph, in 1800 lamenting Jupiter's death: "he leaves a void in my administration which I cannot fill up." Jefferson then looked to his daughter Martha and son-in-law Thomas to oversee the bottling operations while he was in Washington.[31]

Along with enslaved laborers, white overseers also managed the orchards and parts of the cider process at Monticello. Edmund Bacon, a white overseer at Monticello from 1806 to 1822, recalled the tedious bottling operations.[32] Bacon remembered that every March he and several house servants/enslaved laborers (Betty Brown, Sally, Critta, Betty Hemings, Nance, and Ursula Granger Hughes, the granddaughter of George and Ursula Granger) bottled all the cider: "Dear me, this was a job. It took us two weeks. Mr. Jefferson was very particular about his cider. He gave me instructions to have every apple cleaned perfectly clean when it was made."[33] Bacon's recollection of Jefferson's expedient and specific instructions are confirmed in a letter from November 15, 1817. "We have saved red Hughes enough from the North orchard to make a smart cask of cyder," Jefferson explained, "They are now mellow & beginning to rot. I will pray you therefore to have them made into cyder immediately. let them be made clean one by one, and all the rotten ones thrown away or the rot cut out. nothing else can ensure fine cyder. I request particular attention to the Coopers that no hindrance may prevent their deliverance of their weekly complement of Barrels."[34] It is obvious that cider was of the upmost importance to Jefferson because of his specific instructions for cleaning, directions for apple selection, and his follow-up correspondence ensuring that the cider be placed into barrels immediately.

Jefferson's family members were also interested in cider making and managing orchards. His oldest daughter, Martha Jefferson Randolph, sometimes tended to the alcohol production. While her father was in Philadelphia in 1793, he received news from Martha that there was an accident with the cider bottles. "I have a terrible account to give you of your cyder," she explained "Of 140 bottles that were put away you will hardly find 12. It flew in such a manner as to render it dangerous going near them. Those that were carelessly corked forced their corks the rest burst the bottles amongst which the havoc is incredible."[35] These likely exploded due to improper bottling and/or a buildup of too much carbon dioxide. (CO_2 is one of the by-products of fermentation.) Martha also assisted with the cider operation when her father was in Washington, DC. In the spring of 1807 Jefferson wrote to his daughter checking on the status of the cider, "I thank you, my dear, for your attention to the cyder, & hope you have had it bottled."[36] Jefferson's granddaughter, Anne Cary Randolph, also helped with importing cider while he was away. On March 18, 1808, she wrote to her grandfather with bad news about the cider shipment. "I am afraid the cider you got of Mrs Clarke this year is bad," explained Anne. "It is said that the summer was so wet that all the apples were watery & the cider also."[37] He also corresponded with Ellen Wayles Randolph Coolidge, one of his favorite grandchildren, about cider only a few months before his death. (Ellen regularly accompanied him on his trips to Poplar Forest, his private retreat and plantation located in eastern Bedford County.) On March 19, 1826, Jefferson sent a dozen cuttings to his granddaughter. He explained that "They are called the Taliaferro apple, being from a seedling tree discover by a gentleman of that name near Williamsburg and yield unquestionably the finest cyder we have ever known, and more like wine than any liquor I have ever tasted which was not wine."[38] This was a nice gift to his favorite granddaughter to carry on his love of the fruit only a few months before his death. Mary Randolph, a member of Jefferson's extended family, published the first regional southern cookbook in 1824. *The Virginia Housewife* featured a recipe for cider wine that called for "Fifteen gallons of cider, fresh from the press; to each gallon, add two pounds of good brown sugar."[39]

Jefferson not only grew apples and made cider at Monticello, but he also purchased it from local planters like Charles Massie, who owned Spring Valley plantation on the southwestern border of Albemarle, and Fanny (Frances) Whitlock Brand who lived at Findowrie in Albemarle County. Massie and his son, Charles, sold apples and cider, and their orchard was known for its Albemarle Pippins.[40] Some of the shipments of cider would be adequate, and others would not be to Jefferson's liking. He found the batch for 1824 to be undesirable, but even after the bad product, Jefferson requested more cider from the Massies.[41] On October 26, 1825, he ordered "about 90. Or 100 galls" and asked that Massie select the very best cider.[42] Jefferson was also particular about his cider purchases with Fanny Brand. In a letter to her on December 16, 1815, he explained that "If your cyder is as good as what I had before I shall willingly take two to three hundred gallons. The quantity will depend on the quality."[43]

Many visitors ranging from politicians to socialites ventured to Monticello to see one of the nation's most interesting Founders, and in the winter of 1815, Francis Gray, an art collector, lawyer, and public official from Massachusetts, stayed at Monticello and gave a vivid account of his dinner, which included cider.[44] The attendees at the dinner included Jefferson, his daughter Martha Jefferson Randolph, her husband Thomas Randolph, and their children, along with Jefferson's younger sister, Mary Jefferson Carr.[45] Gray described the scene at the table: "The drinking cups were of silver marked G.W. to T.J—the table liquors were beer & cider & after dinner wine."[46]

George Washington

George Washington, like Jefferson, was a cider lover, too. He appreciated quality alcohol and greatly enjoyed Herefordshire cider, which he regularly purchased from England.[47] This popular West Midlands beverage, made from Redstrake or Redstreak, was one of the most desired beverages of the seventeenth and eighteenth centuries. It was equal or better than some of the finest European wines and was regularly exported to the colonies.[48] Also like Jefferson, Washington would use his plantation to create orchards for cider production.

He purchased apple trees throughout his life and began grafting by 1760. Washington regularly bought scions from his neighbors William Digges and George Mason and his plantation included varieties like Redstreaks, Maryland Redstreaks, Gloucester Whites, Golden Pippins, and Newtown Pippins.[49] He built a large orchard dedicated to cider on his property at Mount Vernon, his eight-thousand-acre estate on the banks of the Potomac River, which included several farms and held more than three hundred enslaved workers.

Each of the farms consisted of an overseer who managed the crops, including the orchards.[50] It's likely that cider was made at several of these locations. Washington's cousin, Lund Washington, was the main caretaker of Mount Vernon starting in 1764, and his duties included managing the overseers. He often checked with them on the status of cider making at two of the farms: Muddy Hole and Clifton's Neck. On August 17, 1767, Lund wrote to his cousin that "the Negroes are all well—Bishup has sew'd half his field in wheat & made two Casks of Cyder." Less than a month later, on September 5, 1767, he reported on both Bishop and Cleveland's progress: "Bishup got done sewing Wheat to Day & has made all his apples into cyder, which is four Casks Cleveland is something more than half done sewing his fourth Cut, & made four Casks of Cyder."[51] Like Jefferson, Washington also relied on skilled enslaved laborers and family members for alcohol production.

It's evident from Washington's lack of correspondence on apples and cider during times of war and later as president that orchard management and alcohol production were not a priority for him during those crucial periods. (The exception was to ensure that his troops were provided the proper ration of alcohol, as discussed in the previous chapter.) In the middle of the Revolutionary War, James Duane (a New York Delegate) wrote to General Washington to see if he would help him identify one of his apples to see if it was a Hewe's Crab. The request never made it to Washington, because Alexander Hamilton (Washington's wartime aide) lost the apple that Duane sent him.

MARTHA AND NELLY WASHINGTON: WASHINGTON'S CIDER LEGACY

Martha Washington had inherited a cookbook from her first husband, Daniel Parke Custis, that included a cider recipe. The book had belonged to Daniel's mother (Martha's mother-in-law), Mrs. Frances Parke Custis. It was common for cookbooks to be passed down to the females of the family. According to a later editor, "apples were beaten, squeezed, and left to stand for at least four days. The juice was then put into a clean vessel, probably a cask, which was left open for a time, until it hath done working [fermenting?]. At this point, a small bag of spices was hung in the vessel and the cask was closed up with a stopper. After six months, the cider was put into bottles and was ready to drink." George likely used this recipe for producing cider at his farms, due to the similarities in the directions. Martha eventually gave the cookbook to her granddaughter, (Nelly) Eleanor Parke Custis, who lived with her and George at Mount Vernon. The careful passing of the cookbook through generations shows that cider-making skills were very valuable in colonial society. It appears that Nelly used the cider recipe for its health benefits. In 1823 (two decades after Washington's death), Nelly wrote to a friend that during an illness she took "aqua fortis & hard cider alternately-sometimes one, & the day following the other-to keep the bile in subjection & am almost worn out with anxiety." Nelly likely used the

recipe to make her son-in-law, Charles Conrad, cider in 1835. "I have just returned from the Cellar where I have been bottling a half a Barrel of Cider made at the farm," explained Nelly "It is for you My Dear Charles, & if it is not good I shall be very sorry, as I am laudably anxious that you should drink some good Cider here."

Sources: *Martha Washington's Booke of Cookery,* ed. Karen Hess (New York: Columbia University Press, 1996), 392–93; Nelly Custis Lewis to Elizabeth Bordley Gibson, October 25, 1823, Mount Vernon Repository A-569.086; Nelly Custis Lewis to Charles M. Conrad, April 8, 1835; Mount Vernon Repository W-1251/A

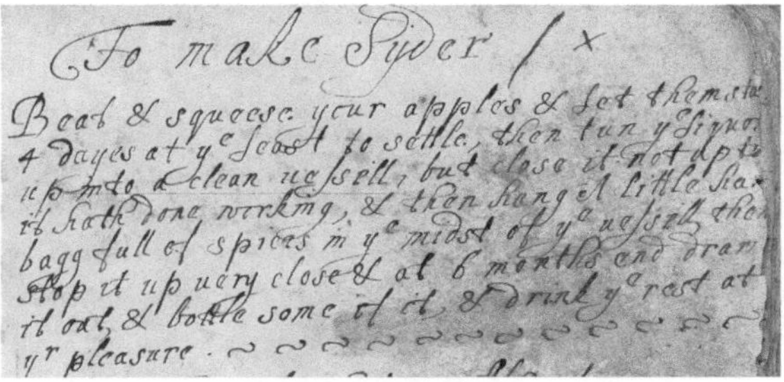

To make Syder / x

Beat & squeese your apples & let them sta
4 dayes at ye least to settle, then tun ye liquor
up into a clean vessell, but close it not up till
it hath done working, & then hang a little ba
bagg full of spices in ye midst of ye vessell, then
stop it up very close & at 6 months end draw
it out, & bottle some of it, & drink ye rest at
yr pleasure.

Cider recipe from Martha Washington's cookbook, which she inherited from her mother-in-law, Frances Parke Custis. (Reproduced with permission from the Historical Society of Pennsylvania)

Hamilton, however, did have two of his soldiers study the piece of fruit before its disappearance and they said that it was clearly not Hewe's, but resembled the common crab-apple.[52] It's clear that this was not the most pressing issue for the Continental Army during the war, or it would have been delivered to Washington.

General Washington's own orchards at Mount Vernon suffered due to his absence during the American Revolution. In 1778, Lund Washington complained that "we have neither apples nor peaches this year."[53] Another crop was lost due to a particular dry year.[54] There is also little correspondence concerning cider during Washington's presidency, but before he left for his first term in 1789, he had a conversation with Senator William Maclay from Pennsylvania about his orchard, and Washington lamented that his fruit that year had been completely lost mainly because of the poor weather.[55] Washington's apple interest also led him to visit the well-known William Prince Nursery in Flushing, New York, in 1789. Robert Prince had established the first commercial apple tree nursery in America in 1737. The nursery was very popular by the late eighteenth century, but Washington seemed less than impressed with the business when he visited on October 10: "I set off from New York, about nine oclock in my barge, to visit Mr. Princes fruit gardens and shrubberies at Flushing. These gardens, except in the number of young fruit trees, did not answer my expectations. The shrubs were trifling and the flowers not numerous."[56] As Washington began his first term as president, his love of cider led to a problem with insufficient storage problems. When he moved into the President's House in Philadelphia in 1790, he had difficulty securing the appropriate amount of space for his cider collection, and his personal secretary, Tobias Lear, wrote that the cellar is too full and "we cannot put a single barrel into the Cellar."[57]

CHAPTER 3

Cider's Downfall and Reemergence

Apples and cider have been connected with Virginia's history and culture since the beginning, but the popularity of cider would hit a few road bumps in the late nineteenth century. Apple growing and cider making in the Commonwealth had remained linked to large planter households and small farms and homesteads through the 1850s, but after the Civil War many orchards began to be abandoned with the migration of rural families into the cities. A major part of the decline of cider popularity concerns the mass exodus of Americans retreating from country homesteads to the comforts of city life.[1] Since fewer people were living on rustic farms, they didn't have access to an abundance of fresh apples to make cider. The Second Industrial Revolution, as well as immigration, also paved the way for mass produced beverages such as lagers.[2] Most of the production of alcoholic beverages was now done through machinery, and many American palates shifted from the bold flavors of handcrafted farmhouse cider towards the clean, crisp, mass produced lagers. The growing demand for lager was mainly due to the increase in German and Northern European immigrants, many of whom were familiar with the beverage and its brewing, and by the end of the nineteenth century lager had swept American tastes, altering the beverage landscape forever.[3]

Thousands of Germans settled in Virginia during the mid-nineteenth century, and by the end of the Civil War, Germans made up about one quarter of the white population in Richmond. It wasn't just the large cities where German immigrants settled, but they also populated rural areas like the Shenandoah Valley, which was similar to the landscape of southern Germany.[4] As this population change occurred throughout the Commonwealth, so did many Virginians' preferred beverage. Englishman David W. Mitchell visited the Old Dominion in the mid-nineteenth century and reported that "[lager] is a new beverage of German origin, but it is used everywhere, by everybody . . . in immense quantities."[5] He was right, as the lager craze would dominate the alcohol market throughout Virginia and the nation. Richmond author Samuel Mordecai confirmed this in his 1856 publication, *Richmond in By-gone Days*. "Lager has raised its head," Mordecai noted, adding that it "has gone ahead of all beverages."[6]

Another reason for the decline in cider is that many farmers transitioned from growing apples mainly for cider production to planting the fruit for the emerging fresh eating market. These tasty varieties began to take hold throughout the country, and by 1872 Charles Downing's *The Fruits and Fruit Trees of America* listed more than 1,000 different kinds of apples that originated in America that could be used for purposes other than cider (dessert, fresh eating, applesauce, etc.).[7] Grafting would provide consumers access to thousands of apple varieties by the turn of the century. These varieties were published by the United States Department of Agriculture in the bulletin *Nomenclature of the Apple: A Catalogue of the Known Varieties Referred to in American Publications from 1804 to 1904.* The author and staff pomologist, W. H. Ragan, explained in the pamphlet that apples "spanned the seasons, offered a rainbow of colors and textures, included a vast array of flavors and aromas, and included apple varieties that could be used to cook, eat raw, store, and feed livestock."[8] The economic move to focus on fresh-eating apples along with industrialization, immigration, and urbanization were all contributing factors that led to the changes to America's cider culture.

The temperance movement and Prohibition have often been cited as the main reason for cider's demise in America, but cider consumption and production were already on the decline by that point. Many of the early opponents of alcohol consumption claimed that alcohol (especially hard liquor) was the cause of many of societies' evils, but these crusaders against the evils of fermented beverages often left cider and small beer out of the debate due to their lower alcohol content. But by the early twentieth century, prohibitionists claimed that all alcoholic beverages were bad for health and society. Some farmers who made cider embraced the temperance movement and swore off alcohol and cider production. Some even took axes to their orchards, destroying the cider-making apples and replacing them with fresh-eating apples. Other farmers switched from making (hard) cider to fresh nonalcoholic cider.[9]

The Eighteenth Amendment abolishing "the manufacture, transportation, and sale of alcoholic liquors except for medicinal and sacramental purposes" wasn't passed until 1919, but Virginia had gone dry before the federal legislation was pushed through.[10] The Virginia Anti-Saloon League and other groups in the Commonwealth vehemently protested the sale and production of alcoholic beverages. By September 1914, these groups persuaded state legislators to hold a referendum on Prohibition, and by March 10, 1916, they passed the Mapp Act, which made it illegal to manufacture, sell, or transport "ardent spirits" in the Old Dominion. The state went dry on November 1, 1916.[11]

The "Noble Experiment," as Prohibition was called, has a problematic legacy. Thousands died because of tainted homemade alcohol. Prohibition also turned otherwise law-abiding citizens into criminals, as large numbers of people continued to drink. It also allowed for gang and bootlegging activities to increase at an unprecedented level, and by the 1930s it was clear that Prohibition needed to be repealed.[12] In the midst of the Great Depression in 1933, under Franklin Roosevelt's leadership, the Twenty-first Amendment was passed, repealing the Eighteenth Amendment.

Prohibition affected cider in different ways than beer. Cider production was done mostly in homes and on farmsteads, while beer began to be mass produced outside the home in factories. But while breweries had seen success, there weren't any large commercial cideries in Virginia during the early twentieth century. Home Brewing Company in Richmond, Robert Portner Brewery in Alexandria, and James River Steam Brewery in Richmond had dominated the beverage landscape in Virginia before Prohibition. Many breweries altered their business plans during Prohibition and sold "near beer," made sodas or other nonalcoholic drinks, or closed. It was very difficult for alcohol producers to make a comeback after the "noble experiment," and by the late 1970s brewery operations had hit an all-time low in the United States. The number had gone from more than 4,000 in the nineteenth century to under 100 by 1979.[13] Virginia craft breweries didn't reemerge until the late 1980s and early 1990s. In Virginia, Legend Brewing Company, Richbrau Brewing Company, and Old Dominion Brewing Company paved the way for the future craft beer revolution that would take off in the twenty-first century. Today, there are more than two hundred breweries in the Commonwealth.

Virginia wine also had a rough road navigating Prohibition. The Monticello Wine Company established in Charlottesville in 1873 had grown to become the largest winery in the South, but it was forced to shut down in 1916 once Virginia voted "dry." Like the brewing industry in Virginia, it took a long time for Virginia wine to recover from Prohibition's effects as well. Barboursville Vineyards, located about fifteen miles northeast of Charlottesville, was established in 1970 and by 1976 Virginia had six wineries. The mid-1990s saw continued growth for Virginia wine as the state's number of wineries moved into the double digits and many were producing quality wine. The state had also started to devote more resources to the blossoming industry. Today there are more than 200 wineries in Virginia.[14]

These trends in wine and craft beer throughout the nation helped to pave the way for cider's reemergence and eventual revival. Before the turn of the century, cideries started to appear in specific apple-growing states like New York and Pennsylvania. Today there are nearly 1,000 cider producers in the United States.[15] New York and California lead the way with over one hundred, but Virginia is in the top seven with around fifty. As of 2020, Bold Rock, located in Nellysford, is second in retail sales behind Angry Orchard.[16] The cider business has grown from a handful of rural cideries in the 1990s to a robust industry featuring urban cideries and an array of business models. Three pioneers of the Virginia cider industry warrant singling out: Diane Flynt of Foggy Ridge, apple hunter Lee Calhoun, and "Professor Apple," Tom Burford.

The Trailblazer of Southern Cider: Diane Flynt

I chatted with entrepreneur Diane Flynt on the phone at the beginning of my cider journey, which made sense since many consider her to be the original torchbearer for the southern cider industry. Diane opened Foggy Ridge Cider in southwest Virginia in 1997, and it became the first licensed cidery in the South solely dedicated to making cider. Located in Dugspur, at an elevation of 3,000 feet on the Blue Ridge Plateau, Foggy Ridge is in a unique location. The high elevation allowed Diane to focus on different types of cider apples, like Harrison, Hewe's, and English cider apples like Dabinett and Tremlett's Bitter that may not grow as well in other parts of Virginia. Due to its elevation, Foggy Ridge is in the southernmost area for zone 5 planting and is thus similar to the upper Hudson River Valley. Flynt sold her first bottle of Foggy Ridge Cider in 2004 and quickly began distributing to more than twenty-five states. Her goal was to build a national brand, and she has accomplished that remarkably. Foggy Ridge ciders have received numerous awards, and Flynt has been nominated repeatedly for the James Beard Award for "Outstanding Beverage Professional"; she made the short list as a finalist in 2017 and 2018. Foggy Ridge was also listed as one of the top dry ciders by the *New York Times.* She did it all: drove the tractor, cleaned the tanks, pressed the apples, made the cider, and paved the way for Virginia and southern cider. In 2018, she retired the cidery after twenty years of operation, but has continued to maintain her orchard. Her focus is now on helping southern cider makers get the best ingredients for their product, and the orchard at Foggy Ridge is still one of the best around to find cider specific and heirloom apples. She has even published a book with UNC Press on southern apples.[17] Her expertise on heirloom apples and all things cider is endless and has earned her a place among apple royalty.

The Savior of Southern Apples: Lee Calhoun

It's not a coincidence that the members of Virginia's apple royalty were all close friends. Diane Flynt was greatly inspired by Lee Calhoun's publication *Old Southern Apples.* In the early 1990s, the apple hunter and historian traveled from his home in North Carolina to Flynt's farm to help select the best cider varieties for her orchard location. Creighton "Lee" Calhoun became interested in apples when he planted a small orchard of Red Delicious at his home site in Pittsboro, North Carolina. Once a neighbor piqued his interest about other southern apples, he went on an apple hunt to see what other kinds he could find.

He ventured on road trips throughout the South to see if he could discover any forgotten apple trees. If he spotted one near a house, he would knock on the property owner's door to see if they would let him cut off a small piece of scion wood and take it back to his home to graft it onto some rootstock. His first nursery catalog identified sixty apple trees on his property, and within five years, this number had grown to more than 300 varieties. His dedication to the craft has earned him the name the "Savior of Southern Apples." The former army lieutenant's passion for adventure saved the day just as many southern apples were threatened with disappearing forever. Commercial growers had switched to fresh eating apples, and homestead sites with orchards had been neglected. Calhoun made it his mission to hunt for apples that had been abandoned and bring them back to life. He passed away in 2018, but his work on southern apples has been preserved through the University of North Carolina Southern Oral History Program. His papers are also held at the University of North Carolina, and his seminal 1995 book, *Old Southern Apples,* continues to serve among the greatest apple resources available. It features more than 1,800 apples of either southern or heirloom varieties. Lee's vast orchard is now maintained by Horne Creek Living Historical Farm, an operation within North Carolina's Division of State Historic Sites and Properties.[18]

Professor Apple: Tom Burford

Tom Burford, who passed away in 2020, dedicated his life to evangelizing heirloom apples and cider. Known to many as "Professor Apple," Burford came from a long line of apple growers in Amherst County, Virginia, and with his brother established the Burford Brothers Nursery. Part of their focus was on rare southern apples. His expertise in all-things-apple led to the publication of two excellent resources for any enthusiast: *Apples: A Catalog of Interna-*

tional Varieties and *Apples of North America: Exceptional Varieties for Gardeners, Growers, and Cooks.* During the course of his career, Burford consulted with a variety of cider makers and growers throughout the South and held numerous workshops on grafting and orchard techniques. With Monticello's Director of Gardens and Grounds Peter Hatch, he also held annual apple tastings at Jefferson's estate, where they would discuss the varieties of apples grown there. "For fifty years I painfully watched the disappearance of the apple culture and the emergence of so-called beautiful apples," he wrote in *Apples of North America.* Due to his efforts, along with those of others like Diane and Lee, Virginia apple culture and cider history has been saved from extinction. His family's legacy lives on in many ways, and especially so in a cider apple called Burford Redflesh. This attractive apple is white-fleshed and speckled with red, and it makes a tasty cider exhibiting a slight red tint.[19]

CHAPTER 4

(Almost) All about Apples

Virginia is fortunate to have varying topographical features ranging from the coastal region to the piedmont to the mountains and valley. Each area produces different tasting apples based on its unique soil and climate, and a rich variety of cider tasting notes are the result. The wine world refers to this as terroir, but it is important to understand that terroir affects the flavor and complexity of cider just as well. This French term denotes the makeup or conditions of the area where the fruit is grown—that is, the soil, climate, and any other natural features of a particular orchard or vineyard.[1] The majority of apples in Virginia are grown in the Blue Ridge Mountains and Shenandoah Valley, but apple trees are found throughout the state. Many orchards thrived in the sandy soil and bay climate of the Northern Neck plantations in the eighteenth and nineteenth centuries. Although it is not an area full of apple trees today, they were quite plentiful in colonial times, and the terroir led to unique apple growth and cider characteristics. Despite the differences in Virginia's diverse regions, one attribute representative of most Virginia apples (like other higher temperature areas) is that they tend to be high in sugar. This elevated sugar level can lead to a product with a higher alcohol by volume (ABV), and some Virginia ciders easily exceed 8 percent ABV when fermented. The soil in each location varies from the lime deposits present in the fertile upper Shenandoah Valley to the coastal region of Eastern Virginia, which is covered by red clay and residual river deposits, while elements of gravel and silt are evident in the mountain region of Appalachia.[2] The hills and valleys in the western part of Virginia (or the Valley and Ridge) are affected by diurnal shift and this can lead to more acidic apples that can alter the taste of a cider. This higher elevation also lends itself to a wider range of temperature between the evening and daytime.[3] As a result of the diverse weather and topography that Virginia has to offer, cider apples from the Old Dominion are some of the most unique and complex.

According to the Virginia Cider Association, "There are over 30 different apple varieties grown specifically for cider production throughout Virginia." I have provided a list of some of the most common apples used for making cider in Virginia. This is not a comprehensive list of all the apples (or cider apples) grown in Virginia, but it covers the primary apples (and my favorites) used for cider production throughout the Old Dominion. Some of these apples are European apples like Dabinett and Ashmead's Kernel, some are New World fruit like Harrison, and some are specific to the mid-Atlantic region like Hewe's Crab.[4] Some are specifically used for cider-making and others are multipurpose apples (fresh eating, cider, dessert, etc.) Each apple produces a unique cider whether the juice is blended with other varieties or used to produce a single varietal beverage, and it is up to the cider maker to make this selection based on each cider's characteristics.[5]

ARKANSAS BLACK

This variety is used at several different cideries as both a single varietal and within a blend. Possibly a seedling of Winesap, this dark red apple (which appears almost black when fully ripe) was first grown in Arkansas in the late nineteenth century. It is a highly acidic apple that produces a full-bodied fruity cider with aromas of lime zest and flavors of pears and peaches.

ASHMEAD'S KERNEL

This muted greenish yellow eighteenth-century English dessert apple is medium sized. It is excellent for both fresh eating and cider due to its sweet, sharp flavor. Some ciders made from this lovely apple can showcase lime and grapefruit zest as well as herbal notes. I have found Virginia varieties to exhibit exceptional levels of tartness.

BLACK TWIG

Black Twig was Lee Calhoun's favorite apple, and it is one of mine as well. Discovered in Tennessee in the early nineteenth century, it was also beloved by President Andrew Jackson and is the state apple for Tennessee. Sometimes called the "greasy apple" because of the waxy film it takes on in storage, this apple makes an exquisite complex single varietal that can express notes of citrus, spices, and earthiness.

BURFORD REDFLESH

Claimed to be descended from the Red Siberian Crab, it was grown and marketed by Burford Brothers Nursery starting in the 1970s. It is still available through commercial nurseries and pays homage to the apple connoisseur himself, Tom Burford. One of the oldest Burford Redflesh trees was found at the property of Patrick Henry's mother, Sarah Henry, in the Piedmont region of Virginia. The apple's interior flesh is strawberry color, with a tart taste that adds depth to cider.[6]

DABINETT

Dabinett is a nineteenth-century English cider apple from Jersey. I had a fresh one once, and it is truly a spitter due to the high tannins. But it is among my preferred English cider apples, as it creates a unique cider with medicinal properties and aromas of orange peels. The taste provides enough perceived sweetness and astringency to stand up to most foods. I was fortunate to attend a special tasting of Dabinetts at Blue Bee Cider during CiderCon 2022. We tasted six different single varietal and blends from throughout the world that featured this special apple. It was a once-in-a-lifetime experience that shows how different areas of the country and world can produce distinct ciders from the same apple based solely on varying terroir and fermentation methods.[7]

ESOPUS SPITZENBURG (SPITZENBERG)

Discovered in the late eighteenth century, this apple comes from Esopus, New York. It became one of Jefferson's main dessert apples, but does better at higher elevations.[8] Peter Hatch describes the apple as "easily identified by its vivid, orangish-red skin. Biting into a Spitz produces an explosion of flavors. The yellow flesh is crisp, firm, spicy, and juicy with an extremely rich, aromatic flavor: the ultimate gourmet apple."[9] One of my favorite fresh eating apples, this tasty variety creates a cider full of peach and mango flavors, followed by a great finish. It is coveted for the spicy aromatic character of its cider.

GOLDEN RUSSET

This medium sized American apple with russet skin, like a potato, is one of the greatest cider apples of all time, but its origins are a little murky. Loaded with sugar, it creates a rich cider with an excellent body and tastes of pear and apricot and even floral notes with tartness. It covers all of the great qualities of a cider: aroma, taste, and finish. Some examples present flavors reminiscent of a lemon tart dessert.

GOLD RUSH

This variety was released in the early 1990s by Purdue University in collaboration with Rutgers and the University of Illinois (otherwise known as the PRI Disease Resistant

Apple Breeding Program). The apple is named for the glistening sun-kissed golden hue on the skin and the flavor rush from the sugar and acidity. (Golden Delicious is the parent of this popular varietal.) Even though this is a more recent creation, they are ideal cider apples and can produce ciders that display tropical and citrus flavors and a high potential ABV due to sugar content. Some single varietals can exhibit notes of peaches and ginger.[10]

GRIMES GOLDEN

This cultivar was planted from a seedling in nineteenth-century Virginia (now Wellsburg, West Virginia, not far from where the apple titan Johnny Chapman [a.k.a Appleseed] pressed juice). By the end of the nineteenth century, the apple was very popular and could be found throughout most nurseries in the South. A truly all-purpose apple, Grimes Golden cider can taste of vibrant stone fruits with hints of caramel and big green apple flavors.[11]

HARRISON

Harrison is among the most admired cider apples in the United States; it likely hails from Essex County, New Jersey. President Thomas Jefferson received shipments of "Newark cider" (which included a blend of Harrison and Canfield apples) from Representative (and later Senator) John Condit. Harrison was also often blended with juice from Graniwinkle apples.[12] It makes for a beautifully colored single varietal cider with sturdy tannins and a little earthiness. William Coxe stated that Harrison was the most prized and expensive apple cultivar available in the New York market in the early nineteenth century. It was thought to be lost, but apple hunters have brought it back, and it is now thriving again. According to Tom Burford, "The juice from Harrison apples makes an extremely dark, rich cider with an exceptional mouth-feel." He also believed that Harrison is not only tasty but also economical

APPLE CLASSIFICATION FOR CIDER PURPOSES

As one of the trailblazers for cider, England has created a taxonomy system for cider apples. The Long Ashton Research Station (LARS) created the English Cider Classification System in the early twentieth century. It groups apples into four general categories based on tannins and acids, the two greatest components for cider production. Tannins, which are in the flesh of the apple (not the skins like grapes), provide depth, mouthfeel, and complexity, while acids provide the twang and bite to the beverage. The balance of these two elements is essential. Bittersweet (high tannin, low acid) and bittersharp (high tannin, high acid) are two of the categories, and these represent the more traditional cider apples that are loaded with tannins. These bitter apples may have fewer uses for fresh eating and cooking due to the higher tannins, and they are known as "spitters" due to their overly bitter taste. (One example of a spitter is the English cider apple, Dabinett. Chuck Shelton

as he has "measured the volume as approximately 18 percent greater than Winesap."[13]

HEWE'S CRAB (HUGHES'S, RED HUGHES, VIRGINIA CRAB) This small light red apple with green specks and a translucent yellow flesh with a strong musky flavor is the most prized cider apple in the South and arguably the most notable American cider apple. Its origins are unknown, but it is likely a cross between a *Malus domestica* from Europe

gave me a Dabinett from Glaize Apples while touring Albemarle CiderWorks, and I took a bite and promptly spit it out.) The last two categories are sharp (low tannin, high acid) and sweet (low tannin, low acid). Apples in these categories lack in-depth tannins but can provide a good base for cider or offer a balance between some of the intensity from bittersharps and bitterweets and the mildness of sweets and sharps. Cider can be made with any apple, but in order to produce a complex cider you must have a good equilibrium of the two main components. Some apples (like Hewe's Crab and Harrison), however, have enough acid and tannin to create a beautiful single varietal on its own.

Sources: Cavallo and Pucci, *American Cider,* 16–17.

and a native crab apple, *Malus angustifolia.*[14] Even though it is unclear of its exact beginnings, Hewe's was mentioned in newspaper advertisements in Williamsburg as early as the mid-eighteenth century.[15] According to Lee Calhoun, "This is the most celebrated cider apple ever grown in the South, making a dry cider unsurpassed in flavor and keeping ability. Trees nearly a hundred years old were found in Virginia by [noted pomologist William] Coxe in 1817."[16] Jefferson, Washington, and other prominent Virginians praised the apple for its cider making characteristics.[17] John Hartwell Cocke, planter, friend of Jefferson, and founder of the University of Virginia, said that Hewe's Crab is "the best cider I have ever seen."[18] The apple was so widespread that northern newspapers even advertised it for sale in the late eighteenth century: The Pennsylvania Gazette on April 7, 1768 published an advertisement: "To be Sold by Ritchie and Clymer, Hughs's Crab Cyder, imported from Virginia, fit for immediate Use, at 35s per Barrel."[19]

The apple makes a very fragrant cider with tropical flavors and possible cinnamon, banana, and pear notes. As a single varietal, it is full-bodied and comparable to some complex white wines with adequate tannins and acidity. The liquid is usually a darker muted yellow. In 2019 Albemarle CiderWorks hosted a Hewe's Crab blind tasting event that featured Albemarle CiderWorks, Big Fish Cider, Blue Bee Cider, Potter's Craft Cider, Sage Bird Ciderworks, and Troddenvale at Oakley Farm. It was a lovely event that featured some of the best single varietals in the state and showed how diverse the aromas and tastes from this prized apple can be. Sage Bird was the winner of that competition, but all of the examples were fantastic. Albemarle CiderWorks 2019 Hewes Virginia Crab went on to win the Governor's Cup Best in Show Cider Award.[20]

HONEYCRISP

Developed in Minnesota in the mid-twentieth century, the Honeycrisp has become one of the most common eating apples in the United States. It has a nice crispness, juicy flesh, and pleasing aroma. Some cideries have explored this as a base for their juice in order to provide a clean apple-forward component to blends.

IDA RED

Another early to mid-twentieth century apple from the Midwest, this multicolored Idaho apple became known for pies, apple sauce, apple butter, and fresh eating, but cider makers have embraced it as a good blending apple. Ida Red ciders can be very fruit forward and slightly acidic. This forms a good balance with the more tannic apples in blends.

JONAGOLD

This hybrid of Jonathan and Golden Delicious creates a delicate but fragrant cider. It was created in the mid-twentieth century by the New York State Agricultural Equipment Station in Geneva, New York. This large fruit with a muted aroma is typically yellow with an orangish-red tint. The cider can present flavors of melon.

KINGSTON BLACK

A traditional cider apple from early nineteenth-century England, this bittersharp apple makes an iconic single varietal cider, but it can also be difficult to grow in parts of the United States. It boasts an excellent acidity, making it tart and tangy, and it has been labeled by many as the "King of Cider" apples.

NEWTOWN PIPPIN/ALBEMARLE PIPPIN

The first commercially successfully apple in North America was discovered in New York along Newtown Creek in 1730, and by the mid-eighteenth century, the Newtown Pippin had spread throughout the colonies.[21] During the Revolutionary War, Dr. Thomas Walker brought scions of the apple tree from the Northeast and planted them at his estate at Castle Hill in Charlottesville (now Keswick).[22] Jefferson also acquired a cutting and started to grow them at Monticello. The Virginia climate transformed this apple cultivar to take on tropical flavors, most notably lime. Jefferson was a huge fan of this citrusy green apple that improved with storage and when comparing the Newtown/Albemarle Pippin to European apples while in France, he claimed, "They [the French] have no apples here to compare with our Newtown pippin."[23] The English agriculturist, Richard Parkinson, in 1799 said that the Newtown Pippin was the New World's "best apple."[24] After Queen Victoria received several barrels of Albemarle Pippins from statesman and US ambassador to England Andrew Stevenson in 1837, she enjoyed them so much that she removed the small crown import tax, so that they could be shipped directly to England without taxation.[25] According to Tom Burford, "Cider made from the fruit is very clear and considered to be of the finest quality." He even referred to it as "Sunday cider."[26] This apple makes a wonderful single varietal that exhibits flavors and aromas of green apples, grapes, citrus and a rich flavor.

NORTHERN SPY

Found in the area of Ontario County, New York, in the early nineteenth century—but believed to have come from seeds/pomace taken from Connecticut—this large apple can do well in the Blue Ridge and Appalachian Mountains. Northern Spy is a very popular blending cider apple and baking apple. The historic apple can make a beverage that is mineral-driven with floral aromas and tastes of ripe yellow and green apples and stone fruits.

POMME GRIS

This is one of my favorite eating apples. It was rated very high at the 2022 Monticello Apple and Cheese Tasting Event. I ranked this delicious French apple (which most likely migrated to Canada from Europe and then south into the United States) as one of my top picks alongside the Ralls Genet and Albemarle Pippin. It is very aromatic and has a beautiful nutty flavor, which can make for a great blending apple for ciders. I understand why Jefferson grew this fruity treat as a dessert apple.[27]

RALLS GENET (RALLS)

This storied southern cider apple originated in the Piedmont region of Virginia in the late eighteenth century. Some historians claim that Edmund Charles Genet, the French minister to the United States, gave Jefferson several scions, and Jefferson in turn donated some to Caleb Ralls's farm in Amherst County. The resulting variety became known as the "Ralls Genet."[28] Tom Burford disagreed with the Genet claim, focusing his attention on the more modern development that it "was imported by the Japanese to establish an apple-breeding program at the Tohoku Research Station in Aomori, Japan," which led in the late 1930s to a cross of Ralls and Red Delicious there bearing the iconic Fuji.[29] If one accepts the Genet claim, however, that implies that Jefferson, lover of historic heirloom apples, inadvertently helped to form one of the most popular modern apples. Ralls Genet is truly a multipurpose apple that can be used for dessert, apple butter, cider, or apple pies, and it tastes great off the tree.

STAYMAN

Sometimes referred to as Stayman Winesap—though Burford argued that it is an entirely new variety and should not be classified as a Winesap—the Stayman was discovered in the late nineteenth century by Joseph Stayman in Kansas and quickly began to be sold at several nurseries. It became very popular in the Southeast because it is easy to grow and relatively disease resistant. It is known as an excellent dessert apple and blending cider apple that can add a good balance of tannins and acidity while providing flavors of honeyed berries.[30]

WICKSON CRAB

The Wickson Crab was created in California in the mid-twentieth century as a cross between Spitzenburg and Newtown Pippin. The creator of this sweet-tasting apple,

TALIAFERRO: THE GREATEST AMERICAN CIDER APPLE THAT EVER WAS

This is probably the most storied apple in the United States but unfortunately has been extinct for several years. It was discovered in the eighteenth century by Major Richard Taliaferro of Williamsburg in the field of his neighbor, Mr. Robertson (Robinson), so the Taliaferro apple is sometimes referred to as Robinson or Robertson. Jefferson mentions the fruit several times in correspondence and explains that it is the best apple to produce cider and that the beverage rivals European fine wines. Jefferson planted it throughout his south orchard. His first planting was in 1778, with "96 Robinson apples from Major Taliaferro. Grafted." And in a letter to his granddaughter, (with an enclosed cutting of scion wood) Jefferson included this note, "They are called the 'Taliaferro' apple, being from a seedling tree, discovered by a gentleman of that name near Williamsburg, and yield unquestionably the finest cyder we have ever known, and more like wine than any liquor I have ever tasted which was not wine."

Although the apple is thought to be missing, there have been several claims to the mysterious apple's rediscovery. In *Apples: The Story of the Fruit of Temptation,* author Frank Browning tracks down where he believes the long-lost apple is hiding. Browning became

interested in the apple when Burford told him that there was a hillside farm in Highland County belonging to a man named Conley Colaw where an apple matching the description of the Taliaferro still grew. And at the time (1994), Burford thought it likely that Colaw's apples were in fact the legendary apple. Browning arrived at Colaw's farm too late for the current year's crop, but Colaw poured Browning some cider that was made from that year's yield, which he called "the richest, fullest-bodied farm cider I'd ever tasted, nearly dry. It had a finish almost like fine sherry but full of apples." It's nearly impossible to determine if this cider was made from the long-lost apple, because the descriptions of the apple are very vague. One of the only descriptions that we have comes from Boston pomologist William Kenrick in 1835: "The fruit is the size of a grape shot, or from one to two inches in diameter; of a white color, streaked with red; with a sprightly acid, not good for the table, but apparently a very valuable cider fruit. This is understood to be a Virginia fruit, and the apple from which Mr. Jefferson's favorite cider was made."

In 1814, Jefferson and Philadelphia horticulturalist James Mease corresponded concerning the apple's history. Jefferson discussed his knowledge of the history

(*continues on next page*)

of the Virginia apple and attested to the superiority of Taliaferro to Hewe's in a letter from June 29. 1814:

> It is not a crab but a seedling which grew along in a large old field near Williamsburg where the seed had probably been dropped by some bird. Major Taliaferro of that neighborhood remaking it once to be very full of apples got permission from the owner of the ground to gather them. From these he made a cask of cyder which, in the estimation of every one who tasted it was the finest they had ever seen. He grafter an orchard from it, as did also his son in law our late Chancellor Wythe. The cyder they constantly made from this was preferred by every person to the Crab or any other cyder ever known is this state, and it still retains its character in the different places to which it has been transferred. I am familiar with it, and have not hesitation in pronouncing it much superior to the Hughe's crab. It has more body, is less acid, and comes nearer to the silky Champaigne than any other. Major Taliaferro called it the Robertson apple form the name of the person owning the parent tree, but subsequently it has more justly and generally been distinguished by the name of the Taliaferro apple, after him to whom we are indebted for the

Albert Etter, named it after his esteemed colleague E. J. Wickson. The small apple is loaded with sugar, which makes it a perfect subject for the cider maker. I love ciders made from Wickson Crab. They are usually lively, slightly tart, and exhibit lemon, grapefruit, and pear notes.[31]

WINESAP

Although its place of origin has never been definitively established, it likely dates to the early 1700s in New Jersey. This small- to medium-sized apple makes for a perfect

> discovery of it's valuable properties. It is the most juicy apple I have ever known, & is refreshing as an eating apple.

Despite the disappointment that one of the best American cider apples is lost, there is still hope, and the search for the mystery apple continues, so stay tuned to see if Virginia growers and cider makers can discover this hidden gem.

Sources: Hatch, *Fruits and Fruit Trees,* 75, 222; *Thomas Jefferson's Garden Book,* 618; Browning, *Apples,* 199; James Mease to Thomas Jeffesron, May 24, 1814, *Founders Online,* National Archives, https://founders.archives.gov/documents/Jefferson/03-07-02-0288 [Original source: *The Papers of Thomas Jefferson,* Retirement Series, vol. 7, *28 November 1813 to 30 September 1814,* ed. J. Jefferson Looney (Princeton: Princeton University Press, 2010), 381–82]. The most important research in recent years, however, is in a hitherto unpublished manuscript by Susan Russ Walker, "Of Lost Letters and Forgotten Fruit: Timothy Pickering, John Taliaferro, and the Mystery Apple of Monticello." Much of that research is reproduced in Hatch, "Malus pumila—'Taliaferro Apple'," Thomas Jefferson's Monticello, https://www.monticello.org/research-education/thomas-jefferson-encyclopedia/malus-pumila-taliaferro/.

snack. The first part of its name, "Wine," suggests that it carries vinous characteristics, which is confirmed by the great apple historian William Coxe Jr., who described it as "the choicest cider fruit." Apple and plum notes can dominate this cider's characteristics along with some citrus flavors and spices, leaving a pleasing lingering mouthfeel.[32]

YARLINGTON MILL

Discovered in Somerset England in the late nineteenth century, this medium sized red apple fits into the sweet

SILVER CREEK AND SEAMANS' ORCHARD

Adam Cooke is in the business of apples. He married into the Silver Creek apple family and hasn't looked back. They have been operating as a commercial orchard since the 1950s, and most of their production has been dedicated to commercial apples like Red and Golden Delicious, and Fuji and Gala, but he reserves about 10 percent of the acreage specifically for cider apples. According to Adam, around ten years ago Diane Flynt and Tom Burford told the growers that they needed to work with cider apples, because this would be the next big thing. They were right. For the past seven years, he's listened to cider makers in the state, and worked with them to grow and maintain cider apples. A significant part of Silver Creek's business is pressing juice for cider makers. Most of the businesses are in-state (about 80 percent), but he also presses juice for several cideries in other southern states too (like South Carolina and Tennessee). They press most of the juice for the cider makers, but businesses like Tumbling Creek Cider Company and Albemarle CiderWorks get their apples sent to them and press them themselves. Adam says that some of the cider makers want organic

to bittersweet cider category. The coveted beverage made from Yarlington Mill is typically a beautiful rich color with hefty layers and complexity. This is not for the faint of heart, it is a chewy cider that pairs great with food. It is one of my favorite cider apples.[33]

cider apples, but it's difficult to do that because they have their cider apples mixed in with the commercial apples. Nonetheless, he says the transition to grow more specific cider apples has worked, and he is impressed with new innovations in orchard management, like sprays coming out of Virginia Tech that allow for minimal carbon footprints. He believes that the future of growing cider apples depends on the cider market. If there is more of a demand for cider apples, then he will increase his number. There's about a five-year window from growing an apple tree to time of fruit yield. Silver Creek and Seamans' aren't the only growers who have taken notice of this trend; there are several other growers who have also taken on the challenge. See the list of apple growers throughout the state below. Descriptions on two of the other major growers dedicated to cider apples are contained in their respective cidery writeups; Glaize Apples is covered in Old Town Cidery and Fruit Hill Orchard is included in Winchester Ciderworks.

Source: Phone interview with Adam Cooke, February 24, 2021.

YORK

Found in York, Pennsylvania, in the early 1800s, this hearty, often lopsided, dessert apple began to be sold commercially by the mid-nineteenth century and spread throughout the mid-Atlantic and the South. Most York ciders display a slight acidity, mild fruitiness, and very soft tannins.[34]

OTHER APPLES USED BY VIRGINIA CIDERIES

Virginia cider makers are innovative and experiment with different apple varieties all the time. Working with growers in their native state and beyond, Virginia cideries strive to bring the best quality products to their consumers by using the best apples available. In addition to those listed above, the following are also currently used in Virginia ciders: Ben Davis, Blue Pearmain, White Winterpearmain, Dolgo Crab apple, Zabergau Reinette, Somerset Redstreak, Coxe's Orange Pippin, Golden Hornet Crab apple, Ribston Pippin, Mutsu, Virginia Gold, King David, Rhode Island Greening, Golden Delicious, Red Delicious, Granny Smith, Magnum Bonum, Parmar, Red Limbertwig, Black Limbertwig, Redfield, Yates, Empire, Ginger Gold, Rambo, Wagener, Roxbury Russet, Pink Lady, Gala, Fuji, Sops of Wine, Geneva Crab, Winter John, and McIntosh.

Growers

Virginia is the sixth-largest apple grower in the nation, but most apples are not grown for cider making but for fresh eating.[35] Despite this, several Virginia growers have seen the benefits of focusing areas of their orchards on specific cider apples.

With more than ninety apple growers in the state of Virginia, we cannot cover them all here. The Virginia Apple Board, however, maintains a list and a map of most of the apple growers on their website.[36]

Among the most notable of Virginia apple growers are the following: Henley's Orchard (Crozet), Cootes Store Farms (Broadway), Chiles Peach Orchard (Crozet), Carter Mountain Orchard (Charlottesville), Countryside Farm and Nurseries (Crimora), Hollin Farms (Delaplane), Morris Orchard (Monroe), Crooked Run Orchard (Purcellville),

Stribling Orchard (Markham), Dickie Brothers Orchard (Roseland), Johnson's Orchards (Bedford), Cullipher Farm (Virginia Beach), Drumheller's Orchard (Lovingston), Great Country Farms (Bluemont), Hartland Orchard (Markham), Mackintosh Fruit Farm (Berryville), Marker-Miller Orchards (Winchester), Graves Mountain Farm & Lodges (Syria), Williams Orchard (Flint Hill), Showalter's Orchard (Timberville), Valley View Farm (Delaplane), Turkey Knob Growers (Timberville), Wood's Orchards (Hampton), Paugh's Orchard (Quicksburg), Glaize Apples (Winchester), Fruit Hill Orchard (Palmyra), and Vintage Virginia Apples (North Garden).

CHAPTER 5

Making It, Tasting It, and Exploring Styles

Cider Making Process

Cider is not brewed, and cider makers are not brewers. The fermentation process of wine and cider are somewhat similar, but they are both different than brewing. These do not need water, heat, or hops although some ciders are hopped for added flavor. All-grain brewing needs hot water for mashing (that is, soaking the grains) to extract the fermentable sugars from the grain. The wort (the liquid that is collected from mashing) is then heated and hops are added to provide flavor. The liquid is cooled, and then yeast is added.

Even though wine and cider production are different than brewing, and they both involve the fermentation of fruit (the conversion of the fruit's sugars into alcohol), the exact fermentation science between the two varies because grapes have more sugar than apples and they get their tannins from the skins of the grapes rather than the flesh of the fruit like apples.[1] Some fermentation and storing methods may also vary between the two. Despite the differences among these beverages, there is one factor that is the same for all these products—you need to start with the finest ingredients. And the best ingredients for cider making begins with finding the best apples.

Harvesting

Harvesting apples can be done by hand or with a machine. It is best to gather apples when the fruit is fully tree ripe. There are a couple ways to test the ripeness of the fruit to see if it's ready to be harvested: (1) Check if the stem easily comes off the branch or (2) wait until some of the apples start to fall. Skin color is not an indicator of apple ripeness, because the sun will affect the skin differently. Cutting open the fruit is also an option. Seeds that are dark brown are good, but a greenish-tan seed means unripe.[2] And of course, taste is also an indicator of readiness. Cider makers (and growers) continuously taste apples to see when the peak time is for selection. An educated cider maker can tell based on taste how well the starches have turned into sugar. While the collection of windfall apples (apples that have recently dropped from the tree) for fresh eating purposes are avoided, they are sometimes preferred in cider making because they enhance ripeness while being protected from potential biological invaders through the subsequent fermentation process; still you don't want to use apples that have been on the ground for a long period of time. Fruit lying on the ground can pick up unwelcome elements from the ground, animals, and fertilizer or other chemicals, which can affect the flavors.[3]

Cider makers are not looking for picture-perfect supermarket apples. This is a big difference between commercial fresh eating apples and cider apples, because ugly apples work great for fermentation. Heritage cider apples (or historic apples) can be particularly unattractive, as they can be small, irregular, and covered with various blemishes. Blotches and scars are fine, and small apples make superb cider, because they offer more concentrated sugars. But badly bruised or cut apples or brown apples are not adequate, so the fruit must be sorted to ensure that no damaged apples are used.[4] Some of the damage can be cut out;

early colonists made notes of how they used blemished apples but made sure to cut out any rot (brown spots) or bruises. Most of the harvesting is completed by hand and apples are picked as early as July and as late as the first snow, depending on the region.

Once the apples are picked and sorted, some cider makers prefer to let their bounty sit before they press them. This is called sweating (or softening), which helps with the

Patrick Collins of Patois Cider foraging at an abandoned orchard. (Patois Cider)

Will Hodges of Troddenvale at Oakley Farm harvesting their first substantial crop of Virginia Hewe's Crab. (Troddenvale at Oakley Farm)

conversion of sugar. Whether sweated or not, the most important thing is that the fruit is indeed ripe, as this will ensure that all the starches are turned into sugar and those sugars can be converted to alcohol.[5]

Milling

After the apples have been harvested, sorted, and washed to ensure removal of all unnecessary bacteria, they are now ready to be milled. In order to extract the juice, the apples must be cut or chopped. (This is another difference between wine and cider making, as apples must be ground.) Traditionally this was done by a mill stone pulled by horses or a mule, but today the fruit is chopped up with machinery.[6] The milling device, whether it is an automatic chopper or a hand-cranked crusher, will chop and crush the apple, seeds, and stems all together and create a mushy paste known as pomace.

Pressing

The next step is to separate the juice from the pulp. The cider maker presses the liquid out of the pomace. Sometimes they will let the mixture sit for up to forty-eight hours, which is known as maceration. This allows solids

Zach Carlson of Sage Bird Ciderworks operating their antique apple grinder and press. (Sage Bird Ciderworks)

to fall to the bottom of the container through the work of gravity, creates a brighter colored cider by letting the pomace oxidize, and yields more intense flavors and aromas while also reducing tannins. Pressing was traditionally done with a wooden press that used horsehair or straw between the pomace to allow it to drain better from the press once the liquid was extracted.[7]

Today, a hydraulic press or bladder press are used. The hydraulic press works by spreading the pomace over several layers of nylon or other material and then a screw mechanism forces a weighted plate to press and push the pomace down. This increases the pressure on the different levels and pushes out liquid from the pomace.[8] Smaller cider operations often use a bladder press, which is less expensive, not as cumbersome and complex, and works by expanding a bladder from tap water. The bladder mechanism presses the juice in a much shorter time; juice can be extracted in under ten minutes depending on the size of the batch. After the liquid is separated from the pulp, the next step is fermentation. The juice is sometimes filtered before fermentation, and the leftover pomace can be used to feed farm animals.[9]

Fermentation

This is where the magic happens. Fermentation is the process of converting sugars into alcohol, and the alcohol potential for cider is determined by the amount of sugar in the apples. Fermentation begins by either adding yeast or allowing the juice to use natural yeasts to ferment. Natural yeasts can be found in the flesh of the apple, the skin of the apple, the cider barn (building), the equipment, and many other locations. A commercial yeast allows for a more controlled fermentation. Many cider makers prefer to use Champagne yeast for their commercial yeast, but almost any yeast can be used like another white wine yeast, a wild yeast or even a Belgian or British ale yeast. Along with alcohol (ethanol), CO_2 is another byproduct during fermentation, and therefore many ciders have at least a slight sparkling effervescence to them. Fermentation is really a two-step process. "Primary fermentation" is the first step where the yeast are very active converting the sugars to alcohol and giving off large amounts of CO_2. Either an airlock is placed on the vessel or the lid is left open, thus controlling the amount of carbonation. After the first step is complete, and once the yeast is less active, the liquid will be transferred to another vessel for "secondary fermentation," which allows the partially fermented liquid

Zach Carlson checking the stainless-steel fermentation tanks at Sage Bird Ciderworks. (Sage Bird Ciderworks)

to continue to ferment in a clean vessel until the desired "dryness" is achieved. Once fermentation is complete, the cider, no longer juice, is racked to a new vessel, where it is "fined" or further clarified. Certain chemicals like bentonite can help clarify the cider. Now the cider is ready for aging in either a barrel, bottle, or keg. Most of the aromas you get from a cider come from the juice, but some can also be present from the yeast as well. The fermentation of cider does best between 59 and 68 °F.[10]

Fermentation Vessels

Glass and plastic carboys, wooden barrels, and stainless-steel tanks can all be used for fermentation. (All equipment should be cleaned and sanitized, and an airlock may be attached to the top of the vessel.) Most ciders will achieve fermentation in less than three months, but some can last up to a year to convert all the sugars. (Wild yeast and natural fermentations may take up to a year.) The length of time is also left up to the cider makers; some choose to stop the process before all the sugars have been turned into alcohol. This will leave what is called residual sugar and can create a sweeter product.[11]

Blending and Maturation

Once the sugars have finished converting into alcohol, then the fermented juice (now called cider) is moved into a clean container, so the cider can mature and develop. (You can tell when fermentation is complete by checking the activity on the airlock or with a scientific measurement device that measures pH conversion.)

Most ciders are blended, but there are also single varietal ciders where only one type of apple is used. Cider makers will choose to make a single varietal if the apple has all the components (tannins, acidity, and sugars) to make a well-balanced beverage, but most are blended.

Blending allows the cider maker to use their creativity to produce a tasty product from using several apples for different flavor characteristics. It is more likely for cider makers to blend the cider after fermentation, but some mix their juice before fermentation. (Additional fruit, hops, spices, and other adjuncts would most likely be added after fermentation.)

Once fermentation is complete, the cider may be further filtered to remove pectin (a natural substance that is found in the cells of many fruits like apples), yeast, and any other sediment. Filtering and refining will ensure a clearer product. Some ciders are cloudy because they lack filtration or were not clarified with pectic enzyme and bentonite during its fermentation—or it could be from the type of juice.

Resting is important to allow the cider to mature, and it can occur in either the fermenting or storage vessel or in the bottle. Some ciders made with very rich tannic apples benefit from a longer maturation to round out the tannins, while more acidic ciders need not rest as long. During maturation, especially in oak barrels, ciders can take on more aromas and flavors from the vessel and/or the previous beverage held in the vessel and possibly a higher ABV.[12]

Carbonation

There will be some level of carbonation to the beverage due to fermentation, as CO_2 is a natural byproduct of the process. Cider makers can also add more CO_2 by using a machine to force CO_2 into the bottle or vessel to ensure carbonation, or they may choose to produce a still product by releasing carbonation. Force-carbonated ciders will lose their bubbles over time, while the Champagne method—that is, initiating a secondary fermentation after bottling—will allow ciders to continue to develop bubbles over time.[13]

Bottles, Kegs, and Cans (Packaging)

There is also much discussion over the proper vessel for cider. Customarily, the beverage was either drunk from a tapped barrel or a bottle. Today most cideries either bottle their products in 750-mL, 22-oz, or 12-oz bottles or can it in 12-oz or 16-oz servings. Since I started my research, I have seen more and more cans enter the market. The 750-mL bottles tend to be the more traditional approach, and some cider makers view this standard-size wine bottle as delivering a Higher Perceived Value (HPV) than a can or normal beer bottle. Most bottled products are capped, but some are corked. Labeling designs vary from cidery to cidery and product to product. Some labels (Troddenvale and Patois) will even signify the specific orchard where the apples were grown and the growing conditions for that year or vintage, like wine labels. There is also a continuing trend to get your cider filled in a growler (64-oz or 32-oz glass jug) or crowler (32-oz can) from the tap system at a cidery or bar.

Cider Styles

Ciders can range from a dry but rich single varietal Dabinett with a smooth finish to a tangy natural fermented blend of crab apples with an acidity that endlessly dances around your taste buds to a habanero cider aged in whisky barrels that will set your mouth on fire with lingering notes of vanilla and oak. Cider styles are a bit like the Wild West for the US market.

Within the United States, and especially Virginia, cider styles can be broken down into three broad categories: non-flavored ciders, flavored ciders, and perry.[14]

Non-flavored ciders can range from fully fermented bone-dry ciders that use a single varietal heirloom fruit to a blend of apples that are not fermented all the way out and leave some residual sugar. Non-flavored cider may

HOME CIDER MAKING

I have a confession to make: I loved beer long before developing a taste for cider and wine. I lived in Germany for a short time after college, and I fell in love with the Germans' craftsmanship of beer, especially Hefeweizen. When I returned to the states in 2005, it was nearly impossible to find good European beer for home consumption, so I began exploring homebrewing. I quickly moved from extract and bottles to all grain and kegs, so that I could make it exactly how the brewers made it. I also attempted some cider making but was never as successful as I would have liked. Home cider making has really taken off in the past decade, however, and novices can get fresh juice from local orchards and produce quality cider. It's a fantastic hobby that continues to grow. Some adventurous individuals will forage for wild apples and press the juice themselves; this allows them to use Virginia's bounty to produce a truly local beverage. If you don't feel like hunting for apples, then you can get a blend of fresh-pressed juice from several Virginia growers or buy a kit at your local homebrew and cider supply store. Simply get the juice, put it in a sanitized five-gallon carboy (plastic or glass) with fermentation lock. (You could also use a

come from a variety of cider apples blended at a small craft cidery or a large commercial cidery.

Flavored ciders exist at almost every Virginia cidery, and there are endless creations. On one of my trips, I encountered a five-gallon glass carboy of cider fermenting with Sour Patch Kids at the bottom of the liquid. This was

small wooden barrel.) Then either pitch a commercial yeast or let it naturally ferment. Make sure that the juice stays at the designated temperature according to the yeast instructions—if it's too cold it could create a stuck fermentation, and a temperature too high could produce off-flavors. Sanitation and temperature control are two of the most important factors for homebrewing and home cider making. After the bubbles (CO_2) stop coming out of the airlock, then you can siphon it to another five-gallon carboy to let it settle. After at least a week or so, then you can bottle or keg it. (Use an airlock or pH device to ensure that fermentation is complete. Some ciders will take longer to ferment completely.) If you would like a bubbly product, then you can either force carbonate with a CO_2 gun or add a sugar mixture to help with carbonation. Within a couple weeks in bottles or kegs, you will be ready to drink your homemade cider.

For more information on home cider making see Christopher and Kirsten Shockey, *The Big Book of Cidermaking: Expert Techniques for Fermenting and Flavoring Your Favorite Hard Cider* (North Adams, MA: Storey, 2020).

a creation by David Biun at Lost Boy Cider for Halloween. I have had ginger ciders that will make you pucker up and hot pepper ciders that pair well with hot wings. Spices, hops, and almost every type of fruit and herbs have been used to enhance ciders.

Perry is technically not a cider, because it is made from

VIRGINIA TECH AND CORNELL TACKLE THE PROBLEM OF CIDER NOMENCLATURE

As much as I hate saying this as a University of Virginia alumnus, Virginia Tech and Cornell University are huge supporters of cider and apple research. In fact, they are leading the way in defining cider styles in America. Both universities are seeking to better understand cider's identity and create a universal cider language. In 2020, Jacob Lahne, assistant professor of food science at Virginia Tech, and Clinton Neill, assistant professor of population medicine and diagnostic sciences at Cornell, received a $500,000 award from the USDA National Institute of Food and Agriculture to create a descriptive sensory language for hard cider. The four-year research project attempts to "create a common descriptive sensory language to help American cider producers communicate their products to consumers." The first part of the endeavor is to set up focus groups at various locations in the largest apple-producing states on the East Coast: Vermont, Virginia, and New York. The venture includes several tasting and group discussions to determine what consumers expect out of cider. After they've conducted their focus groups, they will then look at standardizing some of the language for cider based on certain descriptors revealed during the sessions. Once the "sensory lexicon" is established, they will conduct tests to see if this new vocabulary affects the consumers' experience. The researchers will then analyze all the data and show cider makers and cider businesses their findings, which will hopefully help those

businesses better market their product to the expectations of consumers.

I was interested in participating in the cider study at Virginia Tech, but I couldn't make the trip from Richmond to Blacksburg on a weekly basis. I was, however, able to join a smaller focus group at Blue Bee Cider in Richmond. Led by Virginia Tech doctoral student Martha Calvert, this session was held on June 7, 2021, and featured an eight-person panel. Martha was trying to figure out what consumers are looking for in cider. What were their expectations? Why they like certain ciders and dislike others? Why do they call one dry and another sweet? Our group blind-tasted three ciders from the local Richmond market, all purchased from Ellwood Thompson's (a popular independent organic store located in Carytown), and then discussed what we liked and disliked about each product. Learning what consumers know about cider, what they expect, and what they dislike is very helpful to the cider producers, so thank you to the Hokies for leading this instrumental research for Virginia cider.

Sources: Alex Hood, "Virginia Tech and Cornell Researchers Team Up to Solve America's Hard Cider Identity Crisis," Virginia Tech News, September 28, 2020, https://news.vt.edu/articles/2020/09/fst-usda-cider.html; Martha D. Calvert, Clinton L. Neill, Amanda C. Stewart, and Jacob Lahne, "Sensory Descriptive Analysis of Hard Ciders from the Northeast and Mid-Atlantic United States, *Journal of Food Science* 88 (2023): 1700–17, https://doi.org/10.1111/1750-3841.16507.

pears rather than apples. There are only a few Virginia cideries that make perry, due most likely to the difficulty of harvesting pears. Patois is one of the only Virginia cideries that makes a perry from 100 percent pear juice. There are several Virginia cideries, however, that make a pear cider—that is, cider with pear juice—but this is not perry. Troddenvale makes a beautiful interpretation of a perry with their Kieffer Country Wine that uses a majority of Kieffer Pears along with a small amount of Dolgo Crabs from Highland County. Perry makers use almost the same process as cider, although pears typically must rest longer than apples before they can be milled, because it takes them longer to ripen. When the pears are crushed and milled, the pomace should sit for at least a day before being pressed, yielding a much cleaner and clearer product. Perry also has a much larger amount of unfermentable sugars (sorbitol) than cider, so it is likely to have more residual sweetness.[15] The beverages' characteristics are very similar, but perries are normally lighter and more delicate. Pear trees can also live to be up to four hundred years old, and they tend to grow much taller than apple trees.[16]

Tasting Cider

Appearance, aroma, and flavor—these are the three essential parts to exploring cider. The tasting experience is not unlike sampling wine due to the similar components.

The first factor is appearance. The initial impression of a beverage is very important to one's understanding of the product. Just by looking at the liquid, you can tell if it is still or carbonated, cloudy or clear, and bright or muted. A cider's appearance varies greatly from a murky gold still liquid to a light-yellow Champagne-like beverage. The appearance can fluctuate due to specific apple type and the type of filtration or clarification process. Some ciders (those made from red flesh apples) can present a ruby red color like a rosé wine. Ditchley Cider Works makes a blush cider from pink and red flesh apples that give it a slightly rosy red tint to the cider.

The next element is aroma. A cider's smell can vary from funky and earthy to citrusy and floral. The aroma changes heavily based on the apple, the yeast or bacteria involved during fermentation, any adjuncts or fruit added, and the storage vessel for the cider. Additional fruit, spices, and hops, along with potential barrel aging, can also have a significant effect. For example, when additional fruit, such as raspberries, is added to the cider, it can take on the sweet-smelling elements of the adjunct, while hopped ciders can give off citrusy and spicy notes, and barrel aging can enhance odors of the liquor (bourbon, rum, brandy) that was contained in the vessel such as scents of spice, vanilla, or oak. Too much of one item can cover up the apples' aroma characteristics and make it unappealing.

The most important tasting component is flavor. If you don't enjoy the taste of what you're drinking, then the appearance and aroma are moot. Cider can be one-dimensional, which is why the majority of products are cider blends. The cider maker can decide how much juice of each type of apple to use to make the beverage more complex. Despite this, there are some apples that have enough tannins and acidity to make a delicious single varietal product. Cider makers attempt to balance the two most important things that the apple provides for tasting purposes: acidity and tannins.

An important aspect of flavor that is often confused is the matter of sweetness. Just as any given wine may be assigned along a scale from dry to sweet, so too may we speak of ciders. It's important to understand that something may seem to be sweet due to the fruitiness of the beverage, but that does not mean that it is *actually* sweet—that is, with a significant sugar content. On the other hand, some ciders have residual sugar, but may not seem as sweet, as that sugar may have been left to balance a very acidic or tannic cider. One of the biggest misconceptions that I hear is that cider is a sweet beverage. Like wine or beer, it can be extremely dry and tannic or as tart as a Lambic or a Berliner Weisse. Flavors like green apple, peach, pear, pineapple, lime, or berries that are sometimes present in the beverage may give the impression of sweetness, but that is just the how our palate perceives it. Some ciders also present flavors that are outside of the fruit realm, which can be a sign of a great product. Mushrooms, butter, vanilla, mint, and other herbs and earthy notes can be flavor indicators of a very well-made beverage. Funky can also be a flavor profile, especially in natural and wild fermentations. This is not necessarily a bad thing, and in many cases, it is a telltale sign of a superb cider.[17]

Cofermentations are also very popular, and this style will take on some characteristics of the other fermentation, whether it comes from honey or additional fruits. Virginia wine is a popular coferment with cider. Potter's Craft Cider does a Concord and Brett with Concord grapes from Waynesboro and a wild yeast. Patois Cider has worked with vidal blanc and petit manseng while Blue Bee Cider cofermented a batch of Hewe's Crab with cabernet franc and then matured it for one year in a Catoctin Creek brandy barrel. Troddenvale worked with Lightwell Survey Wines where the winery contributed petit manseng and vidal blanc grapes and the cidery contributed Harrison and Golden Russet apples. That blend included 50 percent grapes and 50 percent apples. Each winery and cidery took half of the combined mixture to their site and fermented it there. Troddenvale fermented it in oak without sulfites and Lightwell Survey fermented in stainless steel and added sulfur dioxide when bottling. All the wines listed in these collaborations are made from grapes that do well in Virginia.

Barrel aging also creates different flavor characteristics that are usually dependent on what was in the barrel.

Cider makers use bourbon, brandy, gin, rum, wine, and any other type of barrel used to age alcohol. Almost every cider resting in a barrel will take on some of the flavors or aromas of the alcohol that was previously held in the container, as well as some oak and vanilla characteristics from the char or wood. The longer the beverage is aged, the more pronounced these flavors will be. Buskey Cider offers several barrel-aged options throughout the year. One of their more unique versions is a cider aged in sherry barrels. It has a "nutty, raisin character with a citrusy finish."[18] Bryant's Cidery & Brewery does three different ciders aged in bourbon barrels including one with peaches, strawberries, and one with spearmint. (The spearmint concoction is a play on the southern cocktail, mint julep.)

Hopped ciders have taken the US market by storm, following the craft beer hophead boom. I'm not a huge fan of this style of cider, but I do appreciate a hopped cider where the flavoring is either subtle or enhances the beverage's characteristics instead of completely changing the cider's makeup. One of my favorite hopped ciders is the 2021 Blue Bee/Ardent Collab Hops Addition. I'm a little partial to this one, because Ardent Craft Ales is among my top ranked breweries. They tested fifteen different hops with a York/Winesap apple blend, and finally agreed on Nelson Sauvin and Mosaic. The dry-hopped product has a rush of tropical flavor including pineapple and citrus, finishing with a smooth fruity flavor and hint of lime. Bold Rock Hard Cider offers a nice hopped cider called Bold Rock IPA (India Pressed Apple, a play on India Pale Ale), which is dry-hopped with Ekuanot Hops, creating a slightly tart cider with flavors of grapefruit, citrus and fresh apples. If you are looking for a hop bomb, then I recommend Wild Hare Cider's Ophelia, which is a dry-hopped cider infused with grapefruit. Big flavors of blood orange and lime dominate with a pleasing hoppy aroma.

Spices are also used extensively with ciders. Ginger,

Hops growing in Justen Kelly Dick's hop yard at Kelly Ridge Farms. (Kelly Ridge Farms/Tumbling Creek Cider Company)

for instance, has become a popular ingredient.[19] Winchester Ciderworks VaGinga is a great example. They add fresh-pressed ginger to their signature cider, Malice, which sports a zesty and spicy finish. I get a lot of flavors from the ginger, especially a slight tingle on the back of my throat—which ginger fans will love. Less gingery is their Wylde Clyde, which is a tart and tangy mix of black currant juice and fresh pressed ginger. Courthouse Creek Cider also has a nice ginger cider called Bella Vita. This tasty beverage gets ample fruitiness from the addition of raspberries; it's not spicy but you still know that the ginger is there. Big Fish Cider Company's Honey Ginger is full of fresh ginger and backsweetened with local honey to create a tart spicy and slightly sweet cider.

Fall and autumn spices (cinnamon, nutmeg, and allspice) are a common addition to spiced ciders. Blue Toad Hard Cider has a seasonal fall blend cider called "Into the Orchard," a molasses amber cider with cinnamon, allspice, and cloves. It is sometimes served heated at Blue Toad as a “Hot Toadie,” a nod to the owner’s nickname (Toad). Coyote Hole Craft Beverages offers a pumpkin cider, “Apparition,” that is infused with fresh pumpkins, along with brown sugar and light spices. In chapter 6 I review Corcoran Vineyards and Cidery’s Sinful Cider, which is a great example of how a little allspice can go a long way in complementing cider.

Aspects of a cider related to its flavor are mouthfeel, texture, and body. When you taste cider, take your time to swirl it around in your mouth and chew on it to try to get a feel for the body. (It’s a very similar process to wine tasting.) Usually more tannic ciders will have more to chew on and lend themselves to a fuller mouthfeel. A more tannic one with a heavier body may be referred to as “rich,” while a lighter airy acidic one may be referred to as “bright.” Tannins are usually what creates the weight of the cider, but other practices like maturation and fermentation methods can alter the body of the finished product.[20]

Serving temperature is also important when tasting alcoholic beverages. Lighter bodied ciders or those lacking bold tannins should be served colder, between 42 and 50 °F. Some higher alcohol cider (7 percent ABV or higher) may benefit from a serving temperature from 48 to 55 °F. These beverages could have more pronounced tannins that would be muted by colder temperatures. Most European cider apple varieties would be best served at 50–60 °F, which would open up their many layers and complex tannins.[21]

There is no specific drinking vessel for cider, so feel free to use anything from an elegant Riedel wine glass to a red Solo cup. I prefer the wine glass, but some occasions may call for a little less formal container. Similar to beer and wine, however, particular ciders may benefit from specialized glasses. A champagne flute would better complement a heavily carbonated bright cider to adequately release the bubbles and allow the consumer to taste and feel the crispness, while a farmhouse style could benefit from something like a curvy Belgian saison glass to round out the tannins and the potential barnyard/earthy funk. For a high tannic cider that presents a full body mouthfeel, try a burgundy wine or brandy glass that allows the beverage to warm up and release the aromas and flavors. It is also helpful to have enough room in the glass, so that you can adequately swirl and aerate the beverage to release its fragrance.

A pour of Potter's Craft Cider. (Potter's Craft Cider)

Distilling/Fortifying Cider

The distillation of fruits and cider has a rich history, and English settlers in North America took part in this venture by turning their pressed fruit juice into a beverage that would have an extended shelf life. Distillation equipment was expensive and took a good deal of knowledge to operate, but despite this the expertise and methods of distilling apple juice into brandy made its way to the colonies. Virginia settlers were creative in how they fortified and distilled their cider to produce a beverage that would last longer.

Apple brandy is simply distilled cider. There is sometimes confusion over the term "applejack" and apple brandy. To create applejack, American colonists increased the alcohol contents of cider by freezing the liquid repeatedly until the water separates from the alcohol (this was known as "jacking"). Unfortunately, sometimes "jacking" did not separate all the good liquid from the bad liquid. By keeping the heads and tails (the bad parts of the distillation) in the beverage it sometimes led to apple palsy or lockjaw. The method for producing apple brandy/applejack is now done through distillation rather than "jacking."[22] Even though the process has changed for making this popular beverage, some distilleries still retain the name "applejack" to pay homage to historic product. According to the Alcohol and Tobacco Tax and Trade Bureau (TTB), distilleries can use the term "applejack" as long as 20 percent of the liquor comes from apple brandy that has been aged for at least two years, the rest can be made of neutral grain spirits.[23]

Cider royal or royal cider is another historic beverage that was touted by the Founders. This is cider that has been fortified by adding apple brandy. (Imagine a port, but instead of brandy added to wine, apple brandy is added

LAIRD & COMPANY: AMERICAS OLDEST COMMERCIAL DISTILLERY

The most famous and oldest apple brandy producer in the United States is Laird & Company. Scotsman William Laird settled in Monmouth, New Jersey, in the late 1600s and used his background and knowledge of the distillation of Scottish whisky to turn America's beverage, cider, into a tasty liquor. In 1780, his grandson Robert Laird started Laird & Company in New Jersey as the first licensed distillery in the United States. Robert was a soldier under the command of George Washington during the Revolutionary War, and when the Continental Army camped in the Monmouth County area, the Laird family supplied them with applejack. Washington was so fond of the beverage that he ended up requesting the recipe, which the Laird family gave to him.

One of the reasons that Laird & Company has a special place in this book is because one of their production facilities is located in North Garden, a community just outside of Charlottesville. (Most of their apples today come from Chiles Orchard in Crozet.) After Prohibition, Laird decided to expand their operations and purchase the distillery in North Garden to meet the growing demand for their product. It also made sense to have a production facility near some of the best apples in the nation in the Shenandoah Valley. (Winesaps are some of the best apples to use for distillation, because of their flavor profile and high alcohol potential.)

Even though this book is about Virginia cider, I thought that it was important to make a special trip to this historic distillery's Virginia location. On a warm spring day, I pulled off a dirt road and entered Laird Lane in North Garden, rounded the corner, and stepped back in time. I met with the head distiller, Dan Swanson, who has been there for more than twelve years and has his hand on all of Laird's products. His family has lived in the area for many years, as his father owned the local gas station store, and he is happy to continue the tradition by working at the distillery. It doesn't appear that much has changed since the Lairds moved in during the 1940s. (The building was previously the Virginia Fruit Distilling Company.) Full copper stills, hand-riveted storage containers, and wooden barrels line the property, and many are still in use. While I was there, I witnessed a group of welders working to bring the distillery into the twenty-first century by updating some of the operations from aged wood to stainless steel. Dan explained that, just like their product, they try to keep things simple. One of my favorite parts of the tour was stepping into the barrel room. More than forty barrels are stacked high, and you can see (and smell!) the history of the building. The top of the brick structure has turned black due to the "angel's share" escaping the barrels and seeping into the upper part of the building. Laird's

(*continues on next page*)

product line ranges from Blended Applejack (apple brandy mixed with neutral grain spirits) to an Old Apple Brandy aged for seven and a half years. Use the Blended Applejack in a Jack Rose cocktail or sip on the Old Apple Brandy 7½ years in a brandy snifter next to the fire. Most of their products can be found at your local Virginia ABC store.

Sources: Frank J. Prial, "One Family's Story: Apples to Applejack," *New York Times,* May 4, 2005, https://www.nytimes.com/2005/05/04/dining/one-familys-story-apples-to-applejack.html; interview with Daniel Swanson at Laird's Distillery, June 2, 2021; phone interview with Lisa Laird on June 2, 2021.

to cider.) The mixture is combined and then bottled and allowed to sit to ensure the flavors meld together.

Pommeau is slightly different than cider royal. This liquor that originated in France is a mixture of fresh unfermented cider with apple brandy. The mixture is then aged in an oak barrel for up to two years.[24]

Calvados is one of the most prized and historic apple brandies, and it can only be made in Normandy. Like the esteem surrounding Cognac (a brandy whose name requires that it come from the Cognac region in France), an apple brandy can only be called Calvados if it is from a certain region of Normandy.[25]

A cyser is a combination of cider and mead. Mead is a fermented honey beverage that predates cider, and many historians argue that it is the oldest alcoholic beverage. Bill Cavender at Black Heath Meadery in Richmond regularly produces an award-winning cyser known as Blue

Angel. He's on his seventh batch as of 2022. This past year's product featured Pink Lady apples and Virginia wildflower honey. He has used Winesap and other Virginia apples in his past cysers.

There are more than sixty distilleries in Virginia, and several of them produce an apple brandy. It would only make sense for distilleries and cideries to collaborate on fruit fermentations and distillations. The Virginia Distillery Company located in Lovingston has a Cider Cask Finished Virginia-Highland Whisky. The whisky finishes in barrels from Virginia cideries like Potter's Craft Cider and Buskey Cider. The liquor is a flavor bomb of honey, vanilla, and butterscotch with aromas of fresh apples and long creamy finish with lingering tastes of baked bread.[26] Catoctin Creek Distilling Company in Purcellville regularly works with Blue Bee on collaborations where Blue Bee provides a blend of cider that Catoctin distills and turns into a fruit brandy. The liquor is then aged in oak barrels and blended with Winesap cider, creating a deliciously warming fortified beverage. (This is also described in the Blue Bee **Try this** section.)

Cider and Food

Ciders make great aperitifs, and what better way to get your palate ready for a meal than a crisp bubbly cider? Try Widow's Watch Sparkling Cider to prepare your taste buds for a scrumptious dinner. The cider maker, Mark Muse, uses a traditional champagne method, and the bubbles are exquisite.

Cider and cheese are also a perfect marriage. Heavy, creamy cheeses like Brie go best with tannic ciders, while an acidic cider may work better with a French goat cheese. A fruit-infused cider may go well with a buttery Havarti.

Earthy mushrooms, beef stew, and steak would go great with a complex tannic cider that has fruit undertones. Try English apple varieties grown here like Potter's Dabinett,

Sage Bird's Ashmead's Kernel, or Blue Bee's Yarlington Mill for some funk that can stand up to meat dishes.

Shrimp and grits, country ham biscuits, and saltier fare could use something with a bit more acidity, like an Albemarle Pippin. Try Albemarle CiderWorks Royal Pippin, Patois Bent Mountain Pippin, or Old Town Pippin Hard Apple Cider to match the saltiness of the dish.

OAK AND APPLE—A CIDER BAR IN THE HEART OF THE VIRGINIA CAPITAL

Ron Morse, Jeb White, and Ryan Koontz are in the business of restaurants and history. Their Richmond-based group, Historical Restaurant Concepts, owns three tasty eateries, including Station 2, located in the former home of Engine Company 2, and Root Stock Provisions. But I was interested in their apple-and-cider-themed restaurant, Oak and Apple, that opened in the Shockoe Bottom area of Richmond in 2019. I sat with Ron and Jeb on Richmond's busy West Main Street enjoying a cocktail called the Smokin' Apple, which used Maker's Mark, cider, muddled orange bitters, and a house-smoked brown sugar simple syrup. Their menu is heavy on smoked meat items (hence the name "Oak"), but they also offer several apple sauces/accompaniments and, more importantly, apple-related beverages. The idea came to them when they noticed how popular cider was at Station 2. Oak and Apple typically has twenty beers

Sweeter items like dessert work with a cider that boasts a higher residual sugar level or a pommeau or Calvados. Try Mt. Defiance Pommeau and Castle Hill Heritage Blend Pommeau with your end-of-meal sweets.

There are a lot of great food options for hopped, spiced, and aged ciders. Hopped ciders go well with hot wings, and ginger-infused cider can enhance the flavors of Thai food,

and at least ten ciders on tap. They have an extensive bottle list with ciders from all over the world, but their focus is clearly Virginia-based. They offer flights, so you can experience all the different styles from Bold Rock Rosè to Potter's Farmhouse. Cider and food are natural pairings, and they have utilized this through their innovative sauces like a barbecue apple sauce that is put on wings and pork barbeque. Apple slices are also used in their coleslaw, which is fantastic. And to top it all off, you can end your meal with an apple dessert from Root Stock Provisions called Dutch Apple, which is topped with bourbon pecans and almond streusel. Oak and Apple is a must-visit for cider lovers.

Source: interview with Jeb White and Ron Morse, Oak and Apple, November 4, 2020.

while a cider aged in bourbon barrels could complement a slice of bourbon pecan pie.

Drink-pairing meals are all the rage, and why shouldn't cider be included? Part of the festivities for CiderCon 2022 Richmond included cider-pairing meals at local restaurants.[27] Chefs and cider makers got creative when selecting pairings for these dinners. Take, for instance, the menu for the cider-pairing dinner offered by Albemarle CiderWorks and Fall Line Kitchen & Bar. I believe that these combinations really speak to the three Cs: complement, contrast, and cut.

First course: oysters- apple mignonette, celery, cider gelee—paired with Brut D'Albemarle

Second course: fluke crudo- pickled granny smith apple, creme fraiche, grapes, nasturtium—paired with GoldRush

Third course: lacquered duck breast- fennel honey, charred cabbage, rutabaga, cherry calimocho—paired with Jupiter's Legacy

Fourth course: sticky cider pudding cake—paired with cider cocktail[28]

Make sure to check with your local cidery to see if they will be participating in any food-pairing meals. It is an experience that you do not want to miss.

CHAPTER 6

A Guide to Virginia's Cideries

The craft beverage landscape is constantly changing, and by the time this book is published there will likely be some Virginia cideries that are no longer in operation and there will be new ones that have started up. As of 2023, only one of the cideries that I visited (Hinson Ford Cider and Mead in Amissville) closed while I was working on the manuscript, but I was able to enjoy some of their tasty cider before they shut down their operation.[1] This section provides a comprehensive list and descriptions of fifty active cider producers in the state. There are in-depth writeups of thirty-three of the cideries that include their history, products, and mission, as well as my recommendation of their product in a **Try this** section. This does not mean that their other products are of lesser quality; I just found these to be some of my favorites or the most unique. I have grouped these cideries according to region: Shenandoah Valley, Blue Ridge and Appalachian, Charlottesville Area, Richmond Area, Chesapeake and Eastern Shore, and Northern Virginia. They are in no particular order within those regions.[2] In addition to these thirty-three detailed descriptions of Virginia cideries, I have also listed seventeen additional cider producers at the end with shorter descriptions. These other cideries have started up only recently, produce limited cider, or cider is a secondary part of their business model. I still recommend that you visit them as part of your Virginia cider tour, but they do not have a detailed write-up in this book. (Please refer to the map on page 2 if you are organizing a cider trip.)

Shenandoah Valley

Winchester Ciderworks

Winchester Ciderworks was the first cidery I visited after I received my book contract. It was my first official trip on this journey of English and American history, and what better place to start than Winchester Ciderworks. Its location is iconic to the story of Virginia cider, because Winchester has been labeled as the "Apple Capital of the World." The city is surrounded by a vast number of orchards; it is one of the largest apple export markets in the nation and the largest apple-producing area in Virginia. Winchester is also home to the annual Shenandoah Apple Blossom Festival, which draws crowds of more than 250,000 each spring. In this area of apple country lies Winchester Ciderworks.

I arrived at the 1900s-era structure that housed the cidery on a cool fall day, and I was greeted with a warm British accent from Stephen Schuurman. Stephen was in the middle of calling distributors, getting quotes for a new canning line, finding aluminum cans, and making cider. His official title is Cider Maker, but he pretty much does everything. He came to the United States from eastern England with a winemaking background. He had always loved cider, and when it didn't look like the winery scene was the best bet for him, he turned to a new venture. Stephen explained that he had been scrumping for apples around Winchester and made a batch of cider that he shared with friends. (Scrumping is the term used for appropriating fruit from orchards or apple trees in a mischievous way.) The product must have been tasty, because his friends convinced him that he should meet with local orchardist Diane Kearns. Diane is a fifth-generation orchardist at Fruit Hill Orchard. Her family started an orchard in Winchester in 1929. (Some of Winchester's specialty ciders are labeled as Thwaite's named after John

Thwaite, the original orchard owner.) In 2015, Fruit Hill started pressing juice for cider makers. The orchard has been a staple in the Virginia apple and cider community, and it covers over two thousand acres and produces over one million bushels of apples each year. The combination of a creative cider maker and an experienced orchardist was just right. After meeting in 2012, they decided to open Winchester Ciderworks and sold their first cider in 2013.[3]

Stephen told me that it took him a few years to expand his offerings, and this is mainly because of some advice he received from the owner of Aspall Cyder in Suffolk, England. The veteran cider maker told Stephen to get one cider right before working on other parts of his portfolio. After four years of tweaking his base cider, he had

"Apple Capital of the World" sign in Winchester, Frederick County. (Winchester-Frederick County Convention & Visitors Bureau)

perfected it. His signature cider, Malice, is a 6.5 percent ABV proper English cider made with a blend of five Virginia apples. See tasting notes below.

Stephen's objective is to educate the American public that cider can be for anyone anytime. There is not just one style. According to Schuurman, there are certain ciders that are more for summertime, such as Malice, and there are others that would work for wintertime, like one of his specialty ciders aged in bourbon, rye, and port barrels—but it's really up to the individual's preference. The Winchester lineup consists of several signature ciders including a ginger-infused cider, blackcurrant cider, pear cider, hopped cider, and a few barrel-aged options.

Try this: Malice is Winchester Ciderworks's signature cider, which took four years to develop. You can find this in many supermarkets throughout Virginia. Blending five Virginia apples, this 6.5 percent ABV product is a lightly effervescent, complex cider featuring pear and tropical flavors, a little funk and a hint of smoke and earth. There is also an element of tartness and a lasting finish that keeps you wanting more. This beverage is a delightful tribute to its English heritage. ABV: 6.5 percent.

"Cider and Black" is a popular drink in England where cider is mixed with black currant juice. The Blackcurrant Cider is Stephen's attempt to recreate this classic beverage. He adds his own blackcurrant juice to the cider after fermentation. The result is a beautiful rose-colored beverage with a floral and berry bouquet bursting with flavors of raspberries, cherries, and spice. The tart and fruity finish makes for a good food-pairing cider. (Think of similar pairings to a rosé wine.) Try it with a salad with blue cheese crumbles and a raspberry vinaigrette. Stephen recommends even using this black current cider to make a light sauce or a drizzle. Fragrant cheeses would also work well. I think a creamy Brie with walnuts and fig jam and some Blackcurrant Cider sounds heavenly. ABV: 6.2 percent.[4]

Old Town Cidery (Glaize Apples)

Old Town Cidery is the brainchild of David Glaize and Philip Glaize III. If you're familiar with apples, then you have heard of Glaize Apples in Winchester. They ship their tasty products throughout the United States (and the world, in fact), and this family-operated apple business has been around since the 1930s. Glaize Apples is headed by Phil Glaize Jr., whose grandfather started the orchard in 1937, and his sons David Glaize and Philip Glaize III are now the fourth generation of Glaizes that have farmed and cared for orchards between the Blue Ridge and Allegheny Mountains. They grow more than thirty varieties, including commercial apples like Golden Delicious and Granny Smith and cider-specific apples like Dabinett. More than a dozen acres have been dedicated to cider apples as a result of the growing demand by cider makers for quality heirloom apples like Ashmead's Kernel, Yarlington Mill, Hewe's, and other varieties. Beyond providing the cider apples, however, Glaize & Bro. Juice Company was established in 2018 to press juice for cider makers. Glaize will work with cider makers to customize their blend to specifications for acidity and sugar. The juicing facility and orchards serve many of the cideries in the Commonwealth and throughout the nation. They provide juice for businesses as far as Minnesota and for larger cider makers like ANXO Cider in Washington, DC.

David doesn't just provide juice and apples to other cideries; he also has a passion for making cider himself. After spending a few years experimenting with fermentations, he and his brother Philip Glaize III (Head of Operations/Sales) opened up Old Town Cidery in Winchester in 2021. Their outdoor taproom was temporaily located in

Ashmead's Kernel apples harvested at Glaize orchards in Winchester. (Glaize Apples)

downtown Winchester, but they make all of their cider at the Glaize Apple orchards facility, so they can continue to provide a superb beverage for Winchester residents and beyond no matter their location.

Since David and Philip are tied up with Glaize Apple and the business side of the cidery, they have enlisted the help of Stephen Kelly as their cider maker. Kelly makes some delicious cider that ranges from a single varietal Albemarle Pippin cider to unique blends like Raspberry Rosé. Old Town's ciders come right from the source with about a third of Glaize orchard dedicated to apples for their own cidery. Old Town is widely distributed throughout the surrounding Winchester area.

This is the perfect business for the "Apple Capital of

the World." David Glaize continues to support the cider and apple community as a member of the board of directors for the American Cider Association. He was elected in 2022 as the Southern region's representative.

As of Spring 2024, Old Town does not have a tasting room, but you can still pick up their cider at several locations throughout Winchester and the state.[5]

Try this: When my wife and I shop for wine at a grocery store or order drinks at a restaurant, it is a given that she will get prosecco; if prosecco isn't available then she will consider a cider. So when we were in Winchester to pick up some of Old Town's cider, I knew that she would be drawn to the Pearsecco, which offers the best of both of her beverages of choice. She's not the only one who enjoys this interesting take on sparkling wine, because it is their most popular cider. The blend of Gold Rush and Greening apples provide an excellent acidity that is then sweetened with Virginia pears. This bubbly beverage is slightly on the sweet side, but has more of a fruity finish to it than sweet. ABV: 6.9 percent.

The magnificently pinkish-yellow-colored Raspberry Rosé blends Ida Red (one of David's favorite varieties) with Empire apples. It is then flavored with Virginia raspberries, and the resulting flavor is full of brambleberries and a tart, refreshing finish. It is not as sweet as the Pearsecco, but still provides a fruit-filled flavor bomb. ABV: 6.9 percent.

Widow's Watch Cider (Muse Orchard)

I've had a lot of wonderful memories on this journey, but my visit to Widow's Watch Cider has to be one of my favorites. As I made my way along I-64 west past Harrisonburg and turned off the Edinburg exit, I ventured down a farm road and approached the lovely estate of Dr. Mark Muse and Gloria Frigola. The charming couple who owns Widow's Watch Cider at Muse Orchard were very gracious hosts. The idyllic setting of their property could clearly be used as a muse for whatever inspiration you needed. The current farmhouse was built in the late 1860s by Jacob Lantz. Lantz owned the local flower mill in Edinburg and also served as the town magistrate. He built the existing homestead after the original home was burned down by Union forces under the command of General Philip Sheridan during the Civil War.

Mark bought the historic property in 2015, because it gave him enough acreage to plant his own orchard and vineyard. Before he moved to Shenandoah, he had worked in Washington, DC, where he made cider and wine in his suburban Maryland basement—but now he could step up his game from amateur neighborhood cider maker for friends (he had even won a gold medal at the 2005 Indy International Wine Competition) to an orchard manager who could produce a farm-to-glass product for sale. Muse Orchard has more than 220 cider trees that include Albemarle Pippin, Hewe's Crab, Kingston Black, Roxbury Russet, Winesap, and many more historic heirloom varieties whose pedigrees date from before the nineteenth century. In addition to the orchard, he also has a small vineyard that's dedicated to Champagne grape varieties like chardonnay, pinot noir, and pinot meunier. The name, Widow's Watch Cider, comes from the widow's watch located at the top of the house where you can see the beautiful grounds along with views of the mountains on all sides. Mark's love of all things bubbly began when he met his partner Gloria, who is from Catalonia. He promised to immerse himself in her culture, which he did for nearly twenty years. One aspect of her Catalan background involved Cava, the Catalan equivalent of Champagne. He practiced medical psychology and lived in the Barcelona area for nearly two decades and became acutely knowledgeable of the elixir. When he returned to the United States in 1998, he tried to recreate the sparkling beverage on American soil, but he became convinced that Virginia was better suited for apples than old-world grapes. Mark then tried to recreate Cava with regional apples. The Méthode Champenoise is applied to his Champagne cider (Brut). Once the apple blend is fully fermented and clarified, then it is bottled for the second fermentation and set to rest in the cellar. During its time at sleep, the bottle is riddled and eventually disgorged. The sparkling ciders are usually aged between one to three years in the cellar. It is an intricate process but definitely worth the added effort.

During my time at Widow's Watch, Mark shared with me the Champagne cider, Brut, and a still product called Two George Cyder. This was one of my most memorable experiences of my journey—not only because of the delicious beverages and serene setting, but also the company. I imagined that this was what Jefferson was talking about when referred to cider as his table drink. Sitting at Mark and Gloria's table, sipping historic cider and looking out the window at the orchard—this was table drinking at its best. Widow's Watch products are true to the historic character of the beverage and should be shared with friends and family who appreciate this journey of cider.

They do not have a tasting room but sell their products at small retailers in Woodstock, Edinburg, Winchester, and Harrisonburg.[6]

Try this: Two George Cyder is named for Colonel George Washington and Colonel George Muse, who served together as commanders at Fort Necessity during the French and Indian War. Mark uses many of the same apples that were available to early Virginians in this historic blend. This still cider is rich and full bodied with tropical flavors and notes of clove and cinnamon with a dry finish. ABV: 8.5 percent.

Brut, a bright sparkling champagne-esque cider, uses only heritage apples for its blend. It is made in the traditional champagne style and rests for over a year on its lees in the estate's underground cellar. There is a ripe apple bouquet aroma and pleasing number of bubbles that make this the perfect aperitif. ABV: 10.5 percent.

Old Hill Cider (Showalter's Orchard)

There is always a lot of confusion when explaining cider in the United States, because most Americans think of cider as nonalcoholic fresh-pressed cider (or juice) purchased from local farm markets. Some of the best nonalcoholic fresh-pressed cider comes from Showalter's Orchard just north of Harrisonburg and west of New Market. People drive from all around just to get some of this sweet nectar. In 1965 Joe Showalter started a farm in Timberville and set up a market for customers to get fresh fruit. Ten years later, Joe added a cider press, so they could press the "ugly" (blemished) apples that were not being sold. This turned into the famous "Showalter's Apple Cider."

In 2010, Joe's son, Shannon, and his wife Sarah believed they could take the farm and the business to the next level by entering the world of "hard" cider. They already had the most important part of cider: good apples and juice. The next logical step would be to ferment the juice and create a delicious "hard" cider, so they began to experiment and found the perfect blends.

Old Hill is a worthy destination. It includes a large orchard with a gorgeous 360-degree view of the valley landscape. They have over thirty different apple varieties on sixty acres, and you can pick your fruit (both peaches and apples) during the season. The apple orchard features cider apples like Jonagold and Stayman, as well as other varieties. There is also a market where you can select from different types of valley homegrown produce. You can even pick up a jug of that famous "Showalter's Apple Cider" and an apple cider doughnut to go.

It was a gorgeous spring afternoon on the day of my visit, and the farm was quite busy. The tasting room is a quaint area where you can sample Old Hill's lineup. I ordered a glass of their Heritage cider and took a seat on a bench outside overlooking the valley. It was truly picturesque. While I sat and stared at a mountain range enjoying a beverage that came from the farm, I observed the steady traffic coming and going from the market. Many locals were picking up bags of apples and other produce to take home. It was such a communal environment for the valley area. (I saw an elderly man drive his truck right up to the hanger bay to pick up his apples like he had been doing this same routine since 1960s.) It's great that Shannon can carry on the family tradition that his dad started more than fifty years ago.

Old Hill makes a wide range of ciders that showcase the valley's character from single varietal ciders that are wild fermented with oak staves to a lighter thirst-quenching Virginia Radler made from apples, freshly squeezed lemons, and hops. (I lived in Germany for a short time and had a few Radlers, but with beer and lemonade. I think I would prefer this version for the summertime.)

If you're visiting from out of town, don't worry—Old Hill has that covered, as they offer multiple overnight lodging opportunities including glamping in a vintage Airstream. The cozy hillside accommodations make the perfect weekend getaway from the city by providing full views of the orchard and mountains. Make sure to take advantage of these idyllic lodgings if you can.

Try this: Heritage was the cider that I had while gazing at the scenic valley view and observing the interactions at the market. This is a hefty beverage at 11 percent, but the alcohol is hidden by the wonderful flavors of stone fruit and honey balanced with an earthy finish. This deep golden-colored cider is quite inviting due to its pleasing floral aroma. ABV: 11 percent.

I'm not a huge fan of sweet cider, but the slightly sweet Betwixt may have converted me. It reminds me of my childhood days drinking freshly pressed apple cider. This is it. Flavors of fresh green apples and aromas that make me think of autumn. This crisp and warming cider makes you imagine that you are exploring an orchard during fall harvest season. ABV: 7 percent.[7]

Sage Bird Ciderworks

Conducting my research in the middle of a pandemic was a bit challenging, but it was nowhere near as challenging as trying to operate a business in the middle of social distancing, shutdowns, and economic collapses. One of my typical questions for cidery owners was "How has the pandemic affected your business?" They usually answered that their patrons are still buying alcohol and many times those numbers have increased, because of people trying to support community businesses. Some cideries did well during the warmer months if they had suitable outside seating, but others struggled if they didn't have adequate distribution or outdoor spaces. When I met with Zach Carlson (owner of Sage Bird Ciderworks in Harrisonburg) at the height of the pandemic, wearing masks and social distancing, I asked him this question, and he said that nothing has changed, because they opened during the pandemic. I can't imagine launching a business in the midst of the pandemic, especially one that relies heavily on customers to experience your product and setting. Despite this major setback, Zach and his wife, Amberlee, successfully opened the first urban cidery in Harrisonburg and have provided the community with an excellent product for cider lovers to imbibe.

Zach and Amberlee are both James Madison University (JMU) graduates. The graphic arts designer (Zach) and teacher (Amberlee) dabbled in mead production in their apartment in Harrisonburg in 2014, but the product was less than palatable. Even though they were discouraged with the failed honey fermentation, they were still interested in exploring the world of converting sugars to alcohol. Zach ventured into homebrewing while Amberlee investigated the wine industry, but they found their calling in cider. They ordered fruit from local orchards and purchased a 700-pound antique wood and cast-iron apple press for $200. After Zach made a few repairs to the antique, they were up and pressing. By 2018, they started sharing their products with friends and even entered a few amateur cider competitions, which they won. Zach took cider classes through Portland State University and learned the ins and outs of the craft beverage industry while still tweaking his homemade ciders. After an internship at Blue Bee Cider, he was armed with the knowledge and a business plan to start a cidery. The next thing was a location, and in the summer of 2019, they signed a lease for a space in a former tire and auto repair center in the northern end of downtown Harrisonburg. For several months they worked on transforming a dingy old garage into a beautiful urban cidery. In the summer of 2020, Sage Bird opened as the first cidery in Harrisonburg.

I visited Sage Bird a few months after they opened, and it was an absolute treat. It was nice to see the revitalization and development of downtown Harrisonburg. Two decades ago, the only craft beverage place in the city was Calhoun's, but a lot has changed for the "burg" since then. Sage Bird is nestled in a perfect location where craft markets are thriving. The former garage is an ideal spot to relax with friends or complete your chemistry homework while watching the world go by through the beautiful front bay door windows. There's also a quaint outdoor space behind the building where visitors can enjoy the valley air.

Zach, the former graphics designer, is obviously very creative and has quoted Potter's as a source of inspiration for testing cider boundaries. He practices traditional cider making methods but with a modern take, which is evident in his lineup. Styles that range from standards like Dry

River Reserve and their flagship hopped cider, Hip Hop, to limited bottlings of their single varietals such as Harrison and Hewe's to fun drinks like their Fresh Squeezed Cider-mosas, which is orange juice blended with their Dry River Reserve. Even though they have a cider that will meet the needs of any challenging cider customer, they stay true to their mission of highlighting the great flavors of Apple-Achia. The word "sage" means wise, and part of their mission is to gain more knowledge about cider and cider history, to respect the traditions established, and move cider forward. I believe this is what Sage Bird is all about.

Try this: Hip Hop is Sage Bird's flagship hopped cider inspired from Zach's homebrewing days. It is a pleasing beverage that appeals to both the cider fan and can work as an alternative to a juicy IPA for the beer lover. This aromatic cider has a slightly red hue due to the addition of rose hips. The dry-hopped cider uses Mosaic and Amarillo hops and is full of tropical flavors of grapefruit and orange, but still retains some herbal flavors from the hops as well. It starts dry but finishes with a good amount of tartness that alters any potential bitterness. ABV: 6.9 percent.

In 2021 Albemarle CiderWorks hosted a blind tasting of six Virginia Hewe's Crab single varietal ciders, and Sage Bird's was the winner of the competition. This cider has everything: bold tannins and balanced acidity that makes it reminiscent of an old-world white wine. (I can see what Jefferson was talking about when he was comparing Virginia Hewe's Crab to fine European wine.) Zach's creation is a brilliantly crafted beverage that has the earthiness and fruit flavors that you would expect from a classic white wine, but it has the weight of a red wine due to the complex tannins. ABV: 10 percent.[8]

Ciders from Mars

What do you get when you blend a love of outer space, David Bowie, and cider? Ciders from Mars, of course!

Dr. Nikki West is a trained geochemist who has not only spent time teaching about outer space but has also participated in an experimental planetary task force. In addition to her love of all things beyond the earth's atmosphere, she is also a musician who performs as the Mars man himself, David Bowie. Her love for Ziggy Stardust and the Spiders from Mars along with her scientific and explorative background form the basis for her style of cider making. Ciders from Mars offers a technically made product with a lot of fun added to the mix that is out of this world.

Nikki's interest in cider began when she was working on her doctorate at Penn State University. She discovered a local cidery and began to appreciate the historic beverage and craft. After meeting regularly with the cider maker and learning the ins and outs of the business, she set out to try the venture herself. Starting with five-gallon carboys and eventually transitioning to fifty-five-gallon drums, she was ready to move her passion into a business. With help from her partner Jeremy Wimpey, they scaled up the operations and established a small cider orchard in western Augusta County. She now had knowledge of fermentation and apple trees, and in 2018, while teaching virtually, she began thinking realistically about starting her own cidery. To accomplish this, she needed a larger production space, and this led her back to the valley, as she and her husband had attended JMU. Staunton, a vibrant food and beer location, was also in need of a quality cidery to fill the void, and this was the perfect opportunity for Nikki, and Jeremy to capitalize on.

They are in a marvelous spot on the wharf in downtown Staunton, at the former location of Blackdog Bikes (across the street from Redbeard Brewing Company). The building has been remodeled and turned into their ideal cider facility. They finished the renovations to the tasting room and deck in May 2021, and Ciders from Mars opened to a great reception from the Queen City. The building's architecture and artwork showcase the idea of a fun and creative space while still covering the modern (scientific/futuristic) theme. Nikki is now consumed full-time by Ciders from Mars, and Jeremy continues to operate Applied Trails Research out of the Shenandoah Valley.

I met with Nikki soon after her opening and sampled her cider lineup. Using new techniques that she learned from coursework at the Cider Institute of North America and her passion for experimentation, she has created an incredible array of ciders. Their flagship products are Pathfinder and Hellas Dry. Both provide a nice range of what Virginia apples can offer. Ciders from Mars offers several other ciders throughout the year like cofermentations and special barrel-aged ciders. There is clearly a science theme at the cidery, as it's a very sterile environment with laboratory glassware serving as the drinking and serving vessels, and the cidery production area is referred to as "the lab." Staunton is a great foodie and drink location. Zynodoa is a fantastic restaurant that serves scrumptious farm-to-table dishes and includes a great drink and cocktail menu where you can find several Virginia ciders. There are also lots of other drinking establishments such as Ox-Eye Vineyards and Redbeard Brewing Company, as well as historic sites and ample lodging, so come check out Ciders from Mars and the rest of what the Queen City has to offer.

Try this: Hazy Lady is a Winesap single varietal in a traditional style with some nice acidity but a dry finish. The flavors are clean with hints of cooked apples, apple skin, and herbs. This cider's name comes from the fact that it retains some haziness due to its fermentation on lees (or on the sediment). This also adds to its complexity. ABV: 6.2 percent.

I love a Helles lager, and Ciders from Mars's flagship dry cider, Hellas Dry, is clearly worthy of the name. *Helles* means "bright" in German, and this is a great identifier for this crisp cider (even though they have a slightly different spelling), which features complex citrus flavors and a pleasing finish that will satisfy your thirst. ABV: 7.1 percent.[9]

Blue Ridge and Appalachia

Tumbling Creek Cider Company

Four friends (Jerry Bresowar, Justen Dick, Tom McMullen, and Mark Finney) who share a common interest in science, community, and agriculture decided to start Tumbling Creek Cider Company in Meadowview in 2018. They grafted cider apple trees and built an orchard and in 2020 opened their community tasting room in downtown Abingdon. Abingdon had always been a city that I wanted to visit, and during the 2021 winter holiday, my family vacationed in the charming city doing all the touristy activities; we stayed at the historic Martha Washington Inn, saw a play at the local Barter Theatre, and took in the idyllic sights and sounds of Southwest Virginia.

But the main reason I was there was to taste some of Tumbling Creek's cider and tour their farm and production facility in nearby Meadowview. I thoroughly enjoyed the tasting room at The Spring House, located in the heart of Abingdon. The head cider maker, Jerry Bresowar, explained that their tasting room is also connected to a tea shop, coffee shop, and coffee roaster. The space is a community effort and a working co-op at its best. Jerry poured me six ciders that ranged from the clean and refreshing Moonshot (which follows the group's mantra to "shoot for the moon") to an aromatic cider flavored with local spruce tips. The ciders are perfect examples of the flavors of Southwest Virginia. I later toured Kelly Ridge Farms in Meadowview, where many of their ingredients come from. Located about six miles northeast of Abingdon, this outpost also acts as their main production facility. The short drive allowed me to take in the gorgeous views of rolling hills and undeveloped land where livestock and orchards pervaded the countryside. Once I arrived at Kelly Ridge Farms, I joined up with the orchard manager, Tom McMullen, who provided an insightful tour. Tom explained that this is just one of a series of farms that have been passed down through the Kelly family since the late eighteenth century. Tumbling Creek has built a cider lover's dream on one of the farms with rows of semi-dwarfed trees covering the land that include numerous cider apple varieties like King David, Hewe's Crab, and Grimes Golden. The property has a hop farm that is used for some of their own products like Hellbender Hopped. There is also a hog farm where they feed the pomace to the animals, and this adds a sweetness to the sausage that they make. When the orchard manager and I drove past the hogs, they went running towards us, because they thought we were delivering the pomace! Tom is not only in the process of planting new trees, but he is also trying to preserve a historic orchard on the property. He showed me the old Kelly orchard across the street with apple trees more than fifty years old that are seeing their last days. Despite this decay, he is attempting to reinvigorate the landscape to better represent the storied apple history of Kelly Ridge Farms. Their goal is to eventually produce all their cider apples on the premises and only import dessert apples. In addition to the farm, I also toured the cider production barn, which was full of tools and machines for pressing and fermenting, including a machine called the Applenator for pressing apples (a nod to one of Arnold Schwarzenegger's best-known characters).

You can clearly see that the group of friends is invested in producing cider that highlights the rich region. They have accomplished this in their array of exquisite ciders. From traditional to hopped, the products represent the finest that rural Southwest Virginia has to offer.

Try this: Their full-bodied Ridgerunner Dry is a blend of Southwest Virginia apples like Limbertwig and Black Twig. The superb mountain fruit creates a delicious tannic cider with a smooth, dry finish, and it makes for the perfect food-pairing cider. Try it with cream dishes like a pasta with vodka sauce or a savory shrimp and grits dish. ABV: 7.1 percent.

I know that I've already mentioned that I'm not a big fan of hopped ciders, but I really enjoyed Hellbender Hopped. This semi-sweet cider is dry-hopped with Cascade hops from Kelly Ridge Farms. I thought that this popular American hop would overwhelm this cider, but that was not the case with Hellbender. It presents strong floral aromas with flavors full of citrus and tropical essence that complement the main attraction of apples. The beverage is beautifully balanced and very refreshing. ABV: 7.2 percent.[10]

Big Fish Cider Co.

The Big Fish building has been an iconic landmark in the mountain town of Monterey in Highland County, which borders West Virginia. The same building used to house the Maple, a restaurant known to have the best trout around, but now the Big Fish represents some of the best cider around.

Kirk Billingsley was born and raised in Monterey. His dad was the town doctor, and he remembers as a child always looking forward to his dad's fresh-pressed (nonalcoholic) cider, but he enjoyed the cider even more after it sat around for a few days. But once his dad stopped making the fresh cider, Kirk could never find anything comparable, so he got a press and started making his own. At one point, he was producing so much fresh cider that he decided to put some of the surplus in his basement to ferment. One night, he had some friends over and they were sitting around talking, and then asked for some fresh-pressed cider. He didn't think he had any, but then remembered about the fermented stash in his basement. He poured a few cups of a slightly effervescent beverage and passed them around. The next thing he knew the group wanted more and more. Their talking increased and the conversation became more and more interesting. He had made a very inviting "hard" cider. This was close to thirty years ago, and he has been a "hard" cider maker ever since.

In 2015, Kirk took his hobby to the next level when he purchased the building that housed the former Maple restaurant (the building had also served as the town's movie theatre) for his new cidery. There was only one problem: Kirk didn't have a name for his cidery. After debating on several names, he simply thought about what he called the building that he was in, "The Big Fish." The name finally stuck, and he decided that "Big Fish Cider Company" would be Monterey's new cidery.

Big Fish now features a cozy tasting room and cider production facility in the rear. I think Kirk's cidery is one

Big Fish Cider Co., in the former Maple restaurant (known for serving fresh trout) in Monterey. (Photograph by Mark Mones)

of the more unique cideries, because of the apples he uses. Due to its elevation, Highland County has very different temperature zones for apple growing than other parts of the state. They may not be able to grow as many apples as other parts of the Commonwealth, but the apples have a unique flavor and an acidity that makes elegant ciders. According to Kirk, the problem is that you never really know how many you'll get. Kirk told me that 2019 was great, but 2020 was horrible for apples due to the frost in the area. He only pressed a fraction of the amount of juice that he had the previous years. He manages three orchards in the region and grows varieties ranging from Hewe's Crab to Roxbury Russet. It's all about the apples for Kirk, as he has studied grafting and orchard management for several years, and some of his favorite apples are wild apples in the community. These apples are perfect for cider because they grow in areas where the trees are left alone, without any human interaction. These pastures are where livestock and animals roam freely and add to the terroir. The unidentified trees, many of them over fifty years old, are free from chemicals that affect their growth and flavor. Kirk forages for wild apples on his own and asks the community to provide apples from their homesteads. This belief is evident in his Highland Scrumpy, a cider made from apples donated during a Community Apple Drive. Kirk presses more than twenty different varieties of apples and uses a wild fermentation with two different wine yeasts. The result is an intricate golden cider with floral and pear aromas. The wonderful balance of crab apples and other wild apples creates a "clean yet creamy mouthfeel, with earthy flavors, and some lingering melon and citrus notes." His lineup consists of other forage creations such as Wild Meadow and unique offerings like a maple-infused cider that is a tribute to what Monterey is really known for, the Monterey Maple Festival.

Try this: The Highland Scrumpy is a delicious cider that pays homage to the Highland community and the idea of scrumping or hunting for apples. The description is listed above in the writeup. ABV: 7.6 percent.

The Allegheny Gold is a fruit-forward cider blending locally grown Harrison, Ashmead's Kernel, and Wickson Crab. This semi-dry cider displays a nice body and mouthfeel due to the tannins from the apples. Notes of citrus, caramel, honey, and pear are clear, while a nice minerality exists because of the unique terroir of Highland County. The cider finishes with a slightly sweet end from the presence of residual sugar. ABV: 8.2 percent.

Kirk shows his innovative side with his Fireside. This high-alcohol (10.5 percent), amber-colored sweet cider is one of a kind. According to Kirk, "We take freshly squeezed cider and heat it over a fire at a Highland County maple sugar camp to evaporate off excess water. This process concentrates the flavors, the sugars and the apple essences. The result is an intensely flavored cider that will warm you, like the fire that it was crafted with." I'm unaware of any cideries in Virginia or even the United States that have embraced this technique to create a sweet high-alcohol cider. The cider works well with desserts and can be used in cocktails. Zynodoa, one of my favorite restaurants (located in Staunton), has included a winter cocktail with the Fireside in it. They have also used Kirk's concoction to make a reduction glaze for one of their desserts. So whether it's in a cocktail or sipping it straight by a fire, you will have to try Fireside. ABV: 10.5 percent.[11]

Troddenvale at Oakley Farm

The translation of Troddenvale is roughly "Valley Road"—trodden (path-walk) and vale (valley). The goal of Troddenvale (at Oakley Farm) cider is to translate this sense of the valley road and the surrounding area of Bath County into the glass. I believe that Will and Cornelia Hodges, the owners of this farm cidery in the Alleghany Mountains, have accomplished this.

Oakley Farm was founded in 1834 as one of the original farms of the Warm Springs Valley. Sitting on top of limestone at an elevation of 2,400 feet above sea level, there is truly no other place in the Commonwealth quite like this. Will and Cornelia knew this when they purchased the farm from the Von Schilling's (Will's grandparents) in 2018. Orchards have existed on the farm throughout its nearly two-hundred-year history, but the remaining trees have faded, so they dedicated more than four acres of new plantings to help with their new cider venture.

Even though Will and Cornelia couldn't use any fruit from their site when I visited, their product is still amazing. (They had their first crops in 2022.) You can still taste the history of the property and the richness of the valley in the glass. They believe in limited interaction during production and use natural fermentation. No sulfites or filtration are used, and they conduct fermentation in wooden barrels. They both come from a wine-making background, and it shows in their complex product. Their lineup consists of traditional single varietal ciders (like Hewe's) to ciders that have been fermented with fruit (like Kieffer pears and plums) from their farm and the surrounding area. Troddenvale (and Patois) have some of the best labels in Virginia, because they feature the areas and farms where the apples come from, types of apples and specific percentages of the blend, and the growing conditions and soil type. It's very similar to a wine label, and their product is clearly capable of reaching that higher perceived value seen in many desirable wines.

Will and Cornelia are planning to plant two thousand apple trees of twenty different varieties for the future. And in 2019, they developed a partnership with Fireside Farm, incorporating their pastured poultry operation within the orchard. Their goal for their farm and their business is to contribute to the rural economy through a closed looped system that benefits both the land and the community. Everything contributes to the farm. The animals can keep the pests out of the orchard, and they fertilize the ground while also benefitting from feeding on the terroir of the valley road. This is all part of the experience of Troddenvale at Oakley Farm.

Many of their ciders may change year to year based on the fruit yield and what's available. They have also just opened a tasting room, so check their website for hours.

Try this: They have a series called the "Grower Series," which focuses on a single orchard. I absolutely loved their 2019 Foggy Ridge Cider Orchard (this is from Diane Flynt's orchard, Foggy Ridge, in Dugspur). The blend of "52 percent Virginia Hewe's Crab, 24 percent Ribston & Cox's Orange Pippins, 12 percent Horse, 8 percent Parmar, 4 percent Graniwinkle" was placed into neutral French oak where it was fermented with native yeasts and malolactic fermentation. The resulting product was a fantastic complex and multilayered cider. The whole tasting experience is quite in-depth with inviting aromatics and flavors of "tropical fruit and sweet doughy pastry." ABV: 8 percent.

The Petite Cider is one of their signature ciders and should be available annually. This single varietal Hewe's Crab comes from orchards in Nelson and Augusta County. The juice was fermented with native yeast in neutral oak. The cider is bottled still and unfiltered, and the lack of bubbles provided a lush mouthfeel and allows the tannins to come through. There are notes of pineapple, mango, and Seville oranges. This is a beautiful expression of Virginia's most famous cider apple. ABV: 8.4 percent[12]

Halcyon Days Cider Co.

"Halcyon" refers to a mythical, idyllic time in the past, evoking a nostalgia for times of happiness and prosperity,

The labyrinth of trees tracing the history of modern American, heirloom American, classic European, and Central Asian apples, set around the pavilion at Halcyon Days Cider Co. in Natural Bridge. (Halcyon Days Cider Co.)

which makes for a pretty good description of my time at this unique cidery in Natural Bridge. My visit to this tranquil spot was not only happy and peaceful because of the comforting cider, but also because I was mystified as I journeyed through a labyrinth of more than two thousand apple trees of fifty different varieties. The 1.7-mile labyrinth is modeled after the labyrinth at the Chartres Cathedral in France, but what is really unique about this unique feature is that it traces the history of the apple from Central Asia to America. "Through an 11-circuit path, you can venture through the modern American, heirloom American, classic European, and Central Asian ancestral apple trees." The apple trees are also labeled to assist the explorer. It's kind of like an exhibit at an outdoor museum that follows the migration history of the apple. In the middle of the labyrinth is a pavilion that provides a stunning 360-degree view of the Alleghany and Blue Ridge

Mountain ranges. Once you reach the center (with your glass of cider in hand) you have achieved the pinnacle of a halcyon day. This remarkable site in Natural Bridge should be explored and savored by cider and nature enthusiasts alike.

The beginning of Halcyon Days Cider Company starts with the owner, Larry Krietemeyer. He wanted to retire and leave the hustle and bustle of professional life in Florida to settle down in the countryside and work with the land, so he and his wife returned to the scenic valley where they could embrace their love of farming. In 2017, after joining forces with his brother, the Krietemeyers decided to open a family-run cidery in Natural Bridge. Their facility and cider are rooted in farming and history (showcased in the apple orchard labyrinth). The building that houses the cidery was previously the home of a large midcentury dairy farm. Larry transformed the 1940s milking barn into their production facility, and the tasting room is a renovated rustic log cabin dating back to the 1860s. As one stands in these historic buildings and tastes their ciders, one gets the full effect of how history and agriculture collide.

Larry's ciders are remarkably wine-like. Their style involves using the natural characteristics of cider apples, using yeasts that enhance (without altering) the flavors of the apples and providing the fermentation and maturation process enough time to work properly. They are intricate with big flavors and a lovely body, and one can tell that he is getting the best apples available for his products. Some of his ciders resemble a deep golden rich buttery chardonnay, or even a grassy citrusy sauvignon blanc. The colors and flavors are vibrant. When I visited Halcyon Days on a nice spring day, I tasted a cider called Midas Touch made from King David and Golden Russet apples. It was similar to a crisp pinot grigio with floral notes. I also enjoyed a cider called Occam's Razor, which was a blend of

WASSAIL

When most Americans think of cider, they think of nonalcoholic fresh cider or hot mulled cider served during the wintertime. This is due in part to the legacy and continued presence of the seasonal Wassail celebrations. Wassail is an Anglo-Saxon word that means "in good health." This winter festivity held in the middle of January pays homage to the pagan belief in nature as a living spirit, and cider enthusiasts bless the trees and pray for a bountiful harvest for the upcoming year. Traditional wassailing in England has included marching through the orchards armed with torches to light the night sky and brandy to warm your cold bones. In many areas, the procession also included a king and queen of the festival, and their subjects sing songs to wake up the trees. Wassail in America has taken the form of a winter celebration that includes drinking a type of spiced cider made of nutmeg, cinnamon, allspice, or any other fall spices. Several Virginia cideries continue this tradition by having annual Wassail festivals. Each winter, Courthouse Creek in Maidens invites guests to help make some noise and wake up the trees, scare evil spirits away, and bless the orchard to bring a good harvest. Big Fish in Monterey also hosts a popular Wassail festival where guests use torches and shouts to bring nature back from its slumber. You can awaken the spirits while drinking their seasonal Wassail cider that features Jonagold, Pink Lady, York, and Stayman apples with traditional mulling spices.

Source: Cook, *Ciderology*, 195–96.

Hewe's and Wickson Crabs. This English-style cider was almost reminiscent of an earthy old-world red wine. It had perfect acidity with a long comforting finish. You also need to check out the artwork on the bottles; they are very creative and can be coveted by collectors for their pop art appeal.

Try this: Jubilance features a single varietal Harrison that spent time in oak for six months and was bottled unfiltered. A small amount of residual sugar balances out the hefty tannins. "Slightly sweet and tart with tangy mouthfeel due to the high tannins of the Harrison apples. Lingering warm finish," the website reads. ABV: 8 percent

The main star in Eureka, an off-dry cider, is Gold Rush apples. Also bottled unfiltered, this lightly carbonated beverage has a "hint of spice with a mellowed tartness." It's a perfect treat to sip as you navigate the labyrinth at Halcyon Days. ABV: 7.6 percent.[13]

Charlottesville Area

Bryant's Cidery & Brewery

If you're planning a beverage tour down Route 151 in Nelson County, my recommendation is to start with Bryant's Cidery & Brewery and work your way north. You don't want to miss this truly farm-to-table beverage stop that has everything an alcohol adventurer could want. Bryant's makes not only ciders and seltzers but also beer, so everyone in your group can find something that works for them. The first time that I drove to Bryant's, I thought I was at the end of the world (or the end of the 151-alcohol corridor), but the drive is worth it to see this charming historic property and imbibe their delicious beverages. The land where Bryant's sits has been a family farm for over 150 years dating back to just after the Civil War, when it was named Edgewood.

In the late 1960s, Hurricane Camille swept through Nelson County, destroying a large portion of the Edgewood farm, including the orchards, and laying waste to other properties in Nelson County. After the storm, Jerry Thornton's grandparents saved the farm by repairing the house and reestablishing the orchards. Today, through six generations, begins a new chapter for the Edgewood farm with Bryant's Cidery & Brewery. Jerry Thornton is preserving that legacy through his commitment and perseverance to the land.

I met Jerry at his beautifully restored farmhouse, an impressive white structure where he had several old family photographs spread throughout the house as he told me his story. Thornton, a former finance director in Northern Virginia, wasn't happy with his job and wanted to spend more time with his daughter while she grew up. Raised by his grandparents on the farm, he had many fond memories of the property from his childhood and decided to make the transition from finance director to farm manager. He built a cidery on the property (and most recently a brewery), and he hasn't looked back. His cider is very good and tests the limits of flavors. Brite Good is a traditional-style cider that is possibly the same type of cider that his family members were making on the farm in Roseland. It's very dry with oak chips added to enhance its tannins. He experiments with different ingredients such as habaneros, botanicals, coffee, and barrel aging. One of his most popular products is Unicorn Fuel, which incorporates rose hips and hibiscus. I have not tried their beer, but if their cider is any indication, then it's definitely worth tasting.

Bryant's has expanded their market to Richmond by opening up a tasting room in Carytown. This location in Richmond paved the way for Bryant's to partner with the Virginia Capital Trail for its official cider, Trail Blazer. Jerry also likes to experiment with specialty ciders and barrel-aged ciders like his bourbon and peach—Still Swingin—brut cider aged in bourbon barrels and finished with an infusion of fresh local peaches.

Try this: Brite Good is their flagship cider with a pleasant dryness and enhanced tannins. It's available at several restaurants and markets throughout Virginia. ABV: 6.9 percent.

Unicorn Fuel is an appropriate name for this blush-colored dry cider infused with rose hips and hibiscus. Rose hips are an ingredient seen more often in recent years, not only in ciders but in other alcoholic beverages as well. It was a traditional addition to English beverages like mead. This cider is made with apples from Nelson County and exhibits a slight citrusy taste. ABV: 6.9 percent.

Another brilliant name and label is Crackberry. This is a special blend of Nelson County apples with cranberries and rosemary. This is one of their most popular expressions, and I can see why, as its taste is refreshing and addictive. The unique balance of berry and herbal notes makes for a flavor bomb. The cider has a pleasant inviting aroma, fruity taste, and dry finish. ABV: 6.9 percent.[14]

Bold Rock Hard Cider

In 2012, my wife and I were on our annual wine trip to Charlottesville and took a detour and stopped by a new cidery in Nellysford called Bold Rock. We were pleasantly surprised when we stumbled across this hidden gem that would eventually become one of the nation's largest cider producers.[15] Brian Shanks, Bold Rock's head cider maker and world-renowned cider connoisseur, began making cider in the late 1980s, and today he's recognized as the father of cider production in New Zealand. Shanks poured us some tasty samples and chatted with us about the property owner, John Washburn, and his plans for a much larger Bold Rock tasting experience. Since 1986, John had been improving the landscape of his property, but he wasn't quite sure what to make of it. Twenty-five years later he found the emerging cider industry to be the perfect opportunity, so he tracked down one of the best cider makers in the world, Brian Shanks, and made him an offer he couldn't refuse. The dynamic duo named their brand Bold Rock, after the name of Wintergreen's black rock as well as a tribute to the company's bold mission and style.

Bold Rock joined forces with Eagle Distributing early on to ensure that their product was marketed and distributed effectively. They projected 8,000 cases in 2012 and sold 48,000 cases. In 2014, their vision for a bold new tasting experience in Nellysford became a reality when John built a $4 million facility along Highway 151. The beautiful rustic structure features reclaimed wood and handmade brick, oak beams, and multiple fireplaces. The building was almost perfect. The only thing that it lacked was sufficient production space.

In 2015, they opened another facility in Mills River,

The beautifully sited and inviting tasting facilities at Bold Rock Hard Cider in Nellysford. (Bold Rock Hard Cider)

North Carolina, in an old vegetable packing center to meet the demand of their growing product. The Mills River production center and tasting room is more of an industrial chic compared to the Nellysford ski lodge feel. The facility is located near Asheville, so it takes advantage of the craft beverage scene in the thriving city along with the apple culture of western North Carolina. Bold Rock makes their own North Carolina Draft and North Carolina Apple with apples from Henderson County, North Carolina.

Some of the biggest news for Bold Rock came in December 2019, when they signed a contract with Artisanal Brewing Ventures (a different ABV) to expand their brand to other regions and increase their footprint and production by using their resources. (ABV is a leading regional craft beverage company that comprises four major beverage brands: Victory, Southern Tier, Sixpoint, and Bold Rock.) Bold Rock has a great portfolio of products from cider and seltzers to cocktails and spirits and hard teas and lemonades. I've been to Bold Rock many times, and their facility is kid-friendly, birthday-party-friendly, and date-friendly, and they have an excellent selection of cider. The lovely tasting room and restaurant overlook gorgeous views of the Rockfish River. Sitting outside with friends, taking in the sights of the valley while drinking a Bold Rock, it's clear that John and Brian have really accomplished their goal by providing perfect place for the community to meet and drink a local tasty beverage.

Try this: Bold Rock is one of the first Virginia cideries to take fruited ciders to the next level. They have several variations including pineapple, pear, and watermelon. The Pineapple is loaded with tropical notes, blending Blue Ridge apples and pineapple juice to create a smooth-tasting beverage that highlights the beauty of Virginia with a citrus flair. Its fruit-forward taste will keep you wanting more from the tap or from a six pack in your fridge. ABV: 4.7 percent.

The Premium Dry is perhaps my favorite of Bold Rock's lineup, and it was also one of the products that we blind-tasted at the Virginia Tech sensory workshop, where it was rated among the highest. This off-dry cider has a good balance of "natural sweetness and acidity," leading to a refreshing finish that begs for another sip. ABV: 6 percent.[16]

Blue Toad Hard Cider

When I met with Todd Rath, otherwise known as "Toad" to his friends, he was in the middle of organizing an album launch party for a local band at his cidery. Todd also recently opened their new Cider Hall building. It was a massive undertaking, but I don't think this bothered him at all, Todd's always trying a new project. After graduating from Purdue University, he and his brother started Rock Bottom Golf, an online discount golf store. His brother still manages the successful golf equipment company, but Todd sold his share to start some new business ventures. He opened a pub in Nelson County, in Afton, right on 151 in 2012, and within three years he launched a second pub in Rochester, New York, where he's originally from. He noticed that their ciders were big sellers, so Todd took the next logical step and started his own cidery in New York. After the success of his pubs and cidery, he looked for a good location for his family to settle permanently, and that's how he ended up in beautiful Nelson County. With his entrepreneurial spirit still kicking, he purchased properties in the surrounding area to manage (including a quaint Afton hotel) and decided to expand his cidery operation to the south. When the former Wintergreen Winery went up for sale, he quickly purchased that property in August 2015 and had it fully operational and licensed by the end of October. The location was exactly what Todd was trying to establish—an idyllic sitting that allows visitors to escape to nature while enjoying a pint of cider made from apples grown in the Blue Ridge Mountains. It's also an ideal site for kids to explore with family activities. (I've witnessed family football games and games of tag and hide and seek being played throughout the property.) Blue Toad is the perfect spot to have a picnic during a trip down 151 and enjoy Virginia's historic beverage with Mother Nature. There is plenty of space and accommodations for large groups and families.

But Blue Toad isn't just about the setting; it's really about the cider. Their ciders use a blend of three to four different apple varieties (mainly from Silver Creek and Seamans' Orchard, grown just down the road in Tyro). Blue Toad's motto is "Old School Values and New World Sensibility." According to Todd, "It's really about farm to tap and this is an all-American product that has come full circle. This land (where the cidery sits) was originally High View Farm where a 300-acre apple farm existed until 1978. It's great to know that this land has apple growing roots in the soil and now we are making cider here."

There are usually at least eight ciders on tap at Blue Toad. These range from their standard bearers like the Blue Ridge Blonde and Flannel Amber (which are simply fermented apples) to their more creative fruited endeavors such as a Hawaii Toad Ohh (pineapple cider) and Orange Crush (cider with Florida orange peels). Each quarter the cidery releases a new and unique barrel-aged cider. They also have a lighter (low-calorie, low-carb) line of ciders that are made with 100 percent Granny Smith apples. Whatever your choice, it will help to enhance your lazy day at the foot of Wintergreen relaxing by the creek. Blue Toad even makes a cider for their brewery friends down the street at Pro Renata Brewing Co. (Cherry Lime and Apple a Day) and Blue Mountain Brewery (Mountain Apple), so if you're visiting Pro Renata for a tasting or grabbling lunch at Blue Mountain, you can still grab a pint.

Try this: Blue Ridge Blonde is their flagship cider. A combination of Golden Delicious, Granny Smith, and Red

Delicious, this cider is crisp and fruit forward. It's very smooth and light and features a bright clean taste of fresh orchard fruit. ABV: 5 percent.

Black Cherry is a blend of apples that are infused with black cherries. This marriage creates a refreshingly mellow tartness. The delicious cherry finish leaves your mouth slightly puckered and wanting more. ABV: 6 percent.[17]

Albemarle CiderWorks

As I traveled around the Commonwealth chatting with different cidery owners and cider makers, there was one question that I was always asked, "Have you chatted with Chuck Shelton at Albemarle CiderWorks?" Chuck Shelton, often referred to as the "Grandfather of Virginia Cider," has helped numerous aspiring cider makers. His knowledge of apples and the fermentation process are endless. Chuck comes from a farming family in Amherst County, and in 1961 when his father, E. R. "Bud" Shelton, took a job at the Department of Forestry, the Shelton family left their Amherst farm and moved to Charlottesville. As Bud and his wife, Mary Shelton, closed in on retirement twenty-five years later, they wanted to return to the farm life, so in the fall of 1986, they along with their children, Chuck, Bill, Charlotte, and Todd, purchased a homestead in southern Albemarle County. This farm in North Garden would eventually become a nursery and a cidery. In 1990, after being inspired by heirloom apples through courses taught by Tom Burford and Peter Hatch, the Sheltons began growing a large number of old apple varieties. Within a few years, they created a successful nursery that provided apple trees to amateur and veteran apple enthusiasts alike. In 2000, Vintage Virginia Apples LLC opened with over one hundred varieties of apple trees. The Sheltons provided educational workshops for community members who wanted to learn more about horticulture and orcharding. In 2009, as their orchard continued to expand, they embarked on a new business venture and created Albemarle CiderWorks.

Albemarle CiderWorks is truly a family affair. Chuck is the cider maker. He's the science guy and fermentation expert behind the operation with degrees in environmental science and zoology. When I caught up with him on a cool fall day, he was busy working on the farm, preparing apples to be pressed. We chatted about his start in the world of cider. He admitted that he knew little about cider making when he first started, but he was willing to learn. He worked with Michael Shaps, the Virginia wine guru, to learn more about the fermentation process. After consulting with Shaps, he produced his first batch of cider, and the rest is history. For the past twelve years, the Sheltons have blazed a trail for aspiring cider makers and helped set the standard for Virginia cider (along with Diane Flynt of Foggy Ridge Cider). Virginia cideries have increased exponentially since Albemarle's start, and much of that growth (and success) is a direct result of Chuck's influence. He has consulted with other cider makers, managed interns (who became future cider makers and cidery owners, like Courtney Mailey, founder of Blue Bee Cider), and provided guidance for the Virginia apple community. His kind personality, dedication to the craft, and willingness to share his expertise has led to the success of the Old Dominion's cider industry.

Chuck's sister, Charlotte Shelton, refers to Albemarle's style as "Fine Cider." I met with Charlotte when she was in the middle of juggling several tasks. Charlotte, the oldest of the Shelton siblings, has worn many hats, including as CEO of Vintage Virginia Apples. Her background in history and finance has helped her not only run a successful business but also provide an excellent educational experience to anyone who wants to learn about cider (and apples). (I can attest to this from attending the 2022 apple-and-cheese pairing event at Monticello where Charlotte led the audience through eight different tastings.) She believes that it's important to let the apples speak for themselves, and one of her main goals for Albemarle is to bring the orchard to glass in the form of a "Fine Cider." Their artisanal style is rooted in history, and you can see this in their portfolio ranging from heirloom cider blends to single varietal creations. They also have an excellent website that is perfect for novice and expert cider lovers interested in learning more about apples and apple growing.

Other members of the family business include Bill Shelton (Charlotte and Chuck's brother) who is the nursery manager for Vintage Virginia Apples and Bill's daughter, Anne Shelton, who is the general manager and assists with the day-to-day operations. Albemarle CiderWorks's tasting room is a lovely farmhouse structure that makes you feel like you are part of the orchard-to-glass experience. Their products are a true testament to the wonderful history behind the storied fruit.

Try this: The amber-colored 1817 cider is well-balanced with lush tropical flavors that come from its blend of three historic apples: Harrison, Hewe's, and Winesap. The recipe is from apple historian William Coxe's book, *A View of the Cultivation of Fruit Trees, and the Management of Orchards and Cider,* published in 1817 (and hence the name). The great cider expert remarked that "The finest liquor I ever have seen, was made from the [Hewe's] crab, with a small portion of the Harrison apple of Newark, and the Winesap of West-Jersey." This full-bodied beverage was and is still an excellent food-paring cider. ABV: 7.6 percent.

Jupiter's Legacy is their flagship cider that changes slightly from year to year based on apple availability and Chuck's preference. A medium-bodied cider blend of more than twenty apples including Albemarle Pippin, Arkansas Black, and crab apples that create a smooth tasting cider with just enough tartness. The name is a tribute to one of Jefferson's enslaved workers, Jupiter Evans, who made cider at Monticello (and who was discussed earlier in chapter 2). ABV: 7 percent.[18]

Potter's Craft Cider

Potter's Craft Cider began with two Princeton college buddies, Tim Edmond and Dan Potter, who had a shared love of homebrewing and transitioned their passion from making beer to fermenting apples. This shift began when their plans for a brewery failed as their barley and hops that they were growing were washed away by a flood along the James River. Despite this setback, they were still determined to pursue their interests in agriculture, fermentation, and experimentation. Dan was living at the historic Tuckahoe Plantation in Henrico County (Jefferson's childhood home), where he made a cider out of some Crozet apples and the brewery equipment that they had purchased. After they tasted this brilliantly vibrant acidic creation that was unlike anything they had ever had, they were sold on cider. They opened Potter's Craft Cider

The tasting room for Potter's Craft Cider at Neve Hall. (Potter's Craft Cider)

in 2011 in Free Union, located in Albemarle County just northwest of Charlottesville, as one of the first cideries in Virginia.

Andy Hannas has been the head cider maker at Potter's since 2013. A chef by trade, Hannas has incorporated his background working with different ingredients to produce truly unique and flavorful ciders that strike a balance between apples and "flavor town" (in Guy Fieri's parlance). He is highly revered in the cider world for his creativity and willingness to work outside of the limits. His style includes Champagne-like single varietal Albemarle Pippin Cuvees to barrel-aged apple blends that are wild fermentations with spices. Potter's also has a series of session ciders that consist of a Grapefruit Hibiscus Session Cider and Petit Cider with only 85 calories per beverage. These ciders usually have a lower alcohol content, are more drinkable, and are available in cans. They have at least twenty offerings for visitors to experience, including a few cocktail creations, so you can try all ends of the spectrum. Potter's mission is to reach audiences by providing a tasty craft product that speaks to Virginia's agriculture, and their diverse lineup can appeal to both wine and beer drinkers. Their hop-forward citrus ciders may suit beer drinkers, while the more delicate expressions feature various flavor profiles to benefit wine drinkers' palates.

As a University of Virginia alumnus, I fell in love with the history behind Potter's tasting room at Neve Hall. Located just a few miles south of the University, the former Episcopal chapel and artist's home is linked to several famous people such as twentieth-century architect Eugene Bradbury, who designed Neve Hall, Keswick Hall, and St. Paul's Memorial Church in Charlottesville. Other famous residents include Lady Astor (Nancy Witcher Langhorne Astor, an American-born British politician who served in Parliament), Erskine Caldwell (novelist and short story writer who was author of *Tobacco Road* and *God's Little*

Acre), and Henry "Pop" Lannigan (UVA's first head basketball coach and the namesake of UVA's Lannigan Field). Potter's acquired the historic building in November 2019 and converted it into a stunning open and airy tasting room that still retains the classical architecture of the structure. The location also includes a beautiful outside space that is the perfect venue to sip a glass of cider and watch the day go by.

Try this: The Haven is one of my favorite nontraditional ciders. I have a passion for Belgian beers, and Potter's take on a Trappist-style cider is spot on. This cider blend has been fermented on dark Candi syrup, figs, and coriander. A Belgian yeast is added, and the resulting beverage is similar to the color of a Belgian Quadrupel with a fruity, spicy aroma. The taste is slight honey, with a balance of acidity and dryness. It is named after the local day shelter for the homeless, for whom the proceeds benefit. A wonderful beverage for a great cause. ABV: 12 percent.

Farmhouse Dry was one of Potter's first ciders, and it remains their signature cider. The word "farmhouse" is sometimes used interchangeably with "traditional" to describe a cider that is naturally fermented with minimal intervention from the cider maker. Potter's version is fantastic. The beverage consists of a mix of Old Virginia Winesap, Gold Rush, and Albemarle Pippin apples that's full of ripe melon and stone fruit flavors. It is a very versatile food-pairing option, so enjoy it with whatever you're craving. ABV: 8 percent.[19]

Patois Cider

Patois is the French word for a regional dialect. This is important to Patrick Collins and Danielle LeCompte, owners of Patois Cider based in Charlottesville, as the regional is what Patois is all about. The goal for them is "for the ciders to reveal fleeting moments from small pockets of Virginia." Patrick, a Washington, DC, native, spent time in various restaurants specializing in beverages and working at commercial cideries. He also worked for three years as the assistant cider maker at Potter's. His love of natural wine and his cidery experience led him to create a unique regional product with Danielle. It's about getting the best products in the region for them, and Patois doesn't back down from a challenge. They like using apple trees that have been untouched, usually on someone's homestead. Foraging at abandoned orchards is one of Patrick's favorite hobbies, but it is difficult and sometimes dangerous. Patrick told me stories of how he climbs up trees to get the fruit and fends off wild animals for the bounty. He's also had to scare off cattle who are waiting at the bottom of the tree to get the fallen apples. Patois embraces a strict natural fermentation process, including practices that are sometimes discouraged at other cideries, like malolactic fermentation. But they prefer to let nature run its course—if it happens it happens. According to Patrick, "The ciders are unfined and unfiltered . . . any carbonation is a byproduct of captured fermentation."

Patois's ciders are in line with what you would expect from a fine natural wine, and they make excellent food-paring beverages. They offer vast complexities with unique and elegant flavors that pair very well with various cuisine. One can truly taste the terroir and patois of Virginia in their creations.

Patois's lineup consists of some single varietal ciders, flavorful blends, and Virginia wine cofermentations with Vidal blanc (a grape that does well in Virginia's climate and one of the more popular Virginia white wines).

The bottle descriptions of their ciders, like Troddenvale's, are an homage to the cider maker's background in the wine world. Each cider description goes into detail about the site where the fruit was harvested, the weather, the soil, and the fermentation process.

Patois's ciders change all the time based on the bounty

that Mother Nature provides. Please contact Patois for tasting and purchase options.[20]

Try this: The Bent Mountain 2019, made from 100 percent Albemarle Pippins that come from Witt Orchard in Roanoke County, is superb. Witt is a noncommercial orchard where the trees are more than forty years old. The cider was placed in an oak barrel on gross lees (or natural sediment) for six months, then racked and refermented in the bottle with its own yeasts and organic sugar. It was then aged for twelve months, and then riddled and disgorged by hand in late April 2021. It's quite wine-like, exhibiting a pleasing floral aroma and complex flavors of crushed strawberry and spice. All of Patois's labels are artistic, and the Bent Mountain bottle is no exception. It features a "cyanotype of 2020 blossoms, reflecting the influence of direct sun on this fruit." ABV: 8.3 percent.

In art, bricolage can be a technique or artistic method, where something is created from several different tools available. The Bricolage 2019 is one of the most exquisite ciders that I have ever tasted. It is great with food or on its own, and it shows the craft of cider making while utilizing the beautiful bounty of Virginia's wild apples. The Bricolage blend changes from year to year, but the 2019 was made from fruit from Albemarle, Nelson, and Augusta counties. According to Patois's website this unique cider "had hints of Violets, mountain mint, caramelized plum, river rocks." Check out future vintages of this fantastic blend. ABV: 7.3 percent.

Castle Hill Cider

One of the benefits to researching the story of Virginia cider is being immersed in the history of the cideries, the farms, and buildings, which is definitely the case with Castle Hill Cider in Keswick. Located about fifteen miles northeast of Charlottesville, Castle Hill is listed on both the US National Register of Historic Places and the Virginia Landmarks Register, and it boasts probably one of the most storied pasts of any beverage facility in the United States. The area where the cidery sits was once part of King George II's land grant, and in 1764, Dr. Thomas Walker, a friend of Peter Jefferson, established an estate and orchard on fifteen hundred acres there. Dr. Walker would become Thomas Jefferson's legal guardian and mentor following Peter's death in 1757.

Dr. Walker also put one of the most famous Virginia apples, the Albemarle Pippin, on the map. He served under George Washington during the Revolutionary War, and after the Battle of Brandywine Creek in 1777, he brought scions of the popular New York apple, the Newtown Pippin, back to Albemarle County. The cuttings were successfully grafted at the site of Castle Hill. By the end of the 1700s, the popular apple was grown widely throughout the Commonwealth, and took the name Albemarle Pippin when grown in the mid-Atlantic

During the nineteenth and twentieth centuries, the estate continued to house prominent families like the Rives and the Potts families. The writer and celebrity, Amélie Louise Rives, after whom the cidery's Sunday Muse is named (Amélie drew a nude self-portrait at Castle Hill, entitling it Sunday Muse), occupied the house, as did an officer who served under Robert E. Lee named Colonel Alfred Landon Rives and the first woman master of foxhounds, Mrs. Gertrude Rives Potts.

Castle Hill Cider was founded in 2010 to bring the historic property back to its apple-growing roots. The orchard at Castle Hill has more than 6,500 apple trees like Black Twig, Burford Redflesh, Hewe's Crab, and Albemarle Pippin. To help with growing conditions, they enlisted the expertise of beekeeper Diego DeCorte of The Elysium Honey Company, who ensures that the bees pollinate the apple trees efficiently.

When I met with cider maker Don Whitaker and general manager Ron Campbell at the beautiful manor, it was clear that their objective for Castle Hill is to make one of the best products possible, and they have accomplished that. They work together to select the perfect apple blend for their ciders so that the finished product will have a good balance of acidity, body/structure, and lush aromatics. They also have a unique method of fermentation for one of their ciders. The process is called qvevri. According to their website, qvevri are terra cotta pots imported from the Republic of Georgia. "The process of underground fermentation in qvevri is roughly eight thousand years old, and Castle Hill is the only cidery in the world actively utilizing them for commercial cider production. Levity ferments in the qvevri underground for about four months at 43 degrees—slow and cold. It then experiences a bottle conditioning; or secondary fermentation; for natural sparkle and must be kept chilled to protect some of its sweetness." It is also important to note that the qvevri process leaves a smaller carbon footprint in comparison to standard cider making practices. This innovative practice is a testament to their mission as they explore the boundaries of cider while keeping things traditional. Their lineup consists of "one of a kind" ciders like Levity to their higher-ABV pommeaus and ports.

Try this: Castle Hill's Levity 2017 is a mixture of ten apples that include Albemarle Pippin, Dabinett, Yarlington Mill, Golden Hornet Crabs, and Rhode Island Greening. (I believe that this is one of the only times that I've seen Golden Hornet Crabs used.) Levity is a wild yeast fermentation in the terra cotta qvevri. It has a natural sparkle due to its bottle conditioning, and it is full-bodied with sharp notes of overly ripe bramble berries and roasted almonds. Its finish is long with a hint of lemon zest. ABV: 7.9 percent.

Castle Hill also has a nice array of fortified drinks. Their 1764 Port is a great sipper for relaxing after dinner by the fireplace. At 18 percent it serves as a delightful digestive and body warmer. Named for the year that Castle Hill was founded, this strong elixir packs a punch from its blend of "slightly fermented cryo-concentrated cider apple juice (mainly Black Twig) and custom-distilled eau de vie." The blend is then "aged in oak barrels and presents a medium-heavy body with intense aromatics and sweetness." Try this with any dessert. Their website recommends caramelized peaches, but I could see it complementing something heavier like a chocolate bourbon pecan pie. ABV: 18 percent.[21]

Richmond Area

Courthouse Creek Cider

My ideal tasting experience involves sitting within the very orchards from which the present beverage originated. This may be ambitious, but it is possible at Courthouse Creek Cider in Maidens. The owners of this Goochland cidery, Liza and Eric Cioffi, met in the picturesque wine region of Central California, and when Eric had an opportunity to move to Virginia in 2012, the couple and their family relocated east to take advantage of the calmer pace that would allow them to accomplish their dreams of growing grapes and making wine. They settled on a charming farm west of Richmond to start their vineyard, but after tasting some Virginia cider that plan shifted to an orchard instead. Within four years they sold their first vintage of Courthouse Creek Cider, and a year later established a tasting room on the property.

Their land has four acres of trees planted with a variety of American, English, and French cider apple trees. Their tasting room, production facility, and home are all nestled together, and this close proximity to the orchard coincides with their belief that terroir is "more than just the nature of the land; it necessarily includes the entire sense of a place." For the Cioffis nature is their lives, and this comes through in their ciders. Their product is free of any preservatives and is fermented in wooden barrels using natural yeast (ambient or wild). One of their slogans is to "embrace the funk." Their ciders are free from sulfites and other additives, free from filtering and fining, and always barrel-aged. They also bottle-condition all their products, which leaves a natural sediment in the bottle. This technique showcases nature's beauty in a bottle.

The Cioffis embrace the terroir in their operation, and they refer to their philosophy as "culterra"—their own twist on "terroir." According to Courthouse Creek, "Culterra embodies the notion that understanding, interacting, and interpreting one's community—and the land it inhabits—enriches the foundation of both. Our lives and land reflect our interactions, partnerships, friends, and community that is Goochland, Virginia."

Try this: The dry barrel-aged blend Rustico is a great expression of the Cioffis' belief in minimal intervention. Similar to sidras (natural Spanish cider), it has a beautiful carbonation and citrus-like acidity that makes for excellent food pairing. ABV: 7.5 percent.

Black Twig is one of my favorite single varietals, and the 2019 Black Twig does not disappoint. The apples come from Henley's Orchard in Crozet to create a big and bold cider that delivers elements of earthiness with a slight tangy acidity. Some of the depth from this multifaceted elixir comes from being aged in bourbon and wine barrels. ABV: 7.7 percent.

I had their Magnum Bonam on my most recent visit to Courthouse Creek in Fall 2022. Magnum Bonam, or Bonam, was a popular southern apple coming from North Carolina in the mid-nineteenth century. Courthouse Creek gets the juice from a single tree in their neighboring orchard. The touted heirloom apple produces a very fragrant cider with earthy notes and scents of pear. The flavors were bold and reminiscent of some English ciders. A tart and fruity finish capped off this complex unique cider. ABV: 7.8 percent.[22]

Blue Bee Cider

The first time I had (craft) cider was in 2012 when I tasted a bottle of Charred Ordinary from Blue Bee Cider in Richmond. This vivid sunny yellow liquid of 8.3 percent ABV was very complex with aromas of honeysuckle and flavors of lemon and butter, and a hint of lime. It tasted closer to a fine wine than a sour apple jolly rancher, which is what I had come to expect from "hard" ciders. But what was most surprising to me was that this style of cider was not new and innovative but a tribute to colonial Virginia's history. Courtney Mailey, former owner of Blue Bee Cider, made Charred Ordinary to replicate the style of cider that was served all day in taverns and ordinaries. According to Mailey, "This was the cider for Virginians of all classes and walks of life—man, woman, child, rich and poor."

Courtney is an entrepreneur. She saw that cider had a lot of potential and a relatively untapped market in the twenty-first century. She didn't have much of a cider or beverage background outside of her uncle being a winemaker in Washington. Despite this, she set out to learn everything she could about apples and cider. After she apprenticed at a few cideries, attended cider-making school at Cornell University, and studied the fermentation process in-depth, she started Blue Bee Cider in Richmond in 2012.

Blue Bee is named after the blue orchard bee that is associated with pollinating apple trees, and it was Virginia's first urban cidery—that is, a cidery that chooses to locate their business closer to their customer base than its crop source. Courtney's enterprising spirit paved the way for more cideries to open in urban landscapes. Blue Bee has operated in three different fantastic urban spaces. From

2012 to 2017, Blue Bee was housed in Old Manchester at 212 W. 6th Street, next door to Legend Brewing Company. Their building had previously contained the Aragon Coffee building, hence the name of their first cider, Aragon 1904. I remember visiting the cidery in the historic area south of the River City on their opening weekend when Courtney's father, Mel, was assisting with the tours. It was an excellent introduction to the world of craft cider and how it can be produced in an urban environment. In the fall of 2018, she moved her business across the river to a former Richmond city stables complex in Scott's Addition. Her belief and intuitiveness that Scott's Addition would turn into the hub of Richmond's food and drink scene was correct. It took over a year for renovations to be made to the 1940s structure, but once complete it melded the metropolitan landscape of this emerging Richmond social scene and the historic character of the city. In 2023, after a successful venture, Courtney decided to turn over her Blue Bee Cider to two longtime staff members Taylor Benson (cider maker) and Mackenzie Smith (event coordinator and assistant general manager). Taylor and Mackenzie have recently set up their operations and tasting room at 4811 Bethlehem Rd., just a few minutes' drive from Scott's Addition.

Blue Bee creates a style of cider that is innovative yet reserved, sticking to traditional cider values. Their lineup consists of single varietal heirloom apples such as Dabinett and Spitzenburg that are part of their orchard potluck series to fruited ciders like Aplomb (cider aged with crushed plums) and port styles.

Try this: Again, Charred Ordinary is what first hooked me on craft cider. It's quite complex with aromas of honeysuckle, flavors of lemon and butter, and a hint of lime. ABV: 8.3 percent.

Aragon 1904 pays respect to Blue Bee's first location at the Aragon Coffee Building (which was built in 1904). This light, crisp cider is a blend of modern and heirloom apples with a very smooth finish, likely due to a healthy dose of Albemarle Pippin. This off-dry cider has 2 percent residual sugar and is the perfect cider for a summer day. It can go well with many different foods, but it thrives with picnic foods—especially barbecue. ABV: 8.6 percent.

Harvest Ration is a port made in collaboration with Catoctin Creek Distilling Company in Purcellville. Blue Bee sends their cider to Catoctin Creek, who then distills it into *eau de vie* (fruit brandy) and then ages it in new American white oak barrels. After about six months in the barrels, the brandy is blended into an early-stage ferment comprised primarily of Winesap apples. The result is a complex fortified beverage with a strong aroma and flavors of honeysuckle, butterscotch, and spice with rich, sweet apple notes in the finish. This is an elixir dedicated to those Virginians who worked the apple harvest and were given a ration of cider and brandy. It makes for a great bottle to give to someone for a present or enjoy yourself after a hard day's work. ABV: 18.5 percent.[23]

Buskey Cider

When I worked at the Virginia Museum of History and Culture, many of the staff members were interested in hosting a festival that featured some of the area's craft beverage producers. This eventually became their annual BrewHaha festival held on the museum's front lawn in August. The inaugural event in 2017 was quite successful and provided an ideal venue for the community to experience the flavors of Virginia with more than ten breweries, cideries, and meaderies. One of my favorite parts of the event was getting to know the owners of the different establishments—it's here where I first met Will Correll, the CEO and founder of Buskey Cider, and his wife, Elle Correll, the co-owner and marketing director. I learned from Will that "Buskey" was a term that Ben Franklin noted while visiting a tavern. "An old drinking word with no known definition," he reports. This makes sense because Benjamin Franklin was a cider lover, who may have used the word to describe some patrons that were having a little too much fun while quenching their thirst at a local tavern.

After that initial meeting, and many stops to Buskey afterwards, I can clearly see how the word "Buskey" is representative of their Scott's Addition operation: it's a historic and fun cidery that makes a brilliant product to share with friends. Will, who hails from Virginia but also grew up in Memphis, caught the fermentation bug when he began making cider while attending Hampden-Sydney in 2012. He worked on his product over the next three years and aspired to create a startup cidery. The economics and commerce major was determined to make his dream come true, so he entered a business competition and won a $10,000 grant to help him turn his craft cidery vision into a reality. Since opening in Scott's Addition in 2016, his operation has grown, and after leasing the building for seven years, he finally purchased the structure from the landlord in 2022.

Buskey has a lovely tasting room with views of one of Richmond's most popular districts for culinary adventures. Buskey has a wide selection of board and card games, so take your pick whether it's a quick round of UNO or a lengthy game of Risk.

Will classifies most of Buskey's cider as "sessionable"—that is, easy to drink and not exceedingly high in alcohol content. They offer several fruited cider options, as well as herb infused ciders and even a jalapeno lime cider that packs some heat but is mellowed by the lime. They have traditional ciders like their RVA Cider and Buskey Dry while also experimenting with barrel aging: Laphroig (a single-malt Scottish whisky) barrels manage to pack in some smoke, while sherry barrels impart a nutty rich flavor.

Buskey also opened a cider outpost called Buskey on the Bay in Cape Charles. Now Eastern Shore folks don't have to drive across the Chesapeake Bay Bridge-Tunnel to get good cider.[24]

Try this: Tart Cherry is a wonderful, fruited cider. Unlike many ciders that infuse cherry, raspberry, or blueberry, this one is not too sweet. Rather, this cider infused with 100 percent Montmorency cherries is more tart than sweet (hence the name), and its lovely balance of Virginia apples and cherries creates a refreshing cider. It also has a beautiful inviting bright blush color due to the French cherries. ABV: 6.5 percent.

The Heritage Blend changes every year depending on what the cider maker prefers. The 2020 product featured Ashmead's Kernel and Gold Rush, while the 2021 blend consisted of Harrison, Winesap, and Gold Rush. It is typically an off-dry flavorful cider that is complex yet refreshing. This is one of Buskey's more old-style ciders and pays tribute to their belief in historic values and delicious products. This is an annual offering, so make sure to check out the Heritage Blend each year. ABV: 6.9 percent.

Coyote Hole Craft Beverages

Opened in 2016 by Chris and Laura Denkers and Michael Baier and Sarah Conine, Coyote Hole is an homage to the mining history of the town of Mineral, near Lake Anna. A "coyote hole" is a blast hole used by miners that resembles a coyote's den. When we arrived at the picturesque country farm on thirty-seven acres off Route 208 at the height of the Covid-19 pandemic, my wife and I were impressed by the property and its perfect accommodations for two weary travelers trying to social distance. There was ample outside seating and even a tiki bar. That's right—a tiki bar!

The tasting room manager was very informative and excited to share Coyote Hole's mission for cider. We enjoyed a fantastic tasting that ranged from sangria ciders to a dry-hopped IPA style cider called Coyote HPA (Hopped Press Apple). It was among the best tasting experiences that I've had on my journey. They offer a fun Ciderita (a play on margarita) and a Cherry Pucker, which indeed caused me to pucker—both are flavorful and very well done. I particularly enjoyed their light cider offerings (a berry cider and an orange cider) with lower ABV and fewer calories; they were dry yet refreshing. The Sangria series was also a pleasant surprise. I'm not typically a fan of cofermentations with wine, but all three sangrias (some mixed with white wine and some with red) worked. They also have barrel-aged ciders aged in Belmont Farm Distillery barrels (very whiskey-esque) and seasonal favorites including their Apparition, a fall cider with fresh pumpkins from a local farm, brown sugar, and light spices.

Coyote Hole is the official cider for the Fredericksburg Nationals (the Single-A Minor League team affiliated with the Washington Nationals), so you can check out a baseball game and grab a pint of local cider. Coyote Hole also tries to create a venue to host community events like a paint night, karaoke, comedy night, car shows, and screening football and movies on a huge screen at the front of the property.[25]

Try this: Oma Smith's is their flagship cider that comes from a blend of three apples. The cider has medium sweetness because of some back sweetening from Granny Smith cider. There are crisp refreshing flavors of green apple with a pleasing mouthfeel and lingering finish. This is an easy drinker that I could have a couple pints of. ABV: 6.9 percent.

Their fruity Sister Sangria starts with their flagship Oma Smith's green apple hard cider, adds Cabernet Franc wine (a grape that grows well in Virginia and is one of the most popular and delightful Virginia wine styles), and infuses the alcohol with cranberries, blackberries, and tangerines. It is a rich and flavorful cider sangria that makes for a great sipper by the water, especially Lake Anna. ABV: 5.6 percent.

Chesapeake and Eastern Shore

Ditchley Cider Works

Out of all my alcohol travels, Ditchley Cider Works is among the most picturesque sites that I've visited. Ditchley is tucked away in the historic Northern Neck, and old, abandoned homes and former fertile farmland accompanies the drive from Kilmarnock to the stately manor house close to the Chesapeake Bay. Located about three miles north of Kilmarnock proper, Ditchley is run by two Navy veterans who wanted something to keep them occupied in retirement. Ironically, this is the only cidery in the Northern Neck, yet the plantations in early Virginia along this stretch of fertile land were filled with orchards. When I met with Cathy Calhoun (co-owner of Ditchley), she apologized about her appearance and said she had been trying to catch a bull on the farm and wash him. There was also a family checking out of Ditchley's recently opened bed and breakfast, and she needed to assist them with that process, but I was very happy that Cathy could spend some time and chat with me about the history of the cidery and their product despite her demanding farm schedule.

The land where the cidery sits was inherited by Hancock Lee in the late seventeenth century. The six-hundred-plus acres were passed in 1735 to Kendall Lee, who built the main part of the current house at Ditchley. The duPont family acquired the manor in 1929 and added onto the historic property. After serving in the Navy as an engineer and a Seabee and managing a successful global trade business, Cathy wanted something to keep herself busy during retirement, so she and her husband, retired Vice Admiral Paul Grosklags, bought the property from the Jessie Ball duPont Fund in 2014. They convinced the foundation that they would be good stewards of this historic estate by laying out their vision for renovations and preservation as well as their plans for a working farm with orchards and cattle and hogs. Their purchase consisted of "the manor house, caretakers house, a beach house, and ~160 surrounding acres." After a few years of renovations, Ditchley Cider Works opened in 2018 in the former caretaker's house. The property now includes a farm incorporating an orchard of more than fifty varieties of cider apples. They continue to experiment with different fruits to see which grow best in the Northern Neck climate. All their cider is produced from apples grown on the Ditchley property. Cathy explained that they do everything in-house: growing, picking, crushing, and pressing the apples, as well as bottling. Part of this self-sufficiency involves orchard pest control from the geese and turkey that eat the bugs. The hogs on the farm are also part of this system, as they are fed the leftover apple pomace. You can imagine how amazing the sausage tastes. (Because of their proximity to the bay, they also use the pig fat to fry oysters!)

Their cider style and product lineup are traditional, but some products like Rivah (consisting of a blend of Hewe's Crab and Sops of Wine) have a modern take with the addition of Australian hops.

Try this: Cathy created Blush for the wine lover. This blend of Geneva Crab and Redfield imparts a pinkish hue to the cider. The wine yeast fermentation is ended early to create a bit of residual sugar that leads to a lasting sweetness to coat your tongue. ABV: 7.5 percent.

G-8 is the aviation callsign of one of their cider makers, and it is a very complex cider blend of Black Twig and Wickson Crab with hints of baked apples and caramel with a crisp finish. ABV: 8.0 percent.[26]

Sly Clyde Ciderworks

Sly Clyde Ciderworks is in the Phoebus neighborhood of Hampton in the former home of mortician H. Clyde Smith, after whom the cidery is named. According to his friends and family, Clyde always had a "wicked sense of humor" and a "sly smile that made you realize that he had a few secrets about life that he was waiting for you to learn." In 2018, two of Clyde's grandsons, Tim and Doug Smith, restored the former home and named Hampton Road's newest craft beverage site after their fun-loving but sly grandfather. The Smith brothers embarked on this new adventure while maintaining full-time jobs. Tim is the fifth-generation manager of R. Hayden Smith Funeral Home in Hampton, while Doug currently works for a global nongovernmental organization (NGO) called Data Friendly Space and several other startup businesses. (Doug also served as vice president at the Montpelier Foundation's Robert H. Smith Center for the Constitution.) Their family had been in business in the Phoebus area for more than one hundred years as "florists, carpenters, and funeral director for generations." After renovating the building, Doug and Tim were able to create another local family establishment in Hampton that offers a pleasing product and provides a setting for members of the community to sit and chat about life while enjoying a craft beverage.

Even though their ciders are widely distributed and can be found at many locations throughout the state and beyond, Sly Clyde is still driven by the idea to "keep it local." When I visited the cidery with my family on a nice September day, we enjoyed a lovely day outside sipping cider, throwing the football, and enjoying the tasty eats provided by the neighborhood food truck. Hampton Roads is full of "fun in the sun" activities and their ciders can be perfect for a beach day. Some of their lineup caters to the warmer weather thirst quenchers like Submersive

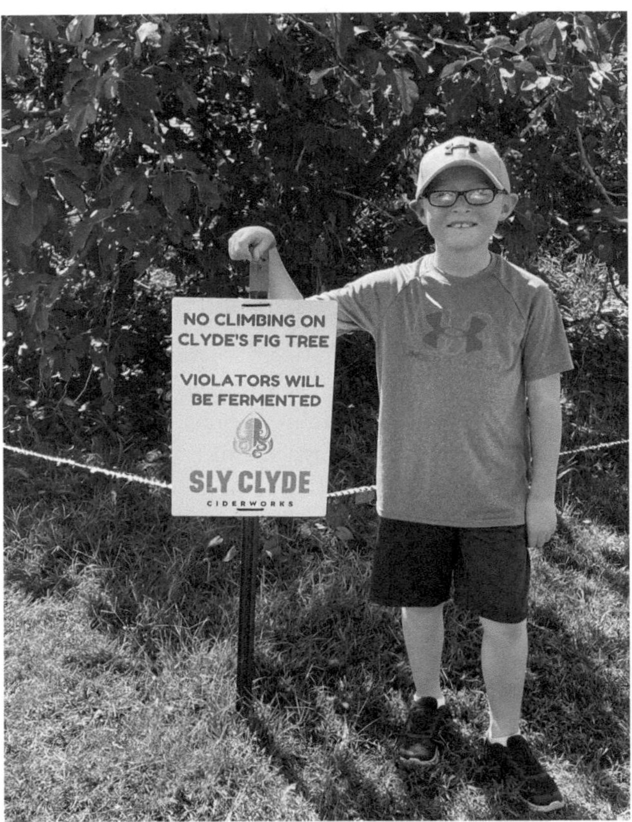

An intrepid explorer (Grant Hansard) on the grounds of Sly Clyde Ciderworks in Hampton. (Photograph by Gregory J. Hansard)

and Inkjet. I think Clyde would be happy to see his former home and business—now a tasting room and production facility—being used as a gathering place for the Chesapeake Bay community.

Sly Clyde's cider ranges from experimental ciders like the habanero and rosemary infused cider, Swinging Compass, to more traditional barrel-aged styles like Dead

Man's Chest that features flavors of vanilla and caramel. Most of their ciders are off-dry to semi-sweet.

Make sure that you check out the photographs and artifacts in the tasting room that tell Clyde's story, and you may see a few jokes too.

Try this: The cherry rose color of Inkjet is quite inviting. The blackberry mint-infused cider offers pleasing fruity and herbal aromas. This mojito-like beverage "deftly combines sweet, savory, and tart." ABV: 6.7 percent.

Submersive is an ideal option for those beachgoers who crave a refreshing semi-sweet cider to quench their thirst on warm day while listening to the crashing waves. This light golden clear cider has aromas of green apple and stone fruit and enough acidity in the apple flavor to balance the sweetness.[27] ABV: 6.7 percent.

Northern Virginia

Fabbioli Cellars

In one of my first cider trips to Northern Virginia (NoVa) I stopped by Fabbioli Cellars, which was a fantastic experience. This winery and cidery operation is the brainchild of Doug Fabbioli and Colleen Berg. In 2000, they purchased twenty-five acres in Loudoun County for a vineyard and family home, and a year later, they began planting merlot and petit verdot, along with building their house. More than twenty years later, Doug has proven himself as a wine pioneer and well-respected vintner and winemaker in Virginia. He has perfected Italian varietals, and the old-world style of his Tre Sorelle Red Blend is outstanding. But his cider is something else entirely. Doug offers two ciders and one perry (pear cider). He explained to me that he has always utilized the fruit on his farm and has tried to be entrepreneurial when considering its potential uses. He's had numerous raspberries, so he made a raspberry port. He had a pear tree, so he pressed some pears to get juice for a pear port wine. A Total Wine representative told Doug that he could sell apple cider in 750 ml bottles, which got Doug's attention. His belief in using all of the bounties of his farm and the growing demand of the cider market led him to start the cider operation for Fabbioli Cellars in 2015.

He knew that he could make a good cider due to his background as a wine maker. Doug purchased some equipment for cider making, specifically CO_2 equipment, so the cider could be effervescent. He had connections to growers in the area, so he acquired fresh Virginia juice from orchards in Lovettsville and the Winchester area and used his old-world wine style to make cider and perry.

The setting of Fabbioli vineyards is stunning. The gorgeous landscape is a reminder that you don't have to drive too far from D.C. to get to the country. Located less than fifty miles from D.C, this is an ideal getaway from the busy city life. The community has been very supportive of his venture into cider, and Fabbioli is currently distributing to several restaurants and pubs in the area. He employs his winemaking background for his cider production and believes that you must get the base cider right first and then you can add fruit and other spices to it. He also includes at least one cider in his wine flights, and a featured cocktail (many of the cocktails incorporate cider as an ingredient). This is the perfect way to market the cider to wine visitors.

Try this: The Ladies Man (labelled as apple raspberry wine and named after one of the winery cats) is loaded with juicy raspberries that come from the farm. The cider is "bright and fruity" with a crisp finish. ABV: 7 percent.

The Attitude Adjuster (apple cider with hops grown from the farm, also named after a resident cat) is a bold "crisp, dry cider made from 100 percent honey crisp apples." It's loaded with Chinook hops that yield notes of grapefruit and a spicy assertiveness at the end. ABV: 7 percent.[28]

Henway Hard Cider

More and more wineries, breweries, and cideries are offering multiple alcohol options to meet patrons' needs. Most of these establishments will have guest taps or wines to meet the demands of all, but it is very rare to find one place that makes all three beverages. One family, the Zurschmeides, have accomplished this and created a trifecta of farm-to-table alcohol ventures in Bluemont. Their four-hundred-acre farm lies about halfway between Leesburg and Winchester, and it is a one-stop shop for all (wine, beer, and cider) with three separate locations for each libation: Bluemont Winery, Dirt Farm Brewery, and Henway Hard Cider. The patriarch of this operation is Bob Zurschmeide, who grew up farming in Indiana and was so invested in the farm life that he says the money he saved to put himself through college was covered in peach fuzz. The Zurschmeide family moved to Loudoun County in the 1970s, and twenty years later they purchased their dream farm in Bluemont. They envisioned growing fruit on their sloping hills, and eventually this vision came true, when they started Bluemont Winery in 2007, Dirt Farm Brewery in 2015, and Henway Hard Cider in 2019. The locations of the beverage production centers and tasting rooms are within just a few yards of each other. The winery and brewery are located on two different hills that provide sweeping views of the valley. The cidery is located at the bottom of the knoll along with Great Country Farms, which provides an opportunity for guests to pick their own fruit and a location to pick up goods from the fresh market. There is also a beautiful pond, rustic cider production area and tasting room, and a restaurant called the Coop.

The cidery's namesake has an interesting story. Bob Zurschmeide's wife, Faye, grew up with a family tradition of Sunday family dinners. Each week her father, Herman Graham Horlander, would serve a chicken from his farm.

He received numerous compliments about the bird, and someone would always ask "What's a hen weigh?" and Graham would respond "About five pounds." According to family members this process was repeated throughout many family dinners, and the name "Henway" became the perfect way to represent a cidery focused on family and agriculture.

During your visit, you can pick blueberries, peaches, and strawberries at Great Country Farms and then drink their blueberry, peach, or strawberry cider. Their offerings include a wide range of ciders from a traditional dry cider to ginger-infused and barrel-aged elixirs and even an apple cider donut inspiration. (They call their cider lineup the "Pecking Order," continuing with the Sunday chicken dinner theme.)

They also feature some terrific events like cocktail classes where the staff teach guests how to create cider concoctions. Bingo and chili nights are regular events, as well as the annual adult Easter egg hunt. (The hunt has incentives of special discounts at the Zurschmeide's establishment and other local businesses hidden in some of the eggs and candy. Admission covers your first pour of cider, which will quench your thirst while you search for eggs.)

It was very clear from my meeting with the Henway team (many of them part of the Zurschmeide and Horlander family) that family, community, and nature is what it's all about. The wonderful flavor of their cider lies in their dedication, which is a testament to the legacy of the two families.

Try this: The Brut is a dry cider reminiscent of Champagne with a golden yellow clear color and hints of baked apples and tropical flavors. This goes very well on its own (possibly as an aperitif) or a breakfast pick-me-up when mixed with fresh orange juice. Cidermosa, anyone? ABV: 7 percent.

The Coop is their flagship cider and will meet the

needs of various cider lovers. It's a semi-sweet and semi-sparkling cider that is bright and crisp and packed with loads of fruit-forward flavors. ABV: 6.9 percent.[29]

Cobbler Mountain Cider

On the way to Cobbler Mountain Cider, one passes by a creek next to an old farmhouse before entering an open field leading to the cidery. It is a beautiful setting, and it's there that I met Daniel Louden in Cobbler Mountain Cider's tasting room. Daniel is the son of the owners, Jeff and Laura McCarthy Louden. He explained that his grandfather purchased the family farm in 1959. Jeff and Laura eventually restored the ninety-acre farm and opened a winery in the cellar of their farmhouse during the summer of 2011. The Loudens found the wine market extremely competitive and made the decision to switch to cider production in 2014, preferring a different business model for another local product that would enjoy a quicker turnaround than wine. (Certain styles of wine will have to sit in the cellar for a much longer period than cider.) Jeff is the cider maker, and his products range from a unique honey-infused cider to a more old-fashioned Jeffersonian dry cider, both of which are well distributed throughout the state. You can find their products in many Virginia markets at local grocery stores, wine shops, and restaurants. They also have fantastic labels that make their brand easily identifiable and feature happy farm and fruit scenes appropriate for this fun beverage. They have recently expanded their lineup to include other fruit-flavored ciders, seltzers, and lemonades, which make for the ideal summertime drink. They even produce an Apple Cider Donut Cider, so you can pair your favorite breakfast sweet dish with this cider that's packed with cinnamon and sugar with hints of apple.

I had an outstanding tasting experience despite the damp spring day. Their tasting room is somewhat like a ski lodge or mountain retreat with surrounding views of Mother Nature. There is an abundance of outside space to enjoy with friends and family. While I sipped my cider, a group of hikers from New York entered the tasting room. They said that Cobbler Mountain is part of their annual camping excursion to Virginia. They pick up several cases for their nutritional needs, and then go out to explore the beauty of the Old Dominion. They've been doing this for several years, and their visit to Cobbler Mountain is always the highlight of their trip.

Try this: What makes a better pairing than honey and cider? The two are intertwined through the work of honeybees pollinating fruit trees. Made with a blend of Fuji, Red Delicious, and Ginger Gold apples, Cobbler Mountain's Honey Cider is brilliantly colored and infused with local Virginia honey. The resulting flavor is smooth with a slightly sweet finish. ABV: 6.8 percent.

Jeffersonian Cider is Cobbler Mountain's take on a traditional colonial cider. By using Red Delicious, Golden Delicious, Ginger Gold, and Fuji apples, they have created a slightly dry cider that is very drinkable. Enough tartness to keep you coming back for more. ABV: 6.9 percent.[30]

Lost Boy Cider

Tristan Wright, owner of Lost Boy Cider, fell in love with cider on a trip to Ireland in 2010, but there was a problem when he returned to the states, as he had a tough time finding good cider. Fast forward to 2015, and Tristan was diagnosed with a serious soy and gluten allergy, so he set out to find a good craft beverage alternative to beer. He remembered his cider experience in Ireland, and since cider is gluten free, Tristan then learned everything he could about cider making. After two years researching the craft and taking classes at various cider institutes and education centers, he left his job in the finance sector and set up his cider operation in Alexandria in 2019. Lost Boy Cider, then, is about his journey to find his way.

When I visited Lost Boy, I had a great tour led by the head cider maker, David Biun. Biun has a diverse background that includes working at both wineries and cideries large and small. (He even worked at a cidery in Sweden called Brännland Cider.) Lost Boy allows David's experimental side to thrive. This was evident when I noticed a five-gallon carboy of juice fermenting with what appeared to be gummy bears, but I soon realized were actually Sour Patch Kids for a fun candy-infused cider for Halloween. Even though he tests the boundaries of fermentation, David comes from a traditional wine makers' background.

Lost Boy Cider's home in Alexandria, very much part of the community. (Lost Boy Cider)

Many of Lost Boy's ciders use both historical and modern-style apples and all-natural ingredients like hops, cranberries, pineapples, and spices. Despite his innovative nature, he is conventional when selecting his apples. He works closely with growers to select the best apples for his juice, and he has created the perfect blend for his signature cider, Comeback Kid. (This is used as the base for almost all their ciders.) The blend is Pink Lady, Stayman, Winesap, and other varieties. He wants the cider to speak for itself, and no matter what the cider is infused with, David believes it should still taste like cider. This is exactly what I found while exploring Lost Boy's lineup.

Located in an industrial area of Alexandria, Lost Boy is the ideal location for an urban cidery. The building is open and full of windows that provide plenty of natural light. There is also a decent amount of space outside to enjoy as an escape from the busy NoVa traffic. Lost Boy is immersed in the community. They hold yoga classes, comedy nights, trivia nights, and much more. Tristan believes in giving back, and he has organized several fundraising events to raise support for various causes including Ukrainian refugees, the LGBTQ community, and other social justice issues.

When you visit Lost Boy, you may be lost in terms of what cider option to select, but trust me—it will be worth the journey. They have something for everyone. Ranging from the Comeback Kid to barrel-aged single varietals to hot-pepper-infused ciders, and most recently seltzers, it is a smorgasbord of tasty fermentations for all.

Try this: Comeback Kid is all about Tristan's journey from a lost boy to a comeback kid and an homage to the rejuvenated Virginia cider industry. This flagship cider makes a fantastic introduction to Virginia cider that is simply Virginia apples and yeast. It's an off-dry blend that is smooth and strikes a balance between acidity and sweetness. Every bottle has the slogan "For Explorers, By

Explorers," so enjoy it with other explorers (friends) to toast a new journey. This cider also won the inaugural Virginia Governor's Cup Cider Best in Show Award in 2021. ABV: 6.9 percent.

Andre the Giant is the perfect name for this cider because right when I walked into the cidery I saw a giant wall graphic of Andre the Giant himself. This blend is naturally fermented and creates an earthy cider that is "simultaneously rustic and elegant" with a zesty, crisp finish. It's a cider so bold and sophisticated that the "Giant" himself would be proud to have his name associated with it. ABV: 6.9 percent.[31]

Valley View Farm

If you're familiar with Virginia wine, then you should recognize the name Philip Carter, the award-winning winery located in Hume. The winery has a rich history, and its CEO, Philip Carter Strother, is a direct descendent of Charles Carter (son of Robert King Carter), who helped put Virginia wine on the map in the eighteenth century.

And if you know anything about Virginia orchards and farms then you've heard of the Strother family's Valley View Farm in Delaplane. The Strother family has served as caretakers of this historic five-hundred-acre farm located in the northern part of Fauquier County since the early twentieth century, and in 2018 Philip Carter Winery and Valley View Farm formed a partnership, where both wine and cider would be produced and offered at the tasting room at the farmstead. The property also features a seasonal pick-your-own fruits, organic vegetables from the Garden at Valley View, and other local products.

There is also a bit of history behind the farm at Valley View. James Ball, a first cousin of Mary Washington, established the homestead in the early eighteenth century. Among the sites' other historic accolades include a stopover for the Underground Railroad during the Civil War.

By the beginning of the twentieth century, the Strother family became the stewards of the farm and in 1997, Charles E. Strother Jr. (Philip Carter Strother's father) inherited the property from his father and expanded the business. He used the site as a retreat for companies and church groups and established a pick-your-own attraction. By 2016 Charles and his son saw an opportunity with the area when they created Valley View Farm winery.

I visited the farm on an overcast day, and as I arrived the clouds began moving into the valley as I took cover in a beautiful old red barn that houses the tasting room and dates to the 1920s. I was greeted by a very energetic and kind tasting manager Kendra Cummings (farm market and events manager) who gave me a peach. I had just been to another Virginia orchard to pick peaches the week before, but this peach was remarkable. It was the juiciest and most flavorful that I had ever had. She then poured me a lineup of ciders and meads that I thoroughly enjoyed. In between sips of cider, I learned about the farmstead and its history. The only other customer that I saw while I was there was one of the resident cats, who was happy to get all the attention. The rustic farmhouse provides a superb tasting experience to enjoy the fruits of the Strother family's labor as they should be enjoyed. When I finished my tasting, I sat on the porch swing and watched the storm move through the valley to give the peach trees and apple orchard a good watering. This was definitely one of the more idyllic settings during my cider journey. And I must not be the only one who believes this, because Valley View Farm inspired the famous artist Andrei Kushnir to spend two years working on landscape paintings of the surrounding Fauquier County area. Over fifty paintings of his document this farmland and the greater region of the county.

Try this: The Virginia Perfection Hard Cider, a delicious blend of Stayman, Red Delicious, and Fuji apples, is very refreshing. It's off-dry with a "floral nose that gives way to a perfect balance between sweet and tart"—a wonderful expression of the magnificent bounty of the Valley. ABV: around 6 percent.

I can attest to the deliciousness of Valley View's peaches first hand, so it is no surprise that their Red Haven Peach Hard Cider, featuring "Stayman and Red Delicious blended with Red Haven Peach concentrate," is a winner. Big peach flavors echo throughout the tasting experience, as well as excellent acidity from the Stayman. ABV: around 6 percent.[32]

Mt. Defiance Cidery and Distillery (Cider Barn)

Marc Chretien spent seven years as a State Department political adviser to combatant commanders in Iraq and Afghanistan before deciding that growing apples and fermenting their juice was a safer and quieter career choice. As an original investor/partner in Stowe Cider, a large Vermont cider company, Marc learned the art of blending different varieties of apples to produce classic cider. In 2014, now equipped with the knowledge of fermentation, he headed south and opened Mt. Defiance in Middleburg. Marc manages the cider operations, and Peter Ahlf runs the distilling side of the business. Together they have two distinct locations and products available in the heart of Loudoun County. (The distillery and cidery are just a few blocks away from each other on Route 50.)

I had a fantastic visit with Marc as we tasted several of his ciders inside the gorgeous Cider Hall. The woodwork, large, vaulted ceilings, and extravagant fireplace and mantles of this building were one of a kind. It is a great facility to meet with friends and family and enjoy your beverage of choice.

Marc focuses on specific cider apple blends and uses mostly Arkansas Black, Ashmead's Kernel, Grimes Golden, and Gold Rush from local growers, but he also uses different fruits and herbs available in their garden on the property. We took a stroll through the quaint garden, and I breathed in the aromatic smells from the different plants that we passed including wormwood, which is used to make the absinthe at the distillery. (I've never had wormwood before, so Marc told me to tear off a leaf and take a bite. It was one of the most bitter things that I have ever tasted. I can clearly see how absinthe received its bad reputation; although I have heard it is very good in cocktails.) There are other liquors that are made at the distillery if the anise-flavored spirit isn't your favorite, and two of their distillations are directly related to apples and cider.

For their apple brandy, they take their cider and distill it twice in a copper still. The liquor is then placed in used whiskey barrels. After resting for two years, the brandy is cut down to 80 proof (or 40 percent ABV). The resulting product is a smooth liquor with a caramel-crusted baked apple pie aroma. Flavors of oak and cinnamon are evident due to the barrel aging.

They also create a pommeau that would make for a wonderful night cap or winter sipper sitting next to the Mt. Defiance fireplace chatting with friends. This blend of apple juice and apple brandy is aged for one year in a bourbon barrel. The magical concoction produces a semisweet nectar that exhibits a fresh apple flavor at the start and finishes with a brandy warmup at the end.

As we ventured back inside from our walk, I was a bit parched, so I opted to try one of their cider sangria specials. This was one of the best sangrias I've ever had. Made with Mt. Defiance cider, fresh fruit, and herbs, it had delightful flavors and aromas that made me think of springtime in the garden. Marc's cider lineup is very diverse and ranges from bourbon-aged ciders to fruited ciders.

Try this: General's Reserve Hard Cider is Marc's tribute to his friend General John Allen, Commanding General of all forces in Afghanistan from 2011 to 2013. This is a bourbon barrel-aged version of their farmhouse cider. According to Marc, the oak barrel "creates a strong, darker colored cider with whiskey notes and hints of vanilla and caramel." ABV: 9.5 percent.

Cider with Blueberries is a great name for this a beautifully colored beverage with a rose hue. The flavors are bursting with notes of berry and citrus fruit. The cider appears to be sweet, but it is dry while still giving some appearance of sweetness due to the fruitiness of the beverage. It's cider with blueberries, after all. ABV: 7.2 percent.[33]

Old Trade Brewery & Cidery

Walking into Old Trade Brewery & Cidery was not what I would have expected out of a farm cidery. There was some serious 1990s alternative music playing that brought me back to my teenage years of angst and slight defiance, and the inside was a little dark due to the time of day and overcast skies. But once I stepped outside with my flight of cider, I was pleasantly surprised at the bucolic, pastoral view of the farm. It's kind of like I went from a Seattle grunge scene to Old MacDonald's farm. (The inside is actually very nice, but the music created a slightly different ambiance, and I liked the music.) While sipping my cider outside, I enjoyed the valley breeze as the chickens and rooster moved through the farm looking for food while noisily making their presence known. After spending a good amount of time taking in the sights and sounds of the homestead, I made it back inside to meet with the owner of Old Trade, Garrett Thayer. The music had picked up a little bit, and I was out of my confusing adolescent mindset and able to get a better picture of what Old Trade is all about. Thayer, a New Englander who went to the University of Massachusetts Dartmouth, comes from a long line of farmers. His family has been farming in New England since the early 1620s, and he is using his entrepreneurial skills to continue the family legacy. After working for the government and living in the DC area, Thayer thought it was time for a change and decided to get back to his roots. He purchased a twenty-acre farm in Brandy Station and immersed himself in the farm life and hasn't looked back since. He created a hybrid farm brewery and cidery in the heart of Culpepper County. His joy of fermentation began when his wife gave him a homebrewing kit for Valentine's Day. He also dove headfirst into the wonderful world of home wine and cider making. After learning the craft, he made his dream come true in 2018 when he opened the doors of Old Trade.

Garrett gets most of his cider juice from Silver Creek and Seamans' Orchard, but he also has an orchard on the farm where he uses bittering cider apples—that is, apples that impart bitterness. The brewery and cidery aren't just all about the drinks, however; they have a restaurant that serves many scrumptious dishes like a duck burger with a duck egg (from the farm) on the patty, which I highly recommend. Garrett's goal for Old Trade is to provide delicious beverages and food while also allowing visitors the opportunity to congregate and immerse themselves in farm life. The location is extremely family-friendly, offering ample entertainment for the kids. There is a huge playground for children that includes a pirate ship, and even an ax-throwing area for adults.

Old Trade features an array of beverages including several different ales and lagers, wine, and at least five ciders on tap. Garrett does all the brewing and cider and wine making. The ciders rotate on a regular basis and include fruit-added ciders like a blackberry and white peach to bourbon barrel-aged ciders. Many of the ingredients for his fruited ciders come from the Old Trade farm. If you were wondering about the origins of the name Old Trade, it is from a lyric in the song "Down in the Valley" by The Head and the Heart.

Try this: Rocky Knoll is a light-yellow sparkling dry cider. This full-bodied cloudy beverage is made from Honeycrisp and other fresh pressed apples from the region. ABV: 6.5 percent.

Emmer is an extremely dry complex cider. It has a hazy appearance with a great mouth feel and pleasing tropical flavors, hint of banana, and a long, lingering finish. This has similar flavor profiles as a Belgian beer (think Tripel), which could be due to Garrett's passion for homebrewing farmhouse style beers. ABV: 11 percent.[34]

Cider Lab

I had never been to this area of Virginia or even heard of the small town of Sumerduck (pronounced "Summer Duck") before my visit to Cider Lab, but I got a great feel for the little town's charm when I stopped by the busy cidery on a Wednesday night. Cider Lab is the brainchild of James and A. J. Rasure. The father-son duo had been fermenting fruit juice together for about five years when they realized that they wanted to test the commercial waters. They opened the first cidery in Sumerduck in the summer of 2020, when the small community showed their support by coming out in droves on opening weekend. The Rasure's were expecting around 150 people, and by the end of Sunday they had poured almost 900 pints.

Cider Lab's name is consistent with the approach taken by its owners, who love the sciences and experimentation. A. J. is a former US Marine Corps musician who works as a physicist at Dahlgren Naval Base, and his dad, James, is a retired US Navy officer who works as a scientist at the National Reconnaissance Office in Northern Virginia. Their platform is unique fermentations of fruit, and they're not afraid to test the waters. For example, the first cider they produced was a mango habanero that packs some serious heat. I tasted the atypical beverage and found that this fan favorite reaches new levels of heat for a pepper cider. (It's not for the faint at heart, so bring some antacids if you're a hot pepper novice like myself.) I also tried their delicious Passion Perry, which utilizes both passion fruit and pears. Their signature cider, however, is Sumerduck Cider, which features a refreshingly lovely blend of berries. The tasting room is a quaint 1600-square-foot building that used to house the Sumerduck Trading Company. The Rasures renovated the building, but also kept some of the traditional town flair, so that it approximates a classy sort of antique store.

Their business plan was originally to sell small five-gallon kegs to restaurants, but they gained a new vision once the community showed their support and demand for cider. Locals wanted a place to bring in a pizza, grab a couple of pints, and then take a growler to go, so they began selling pints to the public and created a cozy place inside their tasting room for groups to meet and mingle. But their experimental vibe is on display with a tap list called "Lab Notes," smaller growlers that look like beakers, and other glassware that may have come from my high school chemistry class. Cider Lab recently expanded their reach by opening up a second tasting room in Spotsylvania.

Try this: I usually tend to side with drier ciders, but Sumerduck Cider is another one of those sweeter ciders that may just convert my palate. I loved this fruity cider with a triple berry blend of blueberries, blackberries, and raspberries. The result is one of the most refreshing ciders that I've ever had. It also has pleasing scents of fresh-cut flowers. ABV: 5 percent.

I'm always interested in trying a perry (pear cider), so their Passionate Perry caught my attention. I just love the flavors that pear juice can bring to the fermentation. With the addition of passion fruit, this beverage combination allows for citrusy flavors with a sweeter but not too sweet finish. ABV: 5 percent.[35]

Corcoran Vineyards and Cidery

Lori Corcoran is one of the founding mothers of the beverage industry in Virginia. In 2002, she and her husband, Jim, started a vineyard on their farm in Waterford just north of Purcellville. After a couple of years growing grapes, they established Corcoran Winery in Loudoun County and served as trailblazers for the wine industry that has since blossomed into more than 300 wineries throughout the Commonwealth. Their love of craft beverages and all things fermented led the Corcorans to open a brewery in 2011 and thus the first winery/brewery combination in the Old Dominion. They soon discovered that the brewery was too large for the farm, so they moved their beer venture to a larger space in Purcellville in 2014. Eventually Corcoran Brewery was absorbed into B Chord Brewing Company to create a more robust and efficient brewing operation. By relocating the brewery operation, they could renovate the area that occupied the farm for a new fermentation project.

Lori decided to use her knowledge in the wine field to start making cider. Continuing with her trailblazer mentality, she became a founding member of the Virginia Association of Cider Makers (now Virginia Cider Association). Her style is reminiscent of Bold Rock, and she credits this to her close friendship with Bold Rock's cider guru, Brian Shanks. Her strategy for making cider is to make it clean, and it shows in her products. All the ciders that I tasted were very good with no off flavors or faults. The juice comes from just down the road in Winchester, about forty-five minutes west. The blend is then fermented in a controlled atmosphere and refined repeatedly until the cider is to her liking. The products are well carbonated, crisp, and refreshing. Her business model now focuses mainly on cider, but also port-style wines that are aged for seven to eight years in the whiskey barrels.

The drive to Corcoran is an interesting one, requiring a jaunt through a suburban residential neighborhood. I met Lori in her tasting room to sample the wares. She is a regular there and is usually on hand to answer her patron's questions. Guests who stop by are treated to delicious beverages and a friendly host. Lori takes her time to chat with anyone who walks through the door. While I was there, I encountered a few locals who stopped by to fill up their growlers and enjoy a glass of cider. There is something for everyone in her lineup and sometimes she mixes cider cocktails as a special treat in the tasting room.

Try this: I love everything about Sinful. The label features a neon sign that you may see in a cabaret with an arrow pointing to the direction where the sinful deeds can be found: "So good it must be a sin." It is a spiced beverage, with just enough cinnamon and allspice to let you know that it's there. It's slightly sweet from the juice, but with a dry finish and a touch of honey that coats your tongue. Sinful is a nicely tart cider that keeps you wanting more. ABV: 5.5 percent.

Another fantastic label may be found on PoPo Peach, as it features a classic police car with a vintage-looking policeman (big shades, mustache, and all). I'm a big fan of peaches, and I've had several members of my family serve in law enforcement, so this cider really sparked my interest. There wasn't an overwhelming amount of peach, just enough, but the apples are the main feature of this concoction. PoPo Peach is a lovely cider to enjoy on a warm day at home. ABV: 5.5 percent.[36]

Wild Hare Cider

Jay and Colleen Clement opened Wild Hare Cider in Bluemont in 2015. They set out to make a delicious product by using local fruit. In December of 2017, they opened a tasting room in historic Loudoun County, but after four years of operating they decided that it was time to allow someone else to take over the reins of the business. In 2018, Chantilly investor Jim Madaj acquired the cidery, and the Clements assisted with the transition by consulting. Jim's sons, Justin and Patrick, are beverage connoisseurs with a background in homebrewing. Justin is the cider maker and runs his cider production out of a warehouse space in Berryville. Wild Hare actually includes four different locations: an 1840s log cabin in historic downtown Leesburg, an 1830s grainery in Old Town Warrenton, a pub in historic Fredericksburg, and most recently, a tasting room in Berryville.

I visited their tasting room at Market Station in Leesburg. One can feel the history immediately upon stepping into the restored log cabin. Justin's homebrewing background comes through in his cider lineup which ranges from the traditional Hatch, with its simply fermented apples, to hopped and spiced ciders and concoctions like a mint julip-like beverage for Kentucky Derby weekend. Several of their ciders highlight beer ingredients, like Bloom, which "evokes the vibe of an orange fruited Belgian White ale, with Orange Blossom Honey, Orange Peel, Coriander, and Azacca Hops." Other ciders include hops but are nicely balanced out by fruit additions. Justin is also a big fan of citrus fruits, as evidenced by the fact that lime is used in most of his products. Pineapple, grapefruit, and lemon are also featured in some of his creations. His creativity and experimentation definitely make Wild Hare stand out.

The Wild Hare Leesburg location has a wonderful outside seating area for taking in the sights, sounds, and smells from the many excellent restaurants in this historic town.

Try this: Made from Shenandoah apples, Hatch is a

"classic dry cider with hints of citrus and stone fruit" that makes for great food pairing. Its crisp carbonation and tartness lend themselves to matching most any cheese. ABV: 7 percent.

VIRGINIA CIDER ASSOCIATION (VCA)

Originally named the Virginia Association of Cider Makers, the VCA is a trade organization of cideries throughout the state of Virginia. In 2018, they had eighteen member cideries in addition to several orchards and growers. Various memberships are offered that allow for companies who have an interest in the cider industry (cideries, orchards, and growers) to receive communications and attend two meetings a year. According to the VCA, "It is the mission of the Virginia Cider Association to provide connections, information, and market exposure to strengthen members' businesses and support the Virginia Cider industry." Virginia Association of Cider Makers to enhance consumer and trade appreciation of cider and perry through education, promotion and publicly recognizable standards of production excellence." Many of their programs revolve around educational and promotional opportunities, and the board acts on behalf of the association to monitor any laws that impact the cider industry and advocate for cider interests. They also coordinate and execute Virginia Cider Week, which runs during the third week of November. This annual event began in 2012 and originally featured Foggy

Willow is a dry cider infused with berries and lime. This single-varietal made from Pink Lady apples presents a "bright raspberry aroma, with a stronger blackberry backbone." ABV: 8.2 percent.[37]

Ridge, Potter's, Albemarle, Bold Rock, Castle Hill, Old Hill, and Blue Bee. That number has grown to more than twenty cideries that participated in events during the 2021 season. Events take place at various cideries throughout the state, with special tastings, tours, and cider-pairing dinners.

Since 2021, the Commonwealth of Virginia has given cider its own category in the Virginia Governor's Cup. Each cider is scored using a 100-point scale, and after the judges taste the entries, the six top-scoring ciders are identified. Then the judges do a blind retasting and rank their favorites from 1 to 6. The highest-rated cider wins the Best in Show Cider. The following list shows the first four winners.

2021: Lost Boy 2020 Comeback Kid
2022: Albemarle CiderWorks 2019 Virginia Hewes Crab
2023: Albemarle CiderWorks 2021 Orchard Blush
2024: Buskey Cider 2022 Ruby Red Crab Apple

Source: Virginia Cider Association, https://www.virginiacider.org.

Other Cideries

The following seventeen cideries have shorter descriptions due to either their limited cider production, their inclusion of cider as merely a secondary part of their operation, or perhaps they have only recently opened. I have visited most of them and tried much of the cider that they offer. Some are small orchards, some are breweries, some are wineries, and others are upstart cideries. The list is no particular order or geographical section. No matter their size or mission, each one has something unique to offer.

Stable Craft Brewing (Shenandoah Valley)

Stable Craft, located in Waynesboro, is an amazing farm brewery that also makes cider. They were established in 2016 in Augusta County as a brewery but have expanded their operation to include a restaurant and cidery. (They also have lodging options as well.) Stable Craft typically has at least three ciders on tap. Their ciders are made with a blend of apples including Granny Smith, Golden Delicious, and Gala, but they also incorporate additional fruit like peaches and apricots. There are plenty of options for the food and drink aficionado as well as indoor and outdoor accommodations for large groups and families. This place would be a great birthday party venue.[38]

Hardywood Park Craft Brewery (West Creek Cider; Richmond Area)

Any Virginia beer fan has heard of Hardywood Park Craft Brewery, the award-winning brewery in Richmond that helped pave the way for the rejuvenation of the Old Dominion's beer industry. Their Gingerbread Stout, in particular, has become a celebrity craft brew. Less known, however, is that they also make a cider available in their taprooms. They started experimenting with cider production in 2017 based on customer interest, and by 2018 they had perfected their West Creek Cider and offered it at both of their locations. The cider is made in small batches at their West Creek facility in Henrico County just west of the city—hence the name. According to Hardywood's president and cofounder, Eric McKay, "West Creek Cider . . . comes from a blend of apples from the Shenandoah Valley, and is fruity, with a lively effervescence and a pleasantly dry finish."[39]

Monroe Bay Winery (Chesapeake and Eastern Shore)

Monroe Bay Winery is a small farm winery and cidery located in Colonial Beach, just east of James Monroe Parkway in the Northern Neck. (It's positioned near Monroe Bay, which leads out to the Potomac River.) The establishment is owned and operated by Kiki Apple—yes, her last name is really Apple, and she makes cider. She caught the fermentation bug when she lived in France and developed an appreciation for wine and terroir. This led her to start her own vineyard and winery and has also added cider to her lineup. She uses a variety of apples for her ciders including some historic apples like Hewe's Crab. Her ciders range from a pumpkin-spice cider to a hopped cider, as well as more traditional options.[40]

Moss Vineyards (Charlottesville Area)

Barry and Ellen Moss have been making wine in Dyke, about a half hour north of Charlottesville, since 2010, but I recently discovered that Moss Vineyards also makes cider. In fact, their Moss Dry Cider earned gold at the 2022 Virginia Governor's Cup. Ian and Cait Moss, the owner's son and daughter-in-law, are the cider makers. This vineyard's signature cider is their Moss Dry Cider, which includes a blend of 50 percent Harrison and 50 percent Arkansas Black apples, and it is fantastic. (I enjoyed a bottle to wash down a bitter taste in my mouth after a UVA loss to the Louisville Cardinals during the 2022 football season.) According to Moss, there are "subtle notes of citrus, pineapple, and grapefruit liken the cider to an almost Prosecco finish. Mid and late season Virginia Glaize apples are used in conjunction with multiple yeast strains to produce a clean, crisp, dry cider." Moss is also a gorgeous property featuring majestic views of valley. They recently planted Harrison and Wickson apple trees on site.[41]

Chateau Morrissette (Blue Ridge and Appalachia)

Located in Floyd in Southwest Virginia, Chateau Morrissette—otherwise known as the wine with the dogs on the label; the website is even thedogs.com—has been around since 1993. Their picturesque winery and grounds are located just off the Blue Ridge Parkway. I've tasted several of their wines before at festivals throughout the Commonwealth, but I had never tasted their ciders. They feature two ciders: a Cherry Ginger Cider and Barrel Aged Cider. These are both widely distributed throughout the Virginia area, and you can pick up some bottles at Total Wine and other stores.[42]

Back Bay Brew House (Chesapeake and Eastern Shore)

Back Bay Brewing Company was founded in 2011 by Virginia Beach native Josh Canada and friends who shared an interest of the sun and nature and hanging with friends. They set out to create a place for the beach community to enjoy craft beverages. In 2017 Back Bay expanded to include a second location known as the Farmhouse that sits on almost nine acres in Kempsville. The brewery also expanded their options by making ciders to meet their customers' needs. They usually have at least two ciders on tap, and their offerings range from old-style cider to pineapple ciders and even a margarita cider (with lime and salt).[43]

Garden Grove Brewing & Urban Winery (Richmond Area)

Garden Grove Brewing & Urban Winery is located right in the heart of Richmond in the popular shopping area of Carytown. They opened in 2015 and have included a diverse lineup of libations since then—in fact, Garden Grove comprises a brewery, winery, meadery, *and* cidery. Their ciders vary but you can usually find both a fruited cider and a traditional blend at their location. Most of their apples come from Winchester, and they use varieties such as Black Twig and Hewe's Crab as single varietals or blends. They are huge fans of Glaize as referenced in their Black Twig descriptions, "Dry, tart and crisp cider with bright, fresh notes of tropical fruit and white grape. Crafted with all Virginia grown, Black Twig apples from the devilishly handsome brothers of Glaize Apples."[44]

The Winery at Kindred Pointe: Life is Hard Cider (Shenandoah Valley)

Located in the heart of the Shenandoah Valley is the Winery at Kindred Pointe. Owners Amy and Bruce Helsley purchased a fifty-eight-acre property in Mount Jackson. Amy turned her attention to horses with the establishment of a stable and barn, and Bruce turned his attention to grapes. They eventually focused on apples and cider and created their brand Life is Hard Cider. Their ciders include both standard and experimental styles. One of their most popular varieties, Cherry Bomb, tastes just like cherry soda with a touch of habanero that delivers a slight heat. They also use barrel aging and other adjuncts like Belgian Candi sugar and ginger for their products. Their barn has been converted into a beautiful tasting room with large glass doors that let you experience the magnificence of the valley.[45]

Teaghlaigh Vineyard: Son of a Bear Ciders (Northern Virginia)

Son of a Bear Ciders is located in Rapidan. Their ciders are produced and bottled by Teaghlaigh Vineyard, which is owned and operated by the McMahon family. "McMahon" means "son of a bear" and "Teaghlaigh" means "family" in Irish Gaelic—and family is what Son of a Bear Ciders is all about. Members of the McMahon extended family live and work at the vineyard and orchard. With family members from the US Air Force, they have several products that carry military names like their flagship cider, Bear Force One. Their cider lineup ranges from semi-dry cider to several barrel-aged ciders and even a rhubarb-infused cider. Their products are available at several local breweries and farmers markets. One of the breweries that they provide cider for is WAR Craft Brewery. US Air Force veteran Brad Stepp opened the brewery/winery/cidery in September 2021 in Rapidan and always has at least five ciders on tap, and some are made by Stepp himself.[46] With the addition of a distillery in 2022, they are now the first "Farm Quad-Fecta in Virginia."

Apocalypse Cidery & Winery (Blue Ridge and Appalachia)

The John family opened Apocalypse Brewery in 2013 in Forest as the first brewery in Bedford County. Nine years later, Doug John is doing it again but this time he's opening a cidery. The former homebrew supply shop owner has been involved in the business of fermentation since the mid-1990s. In the summer of 2022, he added to his alcohol footprint in Bedford by opening Apocalypse Cidery & Winery at the former location of his homebrew store. He has worked with Adam Cooke at Silver Creek and

Seamans' Orchard to create a delicious cider blend that includes Harrison (his favorite cider apple). They make two flagship ciders: Legacy Natural, a traditional beverage with just juice and yeast, and Legacy Hopped, a Hallertau Blanc dry-hopped version of Legacy Natural. He plans on eventually adding more ciders (both dry and sweet) to his lineup that will provide customers a diversified lineup of flavors to meet the mountain community's palates.[47]

Henley's Orchard Estate Cidery (Charlottesville Area)

Another orchard with a historical legacy near Charlottesville is Henley's. Started in 1932 by Joseph T. Henley Sr., the farm has remained within the Henley family and has expanded throughout the years. It is now run by Tim Henley and his wife, Sarah, along with their children, Jacquelyn, Brook, and Steele. Their retail space in Crozet, The Shed, carries over twenty-five apple varieties, including cider apples like Black Twig, Jonagold, Winesap, Grimes Golden, and even a Henley's Golden that is supposedly good for pressing. Henley's Orchard Estate Cidery opened in 2022 and produces three ciders: Jubilee, 87, and Harvest Gold. It's a wonderful place to stop and pick up some fresh wares from Central Virginia and grab a glass of cider to drink on the farm or a bottle of cider to go.[48]

Zoll Vineyards (Chesapeake and Eastern Shore)

Located on the border of Gloucester and Mathews counties sits Zoll Vineyards. The 11-acre property consists of a large vineyard with more than 2,500 vines, as well as a farm-to-table garden. They are a winery at heart, but their beverage list includes two cider options, along with cocktails like a Cranberry Apple Cider that is served warm and an Apple Cinnamon Honey Sangria. They also offer a lovely food menu that highlights specialty sandwiches, charcuterie, and various tempting desserts.[49]

Mountain Run Winery (Northern Virginia)

Opened in 2016, this farm winery situated just outside downtown Culpepper is anything but new. The site has been a homestead for over 125 years, and the tasting room is housed in a 1950s-era corncrib. Typically producing up to twenty wines a year, Mountain Run only makes one cider. This 6-percent ABV off-dry cider has a proven track record since it won "Best Cider in Virginia" at the 2019 State Fair Competition.[50]

Notaviva Farm Brewery and Winery (Northern Virginia)

Located in Western Loudoun on the eastern slope of the Blue Ridge Mountains, this farm craft beverage producer with a curious name offers cider selections ranging from Cherry Cider and Pear Cider to Cranapple Cider. What is Notaviva? According to their website, "It is the intrinsic effect of music upon human emotion, or put simply, it is the feeling you get when you hear your favorite song." The objective of Notaviva Farm Brewery and Winery is to encapsulate those emotions and put them in their products.[51]

Rockfish Brewing Company (Charlottesville Area)

Charlottesville has no lack of craft breweries, but Rockfish Brewing Company has set themselves apart by producing not only quality small-batch specialty beers, but also mead and ciders. With locations at the Downtown Mall and Preston Avenue, this unique business has become a fan favorite among alcohol aficionados in the Charlottesville area. The cider offerings range from a Hüell Melon Cider (a lightly hopped version of their standard dry cider) to a Blueberry Hibiscus Grapefruit Cider.[52]

Crooked Run Fermentation (Northern Virginia)

Crooked Run Fermentation has a large portfolio of craft products that highlight “traditional beers, coolship sours, natural wines, ciders, and seltzers.” They opened in Leesburg in 2013, but over the past ten years they have expanded to two other locations: Sterling (where their main production facility rests) and Washington, DC. Cider offerings vary, but they focus on natural fermentation and have made a single varietal using Albemarle Pippins along with producing blended ciders as well.[53]

Loudoun Cider House (Northern Virginia)

Loudoun Cider House is a new cidery located in the Lucketts area of Leesburg. As of late 2024, they are open for tasting by appointment only, but you can purchase their ciders online or at farmers’ markets in the area. They have two cider options: the first one is a Gold Rush single varietal with a “rich, complex, and not overly sweet” flavor profile, and the second option is a farmhouse-style featuring a “mix of Virginia apples,” with “bright flavors” and is “fruit-forward.”[54]

Conclusion

Each cidery has their own unique story, from the urban businesses like Blue Bee Cider in the heart of Richmond and Lost Boy Cider in busy Alexandria to the rural producers like Halcyon Days Cider Company in the shadow of the Shenandoah Valley and Troddenvale at Oakley Farm tucked away in Bath County. They produce their own style, but much of that approach is based on historic apples, recipes, and methods. And as cider events and cideries continue to grow and spread the knowledge and history of this delicious beverage throughout the Commonwealth, the state of cider in Virginia is very good. Cideries continue to evolve their offerings by looking to the past, growers are working to test the boundaries of old and new apples to meet demands, and consumers embrace both these attempts and the fact that craft cider is historic cider. As a historian, I have attempted to illustrate the importance of this lesser-known Virginia product to the reader. I hope that you have found it to be a fruitful experience.

My good friend and beer historian, Lee Graves, helped inspire me to pursue this adventure to track down Virginia's rich cider history and to tell the story of the cider makers, growers, and advocates of southern apples. In the conclusion of his book *Virginia Beer,* he talks about visiting Old Trade Brewery and meeting patrons from outside of the Commonwealth who commented about why Virginia has so many different beer styles, and his answer was that he believes Virginia's brewing strength is in its diversity. Such a conversation could just as easily be held within a cidery—in fact, Old Trade Brewery is also a cidery!—about the diversity of Virginia ciders. Like other craft beverage makers, Virginia cider makers are creative, and what the apples and other materials they use form a diverse product. The Virginia cider industry is innovative, using adjuncts, spices, and fruits that have been popular with other beverage industries, and it continually tests the limits of our palates with unique fermentation methods and aging practices. I think that what we are seeing in the cider industry is not necessarily a revival, but a continuation of colonial Virginia's beverage of choice. For over four hundred years Virginians have enjoyed the fermented juice of apples, and at present there are no indications that our thirst is quenching any time soon. As each of the cideries profiled herein continue to develop their offerings, and as new cideries pop up in both the countryside and urban neighborhoods, I hope that this book may continue to accompany your cider explorations throughout our great Commonwealth.[1]

APPENDIX A

Beyond the Apple Press FAQs

How many cideries are there in Virginia?

As of 2024, there are around fifty establishments that produce cider in Virginia.

When is Virginia Cider Week?

Virginia Cider Week takes place in the fall—typically launching at the end of the second week of November and lasting through the third week of November. It started in 2012 when the Virginia House of Delegates and the State Senate passed House Joint Resolution 105 to allocate the week before Thanksgiving as Virginia Cider Week. Exclusive events, tastings, and special releases take place at various cideries and businesses throughout the state.

What is the largest Virginia cidery?

Bold Rock Hard Cider located in Nellysford is the largest cidery in Virginia and ranked second nationally in retail sales at $31.9 million in 2020. (Angry Orchard in New York is the largest in the nation.)[1]

What is the Virginia Cider Association?

This organization looks to"enhance consumer and trade appreciation of cider and perry through education, promotion and publicly recognizable standards of production excellence." Originally set up as the Virginia Association of Cider Makers, it was rebranded in 2020 as the Virginia Cider Association. The group has a board of directors that works to monitor and influence state and federal legislation that affects the cider community. They also provide both "educational and promotional programs with other regional entities that share similar goals" related to cider including planning and executing Virginia Cider Week.[2]

What are some of the annual cider festivals and events that take place in Virginia?

Some annual events include the Lake Anna Cider Festival (November), Alexandria Cider Festival (November), Fredericksburg's Virginia Cider Festival (September), and Hampton's Coastal Virginia Cider Festival (October).

Where are most of the cideries located in Virginia?

Cideries are located throughout the Commonwealth, though Northern Virginia and the Charlottesville area include more than half of the cideries. Please check the map to see specific locations for all of your favorite cider makers.

What beverages other than cider are made at cideries?

Some cideries also make fortified beverages like pommeau. There are several beverage establishments that make cider and beer, wine, mead and/or liquor. Some cideries also produce non-alcoholic "sweet" cider.

Do all cideries have orchards?

No, not all cideries have orchards. Like urban wineries, many urban cideries do not grow large amounts of fruit on their property. Most cideries in Virginia get their cider apples from apple growers throughout the Commonwealth. Very few cideries produce cider (solely) from apples grown on their property.

What is the difference between culinary and cider apples?

The great majority of apple varieties today are for eating or cooking. Such culinary apples are soft on the palate with a simple, uniform, uncomplicated taste; they are low in sugar content and, when used in cider making, ferment out at a lower ABV. Sweeter ciders are largely made from culinary apples, whereas dry ciders tend to come from heritage apples, which are more complex in taste and high in natural sugars that ferment to 8 to 9 percent.

APPENDIX B

Virginia Cideries

Shenandoah Valley

Ciders from Mars
121 S. Lewis Street, Staunton, VA 24401 • (540) 416-2120
www.cidersfrommars.com

Life is Hard Cider (The Winery at Kindred Pointe)
3575 Conicville Road, Mount Jackson, VA 22842 • (540) 477-3570
www.kindredpointe.com/

Old Hill Cider (Showalter's Orchard)
17768 Honeyville Road, Timberville, VA 22853 • (540) 896-7582
www.oldhillcider.com/

Old Town Cidery (Glaize Apples)
212 W. Commercial Street (production facility), Winchester VA 22601 • (540)-662-6251
www.OldTownCidery.com and www.GlaizeApples.com

Sage Bird Ciderworks
325 N. Liberty Street, Harrisonburg, VA 22802 • (540) 607-8084
www.sagebirdciderworks.com

Stable Craft Brewing
375 Madrid Road, Waynesboro, VA 22980 • (540) 490-2609
www.stablecraftbrewing.com

Widow's Watch Cider (Muse Orchard)
533 Lantz Road, Edinburg, VA 22824 • (240) 723-0672

Winchester Ciderworks
30 E. Piccadilly St. Winchester, VA 22601 • (540) 686-7632
www.winchesterciderworks.com

Blue Ridge and Appalachia

Apocalypse Cidery & Winery

1219 Burnbridge Road, Forest VA 24551 • (434) 252-4196
www.apocalypseciderayandwinery.com

Big Fish Cider Co.

59 Spruce Street, Monterey, VA 24465 • (540) 468-2322
www.bigfishcider.com

Chateau Morrisette

291 Winery Road SW, Floyd, VA 24091 • (540) 593-2865
www.thedogs.com

Halcyon Days Cider Co.

4135 S. Lee Highway, Natural Bridge, VA 24578 • (540) 291-1340
halcyondayscider.com

Troddenvale at Oakley Farm

170 Oakley Farm Lane, Warm Springs, VA 24484
www.troddenvale.com

Tumbling Creek Cider Company

30558 Old Saltworks Rd. (production facility), Meadowview, VA 24361
238 W. Main Street (tasting room), Abingdon, VA 24210 • (276) 477-9184
www.tumblingcreekcider.com

Charlottesville Area

Albemarle CiderWorks

2545 Rural Ridge Lane, North Garden, VA 22959 • (434) 979-1663
www.albemarleciderworks.com

Blue Toad Hard Cider

Cidery at High View Farm, 462 Winery Lane, Roseland, VA 22967 • (434) 760-9200
www.bluetoadhardcider.com

Bold Rock Hard Cider

Carter Mountain Orchard: 1435 Carters Mountain Trail, Charlottesville, VA 22901 • (434) 982-8942
Chiles Peach Orchard: 1351 Greenwood Road, Crozet, VA 22932 • (434) 823-1583

Nelson County: 1020 Rockfish Valley Highway (Rt. 151), Nellysford, VA 22958 • (434) 361-1030
www.boldrock.com

Bryant's Cidery & Brewery
The Farm: 3224 E. Branch Loop, Roseland, VA 22967 • (434) 818-1215
www.bryantscider.com/ciders/

Castle Hill Cider
6065 Turkey Sag Road, Keswick, VA 22947 • (434) 296-0047
www.castlehillcider.com

Henley's Orchard Estate Cidery
2192 Holly Hill Farm, Crozet, VA 22932 • (434) 823-7848
www.henleysorchard.com

Moss Vineyards
1849 Simmons Gap Road, Dyke, VA 22935 • (434) 990-0111
www.mossvineyards.net

Patois Cider
1740 Broadway Street, Charlottesville, VA 22902
www.patoiscider.com

Potter's Craft Cider
1350 Arrowhead Valley Road, Charlottesville, VA 22903 • (434) 244-2767
www.potterscraftcider.com/

Rockfish Brewing Company
Downtown Mall: 201 West Main St., Charlottesville, VA 22902 • (434) 566-0969
Preston Avenue: 1020 R 900 Preston Ave, Charlottesville, VA 22901 • (434) 566-0969
www.rockfishbrewcompany.com

Richmond Area

Blue Bee Cider
4811 Bethlehem Road, Suite A, Richmond, VA 23230
www.bluebeecider.com

Bryant's Cidery & Brewery
RVA Tasting Room: 3423 W. Cary St. Richmond VA 23221 • (804) 799-0401
www.bryantscider.com/ciders/

Buskey Cider
2910 W. Leigh Street, Richmond, VA 23230 • (804) 355-0100
www.buskeycider.com

Courthouse Creek Cider
1581 Maidens Road, Maidens, VA 23102 • (804) 543-3157
www.courthousecreek.com

Coyote Hole Craft Beverages
225 Oak Grove Drive, Mineral, VA 23117 • (540) 894-1053
www.coyotehole.com

Garden Grove Brewing and Urban Winery
3445 W. Cary Street, Richmond, VA 23221 • (804) 918-6158
www.gardengrovebrewing.com

Hardywood Park Craft Brewery
Pizza Kitchen & Taproom: 2410 Ownby Lane, Richmond, VA 23220 • (804) 418-3548
West Creek Cider: 820 Sanctuary Trail Drive, Richmond, VA 23238 • (804) 418-3548
www.hardywood.com/

Chesapeake and Eastern Shore

Back Bay Brew House
Beach House: 614 Norfolk Avenue, Virginia Beach, VA 23451 • (757) 531-7750
Farmhouse: 1805 Kempsville Road, Virginia Beach, VA 23464 • (757) 531-7750
www.backbaybrewingco.com

Buskey Cider on the Bay (Outpost)
109 Mason Avenue, Cape Charles, VA 23310 • (757) 695-3412
www.buskeycider.com

Ditchley Cider Works
1571 Ditchley Road, Kilmarnock, VA 22482 • (804) 435-3851
www.ditchleyciderworks.com

Monroe Bay Winery
10 Washington Avenue, Colonial Beach, VA 22443 • (804) 410-5628
www.monroebaywine.com

Sly Clyde Ciderworks
207 E. Mellen Street, Hampton, VA 22663 • (757) 755-3130
www.slyclyde.com

Zoll Vineyards
9744 Dutton Road, Dutton, VA 23050 • (774) 275-7581
www.zollvineyards.com

Northern Virginia

Cider Lab
Sumerduck Tasting Room: 5344 Sumerduck Road, Sumerduck, VA 22742 • (540) 212-9745
Spotsylvania Tasting Room: 7501 Graham Street, Suite 128, Spotsylvania, VA 22407 • (540) 699-0605
www.cider-lab.com

Cobbler Mountain Cider
5909 Long Fall Lane, Delaplane, VA 20144 • (540) 364-2802
www.cobblermountain.com

Corcoran Vineyards and Cidery
14635 Corkys Farm Lane, Waterford, VA 20197 • (540) 882-9073
www.corcorancider.com

Crooked Run Fermentation
Washington, DC: 550 Morse St NE Ste #120, Washington, DC 20002 • (202) 355-9010
Sterling: 22455 Davis Dr Ste 120, Sterling, VA 20164 • (571) 375-2652
Leesburg: 205 Harrison St SE Ste B, Leesburg, VA 20175 • (571) 918-4446
www.crookedrunfermentation.com/

Fabbioli Cellars
15669 Limestone School Road, Leesburg, VA 20176 • (703) 771-1197
www.fabbioliwines.com

Henway Hard Cider
18780 Foggy Bottom Road, Bluemont, VA 20135 • (540) 837-4000
www.henwayhardcider.com/

Lost Boy Cider
317 Hoofs Run Drive, Alexandria, VA 22314 • (703) 566-5737
www.lostboycider.com

Loudoun Cider House
43372 Spinks Ferry Road, Leesburg, VA 20176
www.loudounciderhouse.com

Mt. Defiance Cidery and Distillery (Cider Barn)
495 E. Washington Street, Middleburg, VA 20117 • (540) 687-8100
www.mtdefiance.com

Mountain Run Winery
10753 Mountain Run Lake Road, Culpepper, VA 22701 • (703) 638-5559
www.mountainrunwinery.com/

Notaviva Farm Brewery and Winery
13274 Sagle Rd, Hillsboro, VA 20132 • (540) 668-6756
https://notaviva.com/

Old Trade Brewery & Cidery
13270 Alanthus Road, Brandy Station, VA 22714 • (540) 729-1740
www.oldtradebrewery.com

Son of a Bear Ciders (Teaghlaigh Vineryard)
22344 Clarks Mountain Road, Rapidan, VA 22733 • (540) 395-3012
www.sonofabearciders.com

Valley View Farm
1550 Leeds Manor Road, Delaplane, VA 20144 • (540) 592-1021
www.valleyviewva.com

Wild Hare Cider
The Grainery: 75 S. 3rd Street, Warrenton, VA 20187 • (703) 402-7956
Tasting Room: 324 1st Street, Berryville, VA 22611 • (703) 402-7956
Pub & Courtyard: 205 William Street, Fredericksburg, VA 22401 • (703) 402-7956
Cider Cabin: 106 South Street SE, Leesburg, VA 20175 • (703) 402-7956
www.wildharecider.com

APPENDIX C

Glossary

acidity Acids are one of the biggest factors when selecting apples for cider. Acidity is found in the juice and provides the twang and bite to the beverage. The balance of acids and tannins are essential for a good cider.

ABV Alcohol by volume, measured in percentages. It is the measurement used to determine the amount of alcohol in cider.

applejack/apple brandy Apple brandy and applejack are different. Apple brandy is really just distilled cider. The term "applejack" is a bit more complicated. Traditional applejack was made by freezing cider repeatedly until the water separates from the alcohol, but now a safer method is used through distillation [1]

apple juice The unfermented juice of apples. This is typically clarified and pasteurized to ensure a longer shelf life.

brix The measurement of sugar in the juice. A higher brix juice can make a higher alcohol cider. This measurement is also regularly used to determine the potential alcohol content in wine too. Sugar is another one of the essential components for cider.

cider The fermented juice of apples. In the United States, this is often referred to as "hard cider." "Cyder" is the Old English form of the word.

cyser This is a hybrid product made up of cider and mead (fermented honey). A honey-and-water mixture is combined with pressed juice and then fermented.

dwarf stock A standard apple tree grows roughly 25 feet tall, and a semi-dwarf tree reaches 12 to 15 feet tall, while a dwarf apple tree grows 8 to 12 feet tall. This all depends on the rootstock. There are advantages and disadvantages to all types. Semi-dwarf fruit trees produce slightly more fruit than dwarf trees, but they're a bit harder to prune and maintain. They also take up more room in your yard. Dwarf fruit trees are not always as hardy as semi-dwarf and standard trees, and they are not recommended for areas with harsh winters. Because they are less substantial, dwarf trees require trellising to protect them from wind and to sustain the weight of the developing fruit.

fermentation The process whereby yeast produces enzymes to break down sugar molecules in the apple juice, producing mainly alcohol and carbon dioxide. Fermentation in its simplest form is the conversion of sugars into alcohol, and the alcohol potential for cider is determined by the amount of sugar in the apples. The fermentation of cider does best between 59 and 68 °F. Cofermentations are very popular in the cider world and can include honey or raisins as well as grape juice and apple juice.

fortify The addition of liquor to wine or cider.

grafting This is the process to ensure that an apple tree will be copied. Orchardists attach a piece of the tree (a scion) that they would like the fruit from to the lower part of an established rootstock. As the rootstock grows, the scion grows over the original stock. There are a variety of grafting methods and almost all commercial orchards use grafting.

heirloom/heritage Heirloom or heritage apples are historic apples that can be traced at least seventy-five to one hundred years. They are the apples that existed before large commercial farming began. Some examples include Spitzenburg and Ashmead's Kernel. Heritage is sometimes used interchangeably with heirloom. Cider makers love to use heritage/heirloom apples due to their sugar content, acidity, and tannins.

keeving Some cider makers utilize a process called keeving to create a bold, naturally sweet cider with some effervescence. To create this complex beverage, a pectic enzyme is added along with calcium chloride before fermentation begins. These chemicals interlink with the yeasts to create a gel that will float to the top of the vessel during fermentation. The gel, which has now taken the form of brown blob that the French call *chapeau brun* will be separated from the clear liquid below. The cider will be put into another vessel or bottled where it continues to ferment eventually producing a low alcohol natural sweet sparkling cider.

Malus domestica This is the Latin word for the domesticated apple tree or orchard apple tree. Today there are more than 7,500 cultivars (types) of domesticated apple trees, and these species vary from the highly commercial Fuji (culinary) apple tree to the wonderful heritage cider apple tree Harrison. Its origins can be traced back to Kazakhstan.

natural cider This is sometimes referred to as "traditional cider." The cider maker decides to have limited intervention with the fermentation of the cider. No preservatives or yeasts are added. Natural yeasts from the apple skins and surrounding environment will ferment the juice. No sulfites are added, and its carbon dioxide comes from the fermentation itself.

orchard An Old English word for yard, "orchard" can denote any planting of fruit trees, but it can also contain nut trees or sugar maples.[2] It is an area of trees or shrubs that is planted for the purpose of food production.

perry An alcoholic beverage made from the juice of pears. Perry has a much larger amount of unfermentable sugars (sorbitol) than cider, so it is likely to have more residual sweetness. Pear cider is different than perry, because pear cider is cider with added pear juice.

pomace Pomace comprises the solid apple remains (skin, pulp, seeds, and stems) after pressing. The leftover pomace can be used for compost and feed for farm animals. It can also be rehydrated and refermented to be distilled into a *grappa* style *eau de vie.*

pommeau A fortified alcoholic beverage made with apple brandy and apple juice. This usually results in a 15–18 percent ABV. Pommeau is typically consumed as an aperitif or after dinner drink with dessert.

residual sugar Basically, how much sugar is left after fermentation is stopped. Some sugars in certain apples and pears cannot be fermented all the way out. Cideries will label this as residual sugar. This does not necessarily mean that the product will be sweet. Some cider makers use residual sugar to balance out an overly tannic or acidic cider.

single varietal A single-varietal cider is a cider made with only one type of apple. Most ciders are blends, but cider makers may choose to make a single varietal if the apple presents enough tannins and acids to create a well-balanced product.

tannin Tannins are another one of the biggest factors when selecting apples for cider. These organic compounds are found in the flesh of the apple (not the skins like grapes) and provide the depth, mouthfeel, and complexity to a cider.

terroir The makeup or conditions of the area where the fruit is grown. This includes the soil, climate, and any other natural features of a particular orchard or vineyard. The same apple grown in different regions will produce different types of cider as a result of the differences in the terroir.

yeast Fermentation begins by either adding or pitching yeast or allowing the juice to use natural yeasts to ferment. Yeasts can be found in the flesh of the apple, the skin of the apple, the cider barn (building), the equipment, and many other locations. A commercial yeast allows for a more controlled fermentation. Most of the aromas you get in a cider come from the juice, but some can also be present from the yeast as well.

Notes

Preface

1. Eliza Smith, *The Compleat Housewife: Or, Accomplished Gentlewoman's Companion,* Williamsburg: William Parks, 1742, 219. Apple trees grown from seeds are referred to as pippins.
2. Watson, *Cider, Hard and Sweet,* 53.

1. Cider's Beginnings and Spread to North America

1. Cornille, Gladieux, and Smulders, et al.'s "New Insight into the History of Domesticated Apple" provides a scientific account of the origin of the domesticated apple. Some wild crab apples are native to the Americas. (Even though the apple is often assumed as the forbidden fruit that Adam and Eve ate in the Garden of Eden, the Bible is not specific on what type of fruit was consumed. The western world typically depicts the fruit as an apple, though the fig, pomegranate, grape, banana, and even psychedelic mushroom have borne this reputation in Jewish and/or Christian tradition.)
2. Gabe Cook's *Ciderology* and Ben Watson's *Cider, Hard and Sweet* present wonderful overviews of the history of apples from a cider enthusiast's perspective. *Malus domestica* spread to Mesopotamia roughly four thousand years ago where Mesopotamians developed a system of grafting. (*M. domestica* is the more modern term for the domestic apple, while *M. pumila* is the older term.) Other apples such as *Malus orientalis* and *Malus sylvestris* are also thought to contribute to the genetic makeup of the domesticated apple. Watson, *Cider, Hard and Sweet,* 8.
3. You cannot simply produce a specific apple by just replanting its apple seed, because the fruit has the characteristics of the two parents. Cook, *Ciderology,* 35.
4. My neighborhood deer could spread the seeds of my tossed Fuji apple and my neighbor's tossed Winesap apple, and that could possibly produce an apple tree, but that tree would not bear the exact same fruit that we consumed. Cook, *Ciderology,* 33.
5. See Schröpfer, Lempe, Emeriewen, and Flachowsky's "Recent Developments and Strategies for the Application of Agrobacterium-Mediated Transformation of Apple Malus × domestica Borkh." A twig of the original tree is pruned and is grafted onto a neutral base rootstock that is disease resistant, thus creating a scion of the par-

ent tree and ensuring the transfer of the original genetics. The new tree now provides further scions for the propagation of the variety.

6. Watson, *Cider, Hard and Sweet,* 13.
7. Cook, *Ciderology,* 34.
8. Pliny, the Elder, *Natural History* 4.19, 257. Cysers are produced by several cideries and meaderies today. Bill Cavender at Black Heath Meadery in Richmond regularly produces an award winning Cyser known as Blue Angel. See chapter 5 for more information on Cysers.
9. Watson, *Cider, Hard and Sweet,* 15.
10. Watson, *Cider, Hard and Sweet,* 18.
11. European settlers also brought with them disease, which killed millions of native peoples in the Americas (including smallpox and bubonic plague). There is little record of Native Americans (pre-Columbian civilizations) consuming fermented apple juice, and the domesticated apple was not indigenous to the Americas. There were some crab and wild apples present, so they could have created alcohol from those fruits, but there are few if any records that indicate this.
12. Watson, *Cider, Hard and Sweet,* 23.
13. *Virginia Company* 3:400. Jamestown was founded by a joint-stock company where wealthy businessmen pooled their money together in hopes of receiving a return on their investments. The Virginia Company's Second Colony of London funded the settlement of Jamestown and was very interested in seeing the colony thrive. The Virginia Company even implemented measures for paving the way for cider production in Virginia to help the economy of the colony.
14. *Virginia Company* 3:53. For more information on the spread of honey bees in North America see Ella Weber's "*Apis mellifera:* The Domestication and Spread of European Honey Bees for Agriculture in North America," *University of Michigan Undergraduate Research Journal* 9 (Spring 2012): https://deepblue.lib.umich.edu/bitstream/handle/2027.42/97006/UMURJ-Issue09_2012-EWeber.pdf. There were other bees that produced honey in North America, but not honeybees. The bees that were brought to Jamestown in 1622 were *A. mellifera* and were used to produce honey and pollinate fruit trees.
15. Hatch, *Fruits and Fruit Trees,* 61; Littletown historical marker; and email correspondence with Leah Stricker, curator at Jamestown Rediscovery, Historic Jamestown. Virginia became a royal colony in 1624. There is evidence that Jamestown colonists carried beer on their ships, and variations of beer were also brewed at the settle-

ment. For more information on brewing in Jamestown, see Lee Graves, *Virginia Beer.*

16. According to historian H. Graham Woodlief, "supplies and provisions included foodstuffs along with 5 1/2 tuns of beer and 6 tuns of cider" were on board the *Margaret.* See H. Graham Woodlief, "History of the First Thanksgiving," https://berkeleyplantation.com/first-thanksgiving/. Also note that one tun could equal one hogshead or between 210 and 252 gallons. This Berkeley Hundred settlement would not last, but it shows how important that cider was to settlement to be included with the initial provisions, and the Virginia government would take note.

17. Once the colony was under the king's authority, the crown took much more of an interest in the success of Virginia's economy. Shenandoah Applelore, "Early History of the Shenandoah Apple," https://shenandoahappleloreblog.wordpress.com/history-of-the-shenandoah-apple/.

18. "Instructions of Berkeley, 1642," *Virginia Magazine of History and Biography* 2, no. 3 (1895): 281–88.

19. Wm. J. Hinke, Report of the Journey of Francis Louis Michel from Berne, Switzerland, to Virginia, October 2, 1701–December 1, 1702, *Virginia Magazine of History and Biography* 24, no. 1 (1916). Francis Michel is also known as Frantz Ludwig Michel. Michel was planning on setting up a Swiss colony but was unsuccessful.

20. Robert and Parrish Beverley and Susan Scott, *The History and Present State of Virginia,* 314.

21. Meacham, *Every Home a Distillery,* 41.

22. Meacham, *Every Home a Distillery,* 53.

23. Joseph Ball was Mary Ball Washington's half-brother. He moved to England permanently after 1743 but was still involved in the management of his Virginia property. Landon Carter and Jack P. Greene, *The Diary of Colonel Landon Carter of Sabine Hall, 1752–1778* (Charlottesville: Virginia Historical Society, 1965), 2:589.

24. William Byrd II, *The Commonplace Book of William Byrd II of Westover,* ed. Kevin Berland, Jan Kirsten Gilliam, and Kenneth A. Lockridge (Chapel Hill: Omohundro Institute of Early American History and Culture, 2001), 121.

25. Only a year after Lord Fairfax made this stipulation regarding these land grants, John Massey planted a hundred apple trees in Frederick County in 1749. See "Early History of the Shenandoah Apple."

26. Meacham, "They Will Be Adjudged by Their Drink," 123.

27. Steven Davison, Jay Merwin Jr., John Capper, Garrett Power and

Frank Shivers Jr., *Chesapeake Waters: Four Centuries of Controversy, Concern and Legislation,* 2nd ed. (Atglen, PA: Schiffer, 1997), 21.

28. Ebenezer Hazard and Fred Shelley, "The Journal of Ebenezer Hazard in Virginia, 1777," *Virginia Magazine of History and Biography* 62, no. 4 (1954): 410. Hazard was appointed surveyor general of the Continental Post Office in 1776, and he traveled throughout the south in 1777 and 1778. He kept a two-volume account of his trips to the South.

29. Theophilus Grew, *The Virginia Almanack for the Year of Our Lord God 1766,* Williamsburg, 1765, n.p. The wealthy planter John Randolph echoed the dangers of drinking fresh water when he wrote to his son to avoid cold water while traveling in the early nineteenth century. He reported that the papers listed "eight deaths in one week by cold water." Rorabaugh, *Alcoholic Republic,* 97.

30. Meacham, *Every Home a Distillery,* 2. According to Meacham, by 1770 "an average white women drank almost two pints of hard cider per day."

31. Edward Kimber, "Observations in Several Voyages and Travels in America," July 1746, *Encyclopedia Virginia.* Virginia Humanities, https://encyclopediavirginia.org/entries/observations-in-several-voyages-and-travels-in-america-by-edward-kimber-july-1746.

32. Meacham, *Every Home a Distillery,* 13. Colonists were unsure of how to stop fermentation of fruit juices and keep it fresh.

33. Colonial Williamsburg Foundation Library Research Report Series, December 9, 1955, 0043, Colonial Williamsburg Foundation Library, Williamsburg Virginia. Queen's Creek Plantation was owned by Daniel Parke II until his death in 1710 and then the property passed on to his daughter Frances Parke Custis in 1714.

34. *The Virginia Almanack for the Year of Our Lord God 1772* (Williamsburg: Purdie & Dixon, 1772).

35. "Notes on an American Dinner, [ca. 4 July?] 1798," *Founders Online,* National Archives, https://founders.archives.gov/documents/Madison/01-17-02-0108 [original source: *The Papers of James Madison,* vol. 17, *31 March 1797–3 March 1801 and supplement 22 January 1778–9 August 1795,* ed. David B. Mattern, J. C. A. Stagg, Jeanne K. Cross, and Susan Holbrook Perdue (Charlottesville: University Press of Virginia, 1991), 160]. Cider was regularly consumed to celebrate Independence Day. What better to toast America than with America's beverage of choice?

36. "Notes on an American Dinner, [ca. 4 July?] 1798," *Founders Online.*

37. "From John Adams to Benjamin Waterhouse, 19 February 1805," *Founders Online,* National Archives, https://founders.archives.gov/documents/Adams/99-02-02-5072.

38. Rebecca Rupp, "The Highs and Lows of Hard Apple Cider History," *National Geographic,* October 8, 2015, https://www.nationalgeographic.com/culture/food/the-plate/2015/10/08/the-highs-and-lows-of-hard-apple-cider-history/. An ordinary is a tavern or inn that served a full meal.
39. Frank Clark, "A Most Wholesome Liquor: A Study of Beer and Brewing in Eighteenth-Century England and Her Colonies," Colonial Williamsburg, 1999.
40. Smith, *Drinking History,* 84. The temperance movement in America really starts in 1784 with Benjamin Rush's publication *An Inquiry into the Effects of Ardent Spirits Upon the Human Body and Mind.* The book opens many American's eyes to the dangers of excessive drinking. Groups start to form throughout America who believe many of societies' ills can be traced back to alcohol like poverty, health issues, and domestic abuse. They make it their mission to curb alcohol consumption, and this movement will pave the way for the passage of the Eighteenth Amendment in the early twentieth century.
41. Taylor, *Arator,* 274. John Taylor was not a proponent of using apples for brandy and said that the distillation of cider can be "precarious, troublesome, trifling and out of his province. But the apple will furnish some food for his hogs, a luxury for his family in winter, and a healthy liquor for himself and his labourers all the year." (Taylor, *Arator,* 273). See also Hedrick, 185.
42. Taylor, *Arator,* 275–76. There is also a cider recipe from Taylor that uses eggs. Eggs were sometimes used to help with clarification of the beverage.
43. "Thomas Jefferson to Vine Utley, 21 March 1819," *Founders Online,* National Archives, https://founders.archives.gov/documents/Jefferson/03-14-02-0144 [original source: *The Papers of Thomas Jefferson,* Retirement Series, vol. 14, *1 February to 31 August 1819,* ed. J. Jefferson Looney (Princeton: Princeton University Press, 2017), 156–58].
44. "Vine Utley to Thomas Jefferson, 10 June 1819," *Founders Online,* National Archives, https://founders.archives.gov/documents/Jefferson/03-14-02-0380 [original source: *The Papers of Thomas Jefferson,* Retirement Series, vol. 14, *1 February to 31 August 1819,* ed. J. Jefferson Looney (Princeton: Princeton University Press, 2017), 419–22]; Colonial Williamsburg Foundation Library Research Report Series—364 John D. Rockefeller, Jr. Library Colonial Williamsburg Foundation; Durand of Dauphiné in Ayres, Fruit Culture," 130–31; *A Frenchman in Virginia: Being the Memoirs of a*

Huguenot Refugee (Durand, 1686), the latter of which is an earlier account showing that moderation is the key. When the French Huguenot Durand (of Dauphiné) visited Gloucester County in 1686 he described a raucous group that imbibed too much one evening. He explained, "It was cider making time. Everywhere we were required to drink so freely that even if there were twenty, all would drink to a stranger & he must pledge them all. They drank also some bottles of rhum much stronger than brandy. When they were not intoxicated they usually let me drink in my own way & generally I just kissed the glass: but when they were drunk they would have me drink at their will. This so muched annoyed me that as soon as I had room, I went no more. The cider made me ill; I think it was too new." He could be referring to cider that had not fermented long enough (or aged long enough to mellow out the flavors.)

45. Meacham, *Every Home a Distillery,* 3. For more information on smaller homestead production of cider by women, see Meacham, *Every Home a Distillery,* 32.

46. Meacham, "They Will Be Adjudged by Their Drink," 118–19; Meacham, *Every Home a Distillery,* 6. Small planter households made up about half of the homes in the Chesapeake. Descriptions of small planter and large planter households come from historian Sarah Meacham.

47. Meacham, "They Will Be Adjudged by Their Drink," 139. See chapter 1 in *Every Home a Distillery* for more information on the historic method to cider production.

48. Small planter households began to become more self-reliant in cider- and alcohol-making by the second half of the eighteenth century when a better-quality press was created, Hewe's Crab was established as a high-quality cider apple, and a three-gallon still was available for distillation that led to better preservation of beverages. Meacham, *Every Home a Distillery,* 4–5.

49. Meacham, *Every Home a Distillery,* 6. Large planter households also consumed 105 gallons of spirits annually. The annual per capita consumption of alcoholic beverages was "fifteen gallons of cider and three and half gallons of distilled spirits" from Meacham pages 7, 22–23.

50. Meacham, *Every Home a Distillery,* 4; Hedrick, *A History of Horticulture in America to 1860,* 104.

51. Thomas Glover, "An Account of Virginia: Its Scituation, Temperature, Productions, Inhabitants and Their Manner of Planting and Ordering Tobacco &c," *Philosophical Transactions of the Royal Society of London* 11, no. 126 (1676): 13–14.

52. Warren Billings, "Sir William Berkeley," *Encyclopedia Virginia*, https://encyclopediavirginia.org/entries/berkeley-sir-william-1605-1677. Berkeley's book *A Discourse and View of Virginia* (1663) argued for a more diversified colonial economy.
53. Hedrick, *History of Horticulture*, 104–5. Fitzhugh had more than 54,000 acres, most of which was used for tobacco. According to Hedrick, the planter owned "an orchard of 2500 apple trees 'of many varieties, such as mains, pippins, russentens, costards, marigolds, kings, magitens, and bachelors,' most of them grated and well-fenced with a 'locust fence'." Meacham also explains that "an apple tree produced from one to twenty bushels. A typical eight-year-old apple tree gave two bushels of apples a year, providing Fitzhugh with an estimated 5,000 bushels of apples. One hogshead of cider (between forty-eight and sixty-three gallons) required twenty to thirty bushels of apples a year. Using the median number of bushels, Fitzhugh's plantation could make at least two hundred hogsheads or a minimum of 9,600 gallons of cider a year." Meacham, *Every Home a Distillery*, 50.
54. Alexander Craig House Historical Report, Block 17 Building 5 Lot 55, originally entitled: "Alexander Craig House" Mary A. Stephenson, 1956, Colonial Williamsburg Foundation Library Research Report Series—1341, Colonial Williamsburg Foundation Library, Williamsburg, Virginia 1999. An entry in William Byrd's diary on Oct. 27, 1709, described his typical day: "We went to court and sat till 4 o'clock. Then we went to dinner and I ate boiled beef for my dinner. In the evening we played at cards and I won £5. We drank some of Will Robinson's cider till we were very merry." Another letter from 1710 from p. 96 of the Colonial Williamsburg report indicates that Bland was also a cider enthusiast. Byrd noted on January 3, 1712, that "Mr. Bland's sloop brought two hogsheads of cider and 66 hides from Williamsburg which were put ashore" (*The Secret Diary of William Byrd of Westover 1709–1712*, ed. Louis B. Wright and Marion Tinling [Richmond: Dietz, 1941]). In July 1710, he described an account where he drank cider with planter and statesman, Richard Bland. According to Byrd, he "prepared to go to Williamsburg . . . rode to Colonel Ludwell's . . . then proceeded to Williamsburg where I arrived in the evening. I drank some cider with Mr. Bland and then went to the Governor's where I found him just returned from Kiquotan." *Secret Diary of William Byrd*, 260, 263. On November 20, 1710, Byrd wrote that "I ate some toast and cider with Colonel Carter (Robert "King" Carter) at Marot's. About I o'clock we went to the capitol where we did very little." Marot was

technically Byrd's next door neighbor. On Nov. 26, 1710, Byrd commented that "I wrote several things till about two o'clock and then went to Marot's to dinner with the burgesses. I ate roast goose for dinner. In the afternoon we sat and drank a bottle of cider till about 5 o'clock and then adjourned to the coffeehouse."

55. Hatch, *Fruits and Fruit Trees,* 61. The list of apples are "Golden Russet, Red Streak, Golden Pippin, and Winter as well as Summer Pearmain."
56. Meacham, *Every Home a Distillery,* 51.
57. Jeffrey Ruggles, "Robert Beverley," *Encyclopedia Virginia,* https://encyclopediavirginia.org/entries/beverley-robert-d-1722.
58. Meacham, *Every Home a Distillery,* 55.
59. Hugh Jones and Richard Lee Morton, *The Present State of Virginia: From Whence Is Inferred a Short View of Maryland and North Carolina* (Chapel Hill: University of North Carolina Press, 1956), 78.
60. Ayres, *Fruit Culture,* 128–29, 33.
61. *The Diary of Colonel Landon Carter,* 2:1134–35. The note about "Miller's Dictionary" refers to *The Gardeners Dictionary* by Philip Miller (1691–1771). The work focuses on gardening and botany plants cultivated in England and was often cited. Landon Carter was the son of Robert "King" Carter and managed much of his father's land on the Northern Neck and tended to his own plantation at Sabine Hall in Richmond County.
62. Meacham, *Every Home a Distillery,* 50. Carter was very wealthy and also had a large collection of bottles for cider. According to Carter, "I bottled a cask of Nominy (Nomini) plantation cyder" and "23 dozen in my own bottles." Nomini Hall or Nomini Plantation is Carter's other plantation that was located in Westmoreland County. (Robert King Carter, vertical file, Rockefeller Library.) He like other large planters sold off any surplus cider for profit. Edmund Berkeley, "Robert Carter," *Encyclopedia Virginia,* October 26, 2022, https://encyclopediavirginia.org/entries/carter-robert-ca-1664-1732/.
63. This disagreement came to a peak in 1763 when they were required to help pay for the debt incurred by the British during the French and Indian War. Ironically, it would be a cider tax imposed on English citizens (living in England) that forced the prime minister of Great Britain to look at taxing colonists to alleviate some of the debt payment. In 1763, Lord Bute (prime minister, 1762–63) pushed through a new tax on cider and perry production in England. The Cider Act placed a duty of 4 shillings on every hogshead of these beverages made in England. Not only did the tax anger these alcohol producers, but excise commissioners could also search

private properties to ensure that the tax was being followed. The Act created outrage throughout England, and riots emerged all over the country soon after the bill's passage that caused Lord Bute to step down as prime minister; George Grenville replaced him. The resistance to the Cider Act by British citizens directly affected the American colonists. Grenville pushed through the Sugar Act (or the American Revenue Act) in 1764, which taxed Americans on several numerated items like lumber and iron. He hoped it would alleviate British aggressions over the Cider Tax, but George Grenville did not stop with the Revenue Act. He then proceeded with the infamous Stamp Act in 1765. This Act created major dissent from Americans and is one of the earliest causes for revolution. Historians would compare Americans' reactions to the Stamp Act to the English reaction to the Cider Act. The chancellor of the exchequer, Sir Francis Dashwood, was the actual person who pushed forward the bill. Fred Anderson, *Crucible of War: The Seven Years' War and the Fate of Empire in British North America, 1754–1766* (London: Faber and Faber, 2000), 614.

64. "Virginia Nonimportation Resolutions, 17 May 1769," *Founders Online,* National Archives, https://founders.archives.gov/documents/Jefferson/01-01-02-0019 [original source: *The Papers of Thomas Jefferson,* vol. 1, *1760–1776,* ed. Julian P. Boyd (Princeton: Princeton University Press, 1950), 27–31].

65. Beer that required wheat and/or grain would start to decline in popularity since the raw product was not readily available in the colonies.

66. Rorabaugh, *The Alcoholic Republic,* 62–68.

67. "General Orders, 8 August 1775," *Founders Online,* National Archives, https://founders.archives.gov/documents/Washington/03-01-02-0173 [original source: *The Papers of George Washington,* Revolutionary War Series, vol. 1, *16 June 1775–15 September 1775,* ed. Philander D. Chase (Charlottesville: University Press of Virginia, 1985), 268–70].

68. "General Orders, 28 August 1775," *Founders Online,* National Archives, https://founders.archives.gov/documents/Washington/03-01-02-0267 [original source: *The Papers of George Washington,* Revolutionary War Series, vol. 1, *16 June 1775–15 September 1775,* ed. Philander D. Chase (Charlottesville: University Press of Virginia, 1985), 370–71].

69. "To George Washington from Brigadier General William Heath, 22–23 March 1776," *Founders Online,* National Archives, https://founders.archives.gov/documents/Washington/03-03-02-0382

[original source: *The Papers of George Washington,* Revolutionary War Series, vol. 3, *1 January 1776–31 March 1776,* ed. Philander D. Chase (Charlottesville: University Press of Virginia, 1988), 513–14].

70. "From George Washington to the Continental Congress Committee to Inquire into the State of the Army, 19 July 1777," *Founders Online,* National Archives, https://founders.archives.gov/documents/Washington/03-10-02-0328 [original source: *The Papers of George Washington,* Revolutionary War Series, vol. 10, *11 June 1777–18 August 1777,* ed. Frank E. Grizzard Jr. (Charlottesville: University Press of Virginia, 2000), 332–37].

71. "General Orders, 22 March 1778," *Founders Online,* National Archives, https://founders.archives.gov/documents/Washington/03-14-02-0237 [original source: *The Papers of George Washington,* Revolutionary War Series, vol. 14, *1 March 1778–30 April 1778,* ed. David R. Hoth (Charlottesville: University of Virginia Press, 2004), 265].

72. Rebecca Rupp, "Applejack. for When Hard Cider Just Isn't Strong Enough," Culture (National Geographic, May 3, 2021), https://www.nationalgeographic.com/culture/article/applejack-for-when-hard-cider-just-isnt-strong-enough; Courtney Roberson, "The Story behind America's Oldest Distillery and Its NJ Roots," New Jersey Digest Magazine, July 16, 2021, https://thedigestonline.com/nj/laird-applejack/. Also, during the Revolutionary War, Washington would stay at Moses Laird's (Robert's uncle's) house during the Battle of Monmouth in 1778. Moses was Washington's guide of the area. "Revolutionary War Sites in Englishtown, New Jersey," Englishtown, New Jersey Revolutionary War Sites, Englishtown, New Jersey Historic Sites, accessed October 28, 2022, https://www.revolutionarywarnewjersey.com/new_jersey_revolutionary_war_sites/towns/englishtown_nj_revolutionary_war_sites.htm#s9. "America's Oldest Distiller," Laird & Company, February 16, 2018, https://lairdandcompany.com/our-history/. Frank J. Prial, "One Family's Story: Apples to Applejack," *New York Times* (May 4, 2005), https://www.nytimes.com/2005/05/04/dining/one-familys-story-apples-to-applejack.html. Washington was also familiar with the distillation of cider, and he sometimes referred to apple brandy as "cyder spirits" in his diary. A diary entry from September 1763 stated that he "Sowed Rye in . . . & began Stilling Cyder" at Mount Vernon. "[September 1763]," *Founders Online,* National Archives, https://founders.archives.gov/documents/Washington/01-01-02-0008-0007 [original source: *The Diaries of George Washington,* vol. 1, *11 March 1748–13 November 1765,* ed. Donald Jackson (Charlottesville: University Press of Virginia, 1976), 313–14]. Washington also distilled grain into whiskey. Laird & Company and applejack are discussed in greater detail in chapter 5.

73. Daniel Okrent, *Last Call: The Rise and Fall of Prohibition* (New York: Scribner, 2010), 47.

74. "A Dinner at Mount Vernon: From the Unpublished Journal of Joshua Brookes (1773–1859)," ed. R. W. G. Vail *New-York Historical Society Quarterly* 31, no. 2 (April 1947): 75; George Washington Parke Custis, Recollections and Private Memoirs of Washington (New York: Derby & Jackson, 1860), 153.

75. Robert J. Dinkin, *Campaigning in America: A History of Election Practices* (New York: Greenwood Press, 1989). James Madison served as a state delegate until 1779, when he became part of the Second Continental Congress. He would also go on to draft the Constitution and serve as the fourth president of the United States.

76. His father was Benjamin Harrison V, who was one of the Founders.

77. Political ephemera began pouring out of the manufactures to capitalize on the marketing campaign. One manufacturer made bottles shaped like replicas of log cabins filled with hard cider. Another company made hip flasks with a portrait of Harrison on one side and an emblem showing a log cabin, a plow, and a cider barrel on the other. Several prints and graphics were made that depicted Harrison as a man of the people. Whig political rallies and parades included large amounts of hard cider. Unfortunately for Harrison, he would have the shortest presidential tenure after dying from pneumonia only 31 days into his term. John Tyler, a fellow Virginian, subsequently became the tenth president. Some historians have argued that the "Hard Cider" campaign lowered the perceived value of cider (Smith, *Drinking History,* 77–78).

2. Becoming Colonial Virginia's Beverage of Choice

1. Hatch, *Fruits and Fruit Trees,* 62. The remaining apples listed were English.

2. Kiana Pontrelli, "Cider-Loving Founding Fathers," *Cidercraft,* February 19, 2018, https://cidercraftmag.com/cider-loving-founding-fathers/.

3. Pontrelli, "Cider-Loving."

4. "From Benjamin Franklin to Charles Norris, 16 September 1758," *Founders Online,* National Archives, https://founders.archives.gov/documents/Franklin/01-08-02-0039 [original source: *The Papers of Benjamin Franklin,* vol. 8, *April 1, 1758, through December 31, 1759,* ed. Leonard W. Labaree (New Haven: Yale University Press, 1965),

155–56]. Norris was also a trustee of the Pennsylvania General Loan Office.

5. "To Joseph Jones from James Madison, 4 September 1794," *Papers of James Monroe,* accessed February 20, 2021, https://monroepapers.com/items/show/724.
6. "To James Madison from John Roane, 7 April 1810," *Founders Online,* National Archives, https://founders.archives.gov/documents/Madison/03-02-02-0373 [original source: *The Papers of James Madison,* Presidential Series, vol. 2, *1 October 1809–2 November 1810,* ed. J. C. A. Stagg, Jeanne Kerr Cross, and Susan Holbrook Perdue (Charlottesville: University Press of Virginia, 1992), 295].
7. "To James Madison from Lekeel Cosmeaux, 21 December 1814," *Founders Online,* National Archives, https://founders.archives.gov/documents/Madison/03-08-02-0387 [original source: *The Papers of James Madison,* Presidential Series, vol. 8, *July 1814–18 February 1815 and supplement December 1779–18 April 1814,* ed. Angela Kreider, J. C. A. Stagg, Mary Parke Johnson, Anne Mandeville Colony, and Katherine E. Harbury (Charlottesville: University of Virginia Press, 2015), 454–55].
8. An English Redstreak was offered for sale by nurseryman Philip Walten of Baltimore in 1788. ("Letter to George Washington from George Mason," *The Papers of George Mason,* vol. 2, ed. Robert A. Rutland [Chapel Hill: University of North Carolina Press, 1970], 823–24.) See also Mason to GW, 5 April 1785, Library of Congress: George Washington Papers. Ginger was known to provide health benefits for digestion and reduce inflammation of the stomach.
9. "Letter to Thomas Halbert from George Mason," *The Papers of George Mason,* vol. 1, ed. Bernard Bailyn and James Morton Smith (Chapel Hill: University of North Carolina Press, 1970), 23–27.
10. Graves, *Charlottesville Beer,* 13. According to the beverage list for taverns, a quart of English Strong Beer was listed at 18 pence while a quart of Virginia cider was listed at 6 pence.
11. Graves, *Charlottesville Beer,* 13. See also Henry S. Randall, *The Life of Thomas Jefferson* (New York: Derby & Jackson, 1858), 1:11.
12. Jefferson to John Adams, June 11, 1812, in The Writings of Thomas Jefferson, ed. Andrew Adgate Lipscomb and Albert Ellery Bergh (Washington, DC: Thomas Jefferson Memorial Association, 1904), 13:160. The Cherokee chief stopped by Shadwell on his way to and from Williamsburg.
13. Kern, *Jeffersons at Shadwell,* 198: "Thomas Jefferson, a small group of Indian artifacts, and the colonial records of Indian activities describe Outassetè at Shadwell, dining in the best room, wearing a

bright blue coat, drinking cider with Peter Jefferson, Fry, Walker, Lomax, Patton, and Timberlake."

14. Kern, *Jeffersons at Shadwell,* 53–54. In 1770, the Jeffersons' house at Shadwell was destroyed in a fire. His mother would have a smaller house built on the property, but Jefferson moved to Monticello where he would carry on his family's love of cider.

15. "Slavery at Monticello FAQs," Thomas Jefferson's Monticello, https://www.monticello.org/slavery/slavery-faqs/property/. Jefferson inherited the plantation from his father and built his house "Monticello" on a hill that he used to explore as a child. Monticello means "little mountain."

16. Hatch, *Fruits and Fruit Trees,* 59.

17. Hatch, *Fruits and Fruit Trees,* 65.

18. Jefferson was enrolled in William & Mary's philosophy school's two-year program from 1760 to 1762, and then studied with George Wythe from 1762 until 1767. According to Jefferson's autobiography, "Mr. Wythe continued to be my faithful and beloved Mentor in youth, and my most affectionate friend through life. In 1767, he led me into the practice of the law at the bar of the General Court." Thomas Jefferson: Autobiography, January 6–July 29, 1821, Thomas Jefferson Papers, Library of Congress.

19. Mary Goodwin, Colonial Williamsburg Foundation Library Research Report Series 210 (Williamsburg: College of William & Mary, 1967). A brief sketch of the main building of the college, and of the rooms to be restored to their eighteenth-century appearance, is on p. 58

20. The palace was built in 1722 and served as home to several Virginia governors including Dinwiddie, Spotswood, Henry, and Jefferson. In 1781, the Governor's Palace was destroyed in a fire. After an archaeological dig unearthed the remains of an original wall, the cellar and other artifacts, palace reconstruction began in 1930s. (The capital would move from Williamsburg to Richmond in 1780.) The drawing includes an inventory from Governor Botetourt's residency at the palace starting in 1770.

21. "From Thomas Jefferson to James Maxwell, 16 December 1790," *Founders Online,* National Archives, https://founders.archives.gov/documents/Jefferson/01-18-02-0116 [original source: *The Papers of Thomas Jefferson,* vol. 18, *4 November 1790–24 January 1791,* ed. Julian P. Boyd (Princeton: Princeton University Press, 1971), 307–8]. and "From Thomas Jefferson to James Maxwell, 20 March 1791," *Founders Online,* National Archives, https://founders.archives.gov/documents/Jefferson/01-19-02-0153 [original source: *The*

Papers of Thomas Jefferson, vol. 19, *24 January–31 March 1791,* ed. Julian P. Boyd (Princeton: Princeton University Press, 1974), 592]. In 1790 Jefferson requested cider from merchant James Maxwell. Maxwell procured Jefferson some Hewe's Crab throughout his tenure in Philadelphia, but sometimes the product was difficult to come by. "To Thomas Jefferson from James Maxwell, 2 April 1791," *Founders Online,* National Archives, https://founders.archives.gov/documents/Jefferson/01-20-02-0009 [original source: *The Papers of Thomas Jefferson,* vol. 20, *1 April–4 August 1791,* ed. Julian P. Boyd (Princeton: Princeton University Press, 1982), 94–95]. When Maxwell couldn't procure the product due to poor conditions, Jefferson looked elsewhere.

22. "From Thomas Jefferson to Adam Lindsay, 15 September 1791," *Founders Online,* National Archives, https://founders.archives.gov/documents/Jefferson/01-22-02-0145 [original source: *The Papers of Thomas Jefferson,* vol. 22, *6 August 1791–31 December 1791,* ed. Charles T. Cullen (Princeton: Princeton University Press, 1986), 148].

23. "From Thomas Jefferson to Adam Lindsay, 20 December 1791," *Founders Online,* National Archives, https://founders.archives.gov/documents/Jefferson/01-22-02-0396 [original source: *The Papers of Thomas Jefferson,* vol. 22, *6 August 1791–31 December 1791,* ed. Charles T. Cullen (Princeton: Princeton University Press, 1986), 425]. (He had difficulty shipping the cider to Philadelphia due to the Coasting Act.)

24. "From Thomas Jefferson to Thomas Newton, 9 November 1801," *Founders Online,* National Archives, https://founders.archives.gov/documents/Jefferson/01-35-02-0477 [original source: *The Papers of Thomas Jefferson,* vol. 35, *1 August–30 November 1801,* ed. Barbara B. Oberg (Princeton: Princeton University Press, 2008), 588–89]. Jefferson received the cider by the end of November, "I have just recieved your favor of the eighteenth and after due thanks for your attention to the procuring the cyder (10 barrels of Hughes Crab)." "From Thomas Jefferson to Thomas Newton, 27 November 1801," *Founders Online,* National Archives, https://founders.archives.gov/documents/Jefferson/01-35-02-0560 [original source: *The Papers of Thomas Jefferson,* vol. 35, *1 August–30 November 1801,* ed. Barbara B. Oberg (Princeton: Princeton University Press, 2008), 734]. "From James Madison to Thomas Newton, Jr., 5 [August] 1803," *Founders Online,* National Archives, https://founders.archives.gov/documents/Madison/02-05-02-0296 [original source: *The Papers of James Madison,* Secretary of State Series, vol. 5, *16 May–31 October 1803,* ed. David B. Mattern, J. C. A. Stagg,

Ellen J. Barber, Anne Mandeville Colony, and Bradley J. Daigle (Charlottesville: University Press of Virginia, 2000), 280–81]. Unfortunately, he found later shipments not to his liking. In August of 1803, Jefferson received another 8 barrels for the winter from Mr. Newton, but some of the barrels were spoiled with water on the voyage, so it was not worth bottling. "To James Madison from Thomas Newton Jr., 19 May 1804," *Founders Online,* National Archives, https://founders.archives.gov/documents/Madison/02-07-02-0232 [original source: *The Papers of James Madison,* Secretary of State Series, vol. 7, *2 April–31 August 1804,* ed. David B. Mattern, J. C. A. Stagg, Ellen J. Barber, Anne Mandeville Colony, Angela Kreider, and Jeanne Kerr Cross (Charlottesville: University of Virginia Press, 2005), 233]. Thankfully, a year later in May 1804, Jefferson received another shipment from Newton that proved to be much better than the last.

25. Newark cider was made of a blend of Harrison and Canfield apples grown in Essex County, New Jersey. It was regularly shipped to Virginia and praised for its high quality. In 1803, Jefferson again asked the New Jersey congressman to order the cider for him. (*Proceedings of the New Jersey Historical Society: A Magazine of History, Biography and Genealogy,* new ser., 3 [1918], 25, 52; *National Intelligencer,* February 9, 1807; TJ to Condit, October 1, 1803). "To Thomas Jefferson from John Condit, 30 December 1802," *Founders Online,* National Archives, https://founders.archives.gov/documents/Jefferson/01-39-02-0209 [original source: *The Papers of Thomas Jefferson,* vol. 39, *13 November 1802–3 March 1803,* ed. Barbara B. Oberg (Princeton: Princeton University Press, 2012), 234–35]. "To Thomas Jefferson from John Condit, 2 April 1804," *Founders Online,* National Archives, https://founders.archives.gov/documents/Jefferson/01-43-02-0146 [original source: *The Papers of Thomas Jefferson,* vol. 43, *11 March–30 June 1804,* ed. James P. McClure (Princeton: Princeton University Press, 2017), 152]. Condit, sent another shipment of cider to Jefferson in 1804 and instructed him that the cider should not be left out in the sun. According to Condit, Jefferson should be given the "earliest Notice of their Arrival, that they may be taken from the wharf, soon after they are Landed, as their lying in the Sun any time may Injure the Cyder I hope it will turn out to be very good, if I am correctly informed, it is of the finest quality—The Barels Marked in Black, were all made by One Man, the One Marked with red, by another person, both Claiming the preference in making good Cyder—the different marks Are for the purpose of knowing which keeps the best through the summer." "To Thomas

Jefferson from Étienne Lemaire, 19 April 1804," *Founders Online*, National Archives, https://founders.archives.gov/documents /Jefferson/01-43-02-0230 [original source: *The Papers of Thomas Jefferson*, vol. 43, *11 March–30 June 1804*, ed. James P. McClure (Princeton: Princeton University Press, 2017), 265–66]. Jefferson did receive the New Jersey cider blend that month and had eight barrels bottled.

26. *American National Biography*, ed. John A. Garraty and Mark C. Carnes (New York: Oxford University Press, 1999), vol. 9. *Dictionary of American Biography*, ed. Allen Johnson & Dumas Malone (New York: Charles Scribner's Sons, 1931), vol. 7. This is the copied letter from Armstrong to Jefferson concerning the apples. "To Thomas Jefferson from John Armstrong, 20 February 1804," *Founders Online*, National Archives, https://founders.archives.gov/documents /Jefferson/01-42-02-0441 [original source: *The Papers of Thomas Jefferson*, vol. 42, *16 November 1803–10 March 1804*, ed. James P. McClure (Princeton: Princeton University Press, 2016), 507–8]:

> "No. 1. 2. 3. & 4 were sent me from detroit two years since. No. 5 & 6 are from bearing trees in my Orchard—
>
> "No 1 Large White apple—tied with a White string
>
> "No. 2 Large Red apple tied with a red string
>
> "No. 3 Pumgray an apple much admired and will keep the year round tied with a blue string
>
> "No. 4 Calvit apple which is without comparison the best apple that ever was Eaten—tied with a green string
>
> "No. 5 Ox Eye striped apple ripe in the fall, highly flavoured weighs from 16 to 20 Oz—tied with a yellow string
>
> "No. 6 Egg Plumb as large as a hens egg light coloured rich & Sweet with a small stone will succeed by engrafting on a Damson, Wild Plumb or Peach stock—
>
> "I generally cut my scions at this Season of the year, and place one end of the cuttings about two inches in the ground in a perpendicular position and there let them remain until the proper season for placing them into the stock—I practice Tounge Grafting, and seldom lose five trees out of one thousand, have had trees to bear the second year after ingrafting them—It would oblige me if thro some of your friends I could obtain a few cuttings of the Virginia Cyder apple generally called Hughes Crab with a description of the fruit—"

Whip and tongue grafting is stronger than a traditional splice graft, "because the interlocking tongues are held under compression by the natural springiness (elasticity) of the wood of both stock and scion." (See "Whip and Tongue Grafting," Cornell University, https://courses.cit.cornell.edu/hort494/mg/methods.alpha/WTMeth.html.) Armstrong calls Calville Blanc d'Hiver simply Calvit. According to Peter Hatch, Jefferson planted some of these apple trees in his orchard.

27. *Thomas Jefferson's Farm Book,* 96.
28. For more information on George and Ursula Granger, see Darlene Hayes's article, "George and Ursula Granger: The Erasure of Enslaved Black Cidermakers from Cider Culture."
29. "George Granger, Sr. 1730–1799, an Enslaved Overseer," Thomas Jefferson's Monticello, https://www.monticello.org/slavery/landscape-of-slavery-mulberry-row-at-monticello/meet-people/george-granger-sr/. Jefferson was in Paris from 1784 to 1789. You can find more information on the Granger's death here in the letter "To Thomas Jefferson from Martha Jefferson Randolph, 30 January 1800," *Founders Online,* National Archives, https://founders.archives.gov/documents/Jefferson/01-31-02-0294 [original source: *The Papers of Thomas Jefferson,* vol. 31, *1 February 1799–31 May 1800,* ed. Barbara B. Oberg (Princeton: Princeton University Press, 2004), 347–48]. *Thomas Jefferson's Farm Book,* 96. By 1796, George Granger Sr. became the only African American overseer at Monticello who received an annual wage and managed the cash crops and farm laborers.
30. According to historian Lucia Stanton, "he [Jupiter] worked as a personal servant to Jefferson, hostler, a coachman, and stonecutter." An account from Lucia Stanton, *"Those Who Labor for My Happiness:" Slavery at Thomas Jefferson's Monticello* (Charlottesville: University of Virginia Press, 2012), 58.
31. "From Thomas Jefferson to Thomas Mann Randolph, 4 February 1800," Founders Online, National Archives, https://founders.archives.gov/documents/Jefferson/01-31-02-0304 [original source: The Papers of Thomas Jefferson, vol. 31, 1 February 1799–31 May 1800, ed. Barbara B. Oberg (Princeton: Princeton University Press, 2004), 359–61]. *Thomas Jefferson's Farm Book,* 17. "From Thomas Jefferson to Martha Jefferson Randolph, 11 February 1800," Founders Online, National Archives, https://founders.archives.gov/documents/Jefferson/01-31-02-0311 [original source: The Papers of Thomas Jefferson, vol. 31, 1 February 1799–31 May 1800, ed. Barbara B. Oberg (Princeton: Princeton University Press, 2004), 365–66]. According to Jefferson, "There is nobody there but Ursula who unites trust and skill to do it. She may take anybody she

pleases to aid her. I am in hopes if any keys had been delivered to Jupiter that they have been taken care of. When I say that Ursula may have anybody she pleases to help her, I mean to except John, who must have nothing to do with drink."

32. "Edmund Bacon 1785–1866, a Hired White Overseer," Thomas Jefferson's Monticello, https://www.monticello.org/slavery/landscape-of-slavery-mulberry-row-at-monticello/meet-people/edmund-bacon/.
33. Isaac Jefferson and Hamilton W. Pierson, *Jefferson at Monticello*, ed. James A. Bear (Charlottesville: University Press of Virginia, 1967), 100.
34. "Thomas Jefferson to Edmund Bacon, [15 November 1817]," *Founders Online*, National Archives, https://founders.archives.gov/documents/Jefferson/03-12-02-0153 [original source: *The Papers of Thomas Jefferson*, Retirement Series, vol. 12, *1 September 1817 to 21 April 1818*, ed. J. Jefferson Looney (Princeton: Princeton University Press, 2014), 192].
35. *Papers of Thomas Jefferson*, vol. 26, *11 May–31 August 1793*, 380–81. Martha Jefferson Randolph married Thomas Mann Randolph Jr. in 1790.
36. "From Thomas Jefferson to Martha Jefferson Randolph, 2 April 1807," *Founders Online*, National Archives, https://founders.archives.gov/documents/Jefferson/99-01-02-5405 (early access document).
37. "To Thomas Jefferson from Anne Cary Randolph, 18 March 1808," *Founders Online*, National Archives, https://founders.archives.gov/documents/Jefferson/99-01-02-7655 (early access document). Bad cider can be used for vinegar. (Note that Randolph later married Charles Lewis Bankhead of Caroline County and became Anne Cary Randolph Bankhead.)
38. "From Thomas Jefferson to Ellen Wayles Randolph Coolidge, 19 March 1826," *Founders Online*, National Archives, https://founders.archives.gov/documents/Jefferson/98-01-02-5969 (early access document).
39. Mary Randolph, *The Virginia Housewife* (London: Dover, 1993); Helen Zoe Veit, *Food in the Civil War Era: The South* (East Lansing: Michigan State University Press, 2015), 199. Here is the full recipe for cider: "Cider Wine-Fifteen gallons of cider, fresh from the press; to each gallon, add two pounds of good brown sugar. When the sugar has dissolved, strain the mixture into a clean cask. Let the cask want two gallons of being full; leave out the bung for forty-eight hours. Put in the bung, leaving a little vent until fermentation

ceases; then bung up tightly. In a year it is fit for use. It needs no straining; the longer it stands upon the lees, the better."

40. "Charles Massie," Thomas Jefferson's Monticello, https://www.monticello.org/site/research-and-collections/charles-massie. Edgar Woods, *Albemarle County in Virginia,* 266–67. Charles Massie's son and Jefferson corresponded from 1812 to 1826.
41. "From Thomas Jefferson to Charles Massie, 21 December 1824," *Founders Online,* National Archives, https://founders.archives.gov/documents/Jefferson/98-01-02-4799 (early access document). Jefferson found this batch of cider to not last, "Your cyder furnished me has kept so badly," complained Jefferson, "indeed one half generally spoiling has fallen off so much in quality for some years past that I must reduce my demand this year to 90. galls."
42. *Thomas Jefferson's Farm Book,* 421. Jefferson told Massie, that "I hope you will chuse formed of your very best."
43. *Thomas Jefferson's Farm Book,* 419.
44. Francis Calley Gray, *Thomas Jefferson in 1814, Being an Account of a Visit to Monticello, Virginia* (Boston: Club of Odd Volumes, 1924), 67.
45. She was widowed in 1773, and she and her six children regularly stayed at Monticello.
46. It's clear that Jefferson trusted Martha to assist with his cider operation, and he ended up gifting her two of the silver cups labeled "G.W. to T.J." that were given to Jefferson by his friend and former teacher George Wythe. "Francis C. Gray's Account of a Visit to Monticello, [4–7 February 1815]," *Founders Online,* National Archives, https://founders.archives.gov/documents/Jefferson/03-08-02-0189 [original source: *The Papers of Thomas Jefferson,* Retirement Series, vol. 8, *1 October 1814 to 31 August 1815,* ed. J. Jefferson Looney (Princeton: Princeton University Press, 2011), 232–38].
47. "Invoice from Richard Washington, 20 August 1757," *Founders Online,* National Archives, https://founders.archives.gov/documents/Washington/02-04-02-0244 [original source: *The Papers of George Washington,* Colonial Series, vol. 4, *9 November 1756–24 October 1757,* ed. W. W. Abbot (Charlottesville: University Press of Virginia, 1984), 376–81]. Also included "12 dozn best Herefordshire Cyder in best Mould Bottles, wyred Corks."
48. Fiona Mac, *Ciderlore: Cider in the Three Counties* (Eardisley, Herefordshire: Logaston, 2003), 2.
49. Mason lived about sixteen miles from Mount Vernon at Gunston Hall and Digges had a plantation in Prince George's County, Maryland, across the Potomac River called Warburton. "Memorandoms—March 21st. [1763]," *Founders Online,* National

Archives, https://founders.archives.gov/documents/Washington/01-01-02-0008-0010 [original source: *The Diaries of George Washington,* vol. 1, *11 March 1748–13 November 1765,* ed. Donald Jackson (Charlottesville: University Press of Virginia, 1976), 315–18]. U. P. Hedrick, *History of Horticulture in America to 1860* (New York: Oxford University Press, 1950). Gloucester may have just been a location where Washington purchased them; they do not exist today.

50. See September 3–4, 1763, August 22, 1763, and October 1, 1764, in *Diaries of George Washington* 1. Mount Vernon was built in 1758 and by 1767 cider was being made from the plantation's orchards. There were three enslaved overseers at Mount Vernon during Washington's lifetime: Davy Gray (who ran Dogue Run Farm [1790], Muddy Hole [1770–1785], and River Farm [1785–1786, 1792–99]), Will (who ran Muddy Hole [1785] and Dogue Run [1792]), and Israel Morris (who ran Dogue Run [1766–94]). See Thompson, *The Only Unavoidable Subject of Regret,* 343–44 and Hayes, "George and Ursula."

51. "To George Washington from Lund Washington, 5 September 1767," *Founders Online,* National Archives, https://founders.archives.gov/documents/Washington/02-08-02-0016 [original source: *The Papers of George Washington,* Colonial Series, vol. 8, *24 June 1767–25 December 1771,* ed. W. W. Abbot and Dorothy Twohig (Charlottesville: University Press of Virginia, 1993), 25–26]. The farms consisted of River Farm (Clifton's Neck), Dogue Run, Muddy Hole, Union Farm, and Mansion House. Thomas Bishop was a white overseer of Muddy Hole farm who had also served as Washington's personal servant in the army in the fall of 1755, and James Cleveland was a white overseer at the River Farm on Clifton's Neck who managed the cider production on their respective farms in the fall of 1767.

52. "From Alexander Hamilton to James Duane, 14 September 1779," *Founders Online,* National Archives, https://founders.archives.gov/documents/Hamilton/01-02-02-0455 [original source: *The Papers of Alexander Hamilton,* vol. 2, *1779–1781,* ed. Harold C. Syrett (New York: Columbia University Press, 1961), 174]. Duane wrote, "I send an apple, a native of our woods, I have never seen Hughes' Crab, from which the fine Virginia Cyder is produced, but from description I believe this to be the same Fruit; be so good as to shew it to his Excellency & enquire from him." Hamilton wrote back to Duane four days later explaining that he lost the apple before he could give it to Washington. "I received your letter of the 10th ins. two days since & with my usual distraction suffered your apple to pass out of my hands and to be lost before it could be seen by the General." One of the most famous Revolutionary War soldiers was Peter Francisco of Buckingham County who was also a cider lover. Francisco (1760–1831) was born in Portugal and moved to Virginia as a young man where he apprenticed as a blacksmith in Virginia before the Revolutionary War. When the war broke out, Francisco joined the 10th Virginia Regiment in 1776 and fought in several key battles. Standing at 6 ft 8 inches and known for his incredible feats of strength, he was referred to as the "Hercules of Virginia." The massive Virginian was also an ardent cider drinker, and his love of fermented apple is evident in a letter written almost a decade after the Revolutionary War. On December 12, 1792, Francisco wrote to his friend John Stuart (also from Buckingham County) requesting that he send him a selection of his best cider. A note at the bottom of the letter indicates that Stuart had sent him cider before. (See Peter Francisco, letter to John Baker and John Stuart, December 12, 1792, Accession 20122, Personal Papers Collection, Library of Virginia, Richmond.)

53. "Lund Washington to George Washington," September 2, 1778, manuscript, Mount Vernon Ladies' Association; typescript, Mount Vernon Ladies' Association, Mary V. Thompson document.

54. George Washington, September 10, 1785, *Diaries of George Washington* 4:192.

55. Senator William Maclay, September 19, 1789, in *The Diary of William Maclay and Other Notes on Senate Debates,* ed. Kenneth R. Bowling and Helen E. Veit (Baltimore, MD: John Hopkins University Press, 1988), 46.

56. Linda Stradley and Brenda, "Apples—History and Legends of Apples," *What's Cooking America,* October 23, 2020, https://whatscookingamerica.net/fruit/apples.htm.

57. It wasn't just George Washington who occupied the house from 1790 to 1797, but he also was joined by Martha, two of her grandchildren (Washington Custis and Nelly Custis), and a household staff of twenty-four including eight enslaved workers. According to Tobias Lear, "Mr Morris (Robert) still occupies the wine Cellar which is the only one in which the masons will suffer any thing to be put until they make their drains. Mr Jefferson and Mr Madison arrived yesterday. The former will not be able to go into his house for some time." Lear rented the Robert Morris house from the Corporation of the City of Philadelphia for Washington. See "To George Washington from Tobias Lear, 21 November 1790," *Founders Online,*

National Archives, https://founders.archives.gov/documents/Washington/05-06-02-0330 [original source: *The Papers of George Washington,* Presidential Series, vol. 6, *1 July 1790–30 November 1790,* ed. Mark A. Mastromarino (Charlottesville: University Press of Virginia, 1996), 678–82].

3. Cider's Downfall and Reemergence

1. 1790s America was a very agrarian nation with most people living on farms and growing their own food. This number will start to be reduced and by 1900 less than half of America's population was living on rural homesteads.
2. Watson, *Cider, Hard and Sweet,* 28.
3. Watson, *Cider, Hard and Sweet,* 29.
4. Graves, *Virginia Beer,* 16–17.
5. Graves, *Virginia Beer,* 17. See Andrea Mehrländer, *The Germans of Charleston, Richmond and New Orleans during the Civil War Period, 1850–1870: A Study and Research Compendium* (New York: De Gruyter, 2011) for more information on Richmond's German community.
6. Samuel Mordecai, *Virginia, Especially Richmond, in By-Gone Days* (Richmond: West & Johnston, 1860), 244: https://quod.lib.umich.edu/m/moa/ACZ8838.0001.001/250.
7. Watson, *Cider, Hard and Sweet,* 25.
8. Summer Whitford, "The Apple: An American Icon," *Daily Meal,* November 29, 2015, https://www.thedailymeal.com/eat/apple-american-icon.
9. Watson, *Cider, Hard and Sweet,* 30–31. They pasteurized their cider and marketed it as apple juice or "sweet cider." Some apples were planted specifically for cider, and some were planted for fresh eating. Some cider apples have too much sugar and/or tannins to be attractive fresh eating apples.
10. Merriam-Webster.com Dictionary, s.v. "prohibition," https://www.merriam-webster.com/dictionary/prohibition. Cider was sometimes an exception to the law, because it was included as part of the "fruit juice" clause that allowed for fermented juice to be produced at home. One of the reasons for this exception was to try and appease the rural voters who regularly produced alcohol from fruit for their own consumption.
11. Graves, *Virginia Beer,* 26. According to Graves, "When the final votes were tallied, Virginians favored going 'dry' by 94,251 to 63,886."
12. This is when Al Capone's bootlegging and racketeering crime syndicate came to power.

13. Graves, *Virginia Beer,* 27–28.

14. Charles M. Holloway, "Romancing the Vine in Virginia, No Wine before It's Time," *Colonial Williamsburg,* Summer 2002.

15. Pucci and Cavallo, *American Cider,* 4.

16. "Retail Sales of the Leading Cider Brands in the United States in 2021 (in Million U.S. Dollars)," https://www.statista.com/statistics/300775/us-leading-cider-brands-based-on-dollar-sales/. Virginia Cider Association, Strategic Plan 2023: https://vaw-public-prod.s3.amazonaws.com/246e90bd2153e52c6ddc78cf4e604d36.pdf. The states with the most cideries (New York, California, Washington, Oregon, Michigan, Pennsylvania, and Virginia) are also some of the states with the most wineries. Also see American Cider Association Nielsen Reports for more specific data on cider economics, https://ciderassociation.org.

17. Diane Flynt, *Wild, Tamed, Lost, Revived: The Surprising Story of Apples in the South* (Chapel Hill: University of North Carolina Press, 2023). Email correspondence and phone interview with Diane Flynt. Stephanie Ganiz, "Godmother of Southern Cider," *Richmond,* January 31, 2022: https://richmondmagazine.com/restaurants-in-richmond/food-news/godmother-of-southern-cider/. Other information from Diane Flynt's keynote address for CiderCon 2022, Richmond, VA, February 3, 2022.

18. Jodi Helmer, "An Appreciation for Lee Calhoun, the Man who Saved Southern Apples," *Civil Eats,* May 25, 2020: https://civileats.com/2020/05/25/an-appreciation-for-lee-calhoun-the-man-who-saved-southern-apples/. Horne Creek Farm, located in Pinnacle, NC, just about twenty miles from the Virginia border, is a North Carolina State Historic Site that belongs to the North Carolina Department of Natural and Cultural Resources. It is a working farm that includes a nineteenth-century farmhouse that was owned by the Hauser family and a working "southern orchard." The orchard has many cider apple varieties that were used throughout Virginia's history and continue to be used today. The site features more than 850 southern apple trees and at least 425 different types of apples. The website is also a great resource for any apple historian or enthusiast. For more information on Horne Creek, see https://historicsites.nc.gov/all-sites/horne-creek-farm/southern-heritage-apple-orchard. More information on Calhoun and his work can be found in his magnum opus, *Old Southern Apples.*

19. Adrien Higgins, "Tom Burford, champion of the heirloom apple, dies at 84," *Washington Post,* April 3, 2020: https://www.washingtonpost.com/local/obituaries/tom-burford-champion-of

-the-heirloom-apple-dies-at-84/2020/04/03/99c7f116-75b2-11ea -87da-77a8136c1a6d_story.html. More information on Burford and his work on North American apples can be found in *Apples of North America.*

4. (Almost) All about Apples

1. Watson, *Cider, Hard and Sweet,* 124
2. Pucci and Cavallo, *American Cider,* 47.
3. Pucci and Cavallo, *American Cider,* 47. One area where this diurnal shift is evident is Highland and Bath Counties, which are nestled between the Shenandoah Mountains to the east and Alleghany mountains to the west. (Big Fish Cider Co. is located in Highland, and Troddenvale is located in Bath.)
4. Information from the Virginia Cider Association website, https://www.virginiacider.org.
5. Information for the apple descriptions come from the following sources: Pucci and Cavallo, *American Cider;* Calhoun, *Old Southern Apples;* Burford, *Apples of North America;* Hatch, *Fruits and Fruit Trees;* Albemarle CiderWorks, https://www.albemarleciderworks.com/orchard/apple-varieties; and The Southern Heritage Apple Orchard at Horne Creek, https://historicsites.nc.gov/all-sites/horne-creek-farm/southern-heritage-apple-orchard/learn-more/apple-variety-information.
6. Notes come from email correspondence with Mark Muse of Widow's Watch Cider and Muse Orchard.
7. See Albemarle CiderWorks: https://www.albemarleciderworks.com/orchard/apple/dabinett.
8. Hatch, *Fruits and Fruit Trees,* 74. Esopus Spitzenburg was found in the early eighteenth century near the Hudson River in Esopus, NY. Jefferson purchased the apple from Virginia nurseries, and he also acquired cuttings from George Divers and John Taylor but had difficulties growing the apple because of Virginia's warmer climate.
9. Hatch, *Fruits and Fruit Trees,* 74. Calhoun describes his first taste of this historic apple, "My first taste of an Esopus Spitzenberg was an apple I sneaked from a tree in Jefferson's restored orchard at Monticello. I found this purloined apple to be delicious, but I know that it reaches its peak of flavor when I store the apples for a couple months in plastic bags in my refrigerator." See also Calhoun, *Old Southern Apples,* 69–70.
10. See Albemarle CiderWorks: https://www.albemarleciderworks.com/our-cider/cider-varieties/goldrush.
11. Burford, *Apples of North America,* 73.

12. "To Thomas Jefferson from John Condit, 30 December 1802," *Founders Online*, National Archives, https://founders.archives.gov/documents/Jefferson/01-39-02-0209 [original source: *The Papers of Thomas Jefferson*, vol. 39, *13 November 1802–3 March 1803*, ed. Barbara B. Oberg (Princeton: Princeton University Press, 2012), 234–35]. Jefferson was very pleased with the blend and requested additional shipments as president. Many apple varieties that were popular in the south originated in New Jersey. This is likely due to similar climate and coastline of eastern New Jersey. See Calhoun, *Old Southern Apples*, 37.
13. Burford, *Apples of North America*, 75. I attended a Harrison single varietal tasting at Sage Bird Ciderworks in Harrisonburg on November 25, 2022. It was a lovely event that featured a diverse array of tasty Virginia beverages that utilized the flavorful characteristics of the historic fruit. The participating cideries included: Sage Bird, Halcyon Days, Big Fish, Potter's, Ciders from Mars, Albemarle, and Blue Bee.
14. "Hewe's Crab Apple," Thomas Jefferson's Monticello, https://www.monticello.org/house-gardens/in-bloom-at-monticello/hewe-s-crab-apple/.
15. Hatch, *Fruits and Fruit Trees*, 74. A "Hughes Crab" is briefly mentioned being grown in 1741 in James City County, and an advertisement in a 1761 Williamsburg newspaper lists a tract of land for sale having "a very good bearing orchard and another 150 Hughes' crabs beginning to bear." See Calhoun, *Old Southern Apples*, 88. According to Hatch, "In property advertisements in the *Virginia Gazette* between 1755 and 1777, the Hewes Crab appeared more times, thirteen, than all other described fruit varieties combined."
16. Calhoun, *Old Southern Apples*, 88.
17. Hatch, *Fruits and Fruit Trees*, 74. Hewe's was listed prominently in Sorsby's and Ellis's nurseries, and they had numerous different listings of Hewe's, denoting the actual person who propagated it.
18. Entry of Nov. 21, 1817, in the Harrison Henry Cocke papers, #1587, Southern Historical Collection, Wilson Library, University of North Carolina at Chapel Hill.
19. Moss, *Southern Spirits*, 42–43. Colonel Roane's account of the origins of Hewe's Crab and the different varieties of Hewe's Crab is mediated by Timothy Pickering in "Some Account of the Virginia Crab Apple," April 7, 1814, in *Memoirs of the Philadelphia Society for Promoting Agriculture* 3:392–95. (The original transcript is in the William Bradford Alwood Collection at Virginia Tech.) Colonel Roane explained that he had known some type of Hewe's Crab

to exist in Williamsburg for over a century. The crab apple that grew on his plantation (Roane's White Crab) is a variety of Hewe's Crab. Pickering included the following postscript: "A few years ago, when general Sumter, of South Carolina, was in the senate, he told me that the juice of his Hughe's crab apples was so rich as to be clammy. Quere, if a transfer of the apples of thin, meagre juice to the South, and those of rich, thick or viscous juice to the North, would not produce a valuable improvement?"

20. The "Hewe's Crab Smackdown" event took place at Albemarle CiderWorks on November 19, 2021. See their calendar for future cider smackdowns and other special tasting events. See also the description of Sage Bird's Hewe's Crab in chapter 6.

21. Watson, *Cider, Hard and Sweet,* 24.

22. There is more information on Dr. Thomas Walker in the Castle Hill Cider description in chapter 6.

23. In 1777, Dr. Thomas Walker brought scions of Newtown Pippin back to Castle Hill where he had them successfully grafted. See information in the description of Castle Hill in chapter 6. ("From Thomas Jefferson to James Madison, 28 October 1785," *Founders Online,* National Archives, https://founders.archives.gov/documents/Jefferson/01-08-02-0534 [original source: *The Papers of Thomas Jefferson,* vol. 8, *25 February–31 October 1785,* ed. Julian P. Boyd (Princeton: Princeton University Press, 1953), 681–83].) The Newtown Pippin was listed for sale in several Virginia nurseries by the 1760s. See Hatch, *Fruits and Fruit Trees,* 70–71.

24. Richard Parkinson, *A Tour in America in 1798, 1799, and 1800: Exhibiting Sketches of Society and Manners, and a Particular Account of the America System of Agriculture, with Its Recent Improvements* (London: J. Harding and J. Murray, 1805).

25. Calhoun, *Old Southern Apples,* 115–16. By the 1920s, Parliament had placed the tax on the fruit again, so the Pippin's international market dropped.

26. Burford, *Apples of North America,* 37.

27. "Pomme Gris," Albemarle CiderWorks, https://www.albemarleciderworks.com/orchard/apple/pomme-gris. I attended the 2022 Apple and Cheese Tasting at Monticello on October 22, 2022. It was held at Tufton Farm and was a wonderful experience for the apple and cheese lover. Eight apples (majority heirloom) were paired with eight cheeses.

28. Burford, *Apples of North America,* 147. There is an advertisement in the *Virginia Gazette,* August 1, 1771 (p. 2), in which Caleb's grandfather, John Ralls, listed his plantation, named Beulah, for sale.

It included more than seven hundred acres and "a very fine Apple Orchard, from which are made seven or eight Thousand Gallons of Cider a Year (that Quantity has been made on an Average ever since the Year 1756) the Trees are of the best Kind of Fruit, and the Cider as good as any on the Continent."

29. Burford, *Apples of North America,* 147. "Ralls," Albemarle Cider-Works, https://www.albemarleciderworks.com/orchard/apple/ralls. Others have claimed that Ralls received the scion directly from Jefferson. Jefferson's summer home, Poplar Forest, was just across the James River from Ralls' farm in Bedford County.
30. Burford, *Apples of North America,* 172.
31. Burford, *Apples of North America,* 200.
32. Burford, *Apples of North America,* 203.
33. Cook, *Ciderology,* 49. Cattaline or Catline is mentioned in Sarah Meacham's book as the apple used for cider in the Chesapeake until Hewe's Crab was created. Calhoun and Coxe both mention the apple is their books too. (Calhoun, *Old Southern Apples,* 190.) According to Coxe "The Catline is an apple rather below the middling size: and is sometimes, in a fruitful year, and on a full bearing tree, quite small . . . it is considered as a good early cider apple, although not sufficiently strong for bottling." (Coxe, *A View of the Cultivation of Fruit Trees,* 114.)
34. Pucci and Cavallo, *American Cider,* 160.
35. USDA, National Agricultural Statistics Service; USApple, https://usapple.org/wp-content/uploads/2022/08/USAPPLE-INDUSTRYOUTLOOK-2022.pdf; "Pickyourown.org," U.S. Apple Crop Facts, accessed October 28, 2022, https://www.pickyourown.org/USapplecrop.htm.
36. Virginia Orchard Board, Orchard Map, https://www.virginiaapples.net/orchard-map.

5. Making It, Tasting It, and Exploring Styles

1. Cook, *Ciderology,* 73.
2. Watson, *Cider, Hard and Sweet,* 65–66.
3. Email correspondence with Mark Muse of Widow's Watch Cider and Muse Orchard.
4. Watson, *Cider, Hard and Sweet,* 67.
5. Cook, *Ciderology,* 77.
6. Cook, *Ciderology,* 81.
7. Cook, *Ciderology,* 81.
8. Pucci and Cavallo, *American Cider,* 21.
9. Cook, *Ciderology,* 81. According to the 2022 Virginia Cider Apple

Report, Only around 24 percent of cideries in Virginia press their own juice. The remaining cideries get their juice from orchards or purchase apple juice concentrate. See 2022 Virginia Cider Apple Report, Virginia Wine, https://vaw-public-prod.s3.amazonaws.com/d4693764daac2ac3f11a452e1f74fa97.pdf, 6.

10. Champagne yeast is preferred by many cider makers due to its consistency to produce products with smooth flavor and no off-putting flavors. See Cook, *Ciderology,* 84; Watson, *Cider, Hard and Sweet,* 111–14; Pucci and Cavallo, *American Cider,* 21–22. Other information from correspondence with Mark Muse of Widow's Watch Cider and Muse Orchard concerning fermentation.
11. There is also a time-consuming process called keeving that some cider makers utilize to create a bold naturally sweet cider with some effervescence. To create this complex beverage, a peptic enzyme is added along with calcium chloride before fermentation begins. These chemicals interlink with the yeasts to create a gel that will float to the top of the vessel during fermentation. The gel, which has now taken the form of brown blob that the French call *chapeau brun,* will be separated from the clear liquid below. The cider will be put into another vessel or bottled where it continues to ferment eventually producing a low alcohol natural sweet sparkling cider. See Pucci and Cavallo, *American Cider,* 23.
12. Notes come from Cook, *Ciderology,* Pucci and Cavallo, *American Cider,* and Watson, *Cider, Hard and Sweet.*
13. Pucci and Cavallo, *American Cider,* 22 and 32.
14. Beer and wine styles are more defined than cider styles. Beer connoisseurs have a pretty good idea of what flavors that you can expect to come from a German Hefeweizen (banana, wheat, bubblegum, etc.) or an American New England IPA (citrusy, piney, hoppy), and wine enthusiasts know what characteristics a California Pinot Noir (cherry, berry, cola) has rather than an Australian Zinfandel (peppery, chocolate, vanilla). The American Cider Association maintains an annual guide to cider families for members and those seeking pommelier certification.
15. Watson, *Cider, Hard and Sweet,* 138–39. Kieffer pears originated in Pennsylvania, but are now found from New England to the southern part of the United States.
16. Similar to today, pears were not as plentiful as apples in Virginia, so perry never really took off in the colonies like cider, but there were still some Virginia colonists who made perry and pear wine. In *William Byrd's Natural History,* the Virginia planter referred to

"excellent" pear juice and apple juice that "in the Summer are much more pleasant, much sweater, and healthier than wine." He also described twenty-nine different pear varieties in his book. Despite Byrd's praise there was very little perry production in Virginia before 1820. Pears took longer to bear fruit than apple trees and were very susceptible to disease. According to Hatch, another reason why perry wasn't as popular is because unlike cider, colonists weren't able to develop and "popularize distinct American varieties." They were mostly European varieties. See also Hatch, *Fruits and Fruit Trees,* 100–101.

17. Pucci and Cavallo, *American Cider,* 28, 29.
18. Buskey Cider, https://www.buskeycider.com.
19. There is an earlier reference to George Mason's recommendation to grate some ginger into the cider to make it easier on your stomach.
20. Pucci and Cavallo, *American Cider,* 30.
21. Pucci and Cavallo, *American Cider,* 25.
22. Watson, *Cider, Hard and Sweet,* 172, 173.
23. Alcohol and Tobacco Tax and Trade Bureau, https://www.ttb.gov.
24. Watson, *Cider, Hard and Sweet,* 168.
25. Watson, *Cider, Hard and Sweet,* 168.
26. Virginia Distillery Company, https://vadistillery.com/product/cider-cask-finished-virginia-highland-whisky.
27. CiderCon is held annually by the American Cider Association (ACA), which is the official organization of cider and perry producers in the United States. The conference provides cider makers, growers, and cider enthusiasts an opportunity to learn more about their craft and passion. Richmond hosted the 2022 CiderCon event, where sessions ranged from local topics like a keynote presentation on southern apples by Diane Flynt to special tastings of Michigan ciders and lectures on the history of English cider. Other highlights included a session on crab apples and an exhibit hall for meeting and mingling with cider lovers, discovering what was new to the cider market (like canning and apple presses), talking with growers, and of course sampling an array of tasty ciders. Several activities were hosted at local Richmond cideries and restaurants, and many area businesses offered special cider tastings, cider-pairing dinners, and other events. One of my favorite events was the special Dabinett tasting experience hosted by Blue Bee, where cider historian Dan Pucci moderated tastings of ten different Dabinetts from around the world.

28. Fall Line/Albemarle CiderWorks Pairing Dinner: https://virginiacider.org/cw_events/cider-pairing-dinner-at-fall-line-kitchen-bar/; Pucci and Cavallo, *American Cider,* 110.

6. A Guide to Virginia's Cideries

1. Visit to Hinson Ford and interview with Dennis Kelly, Owner, on September 18, 2020. John Hagarty, "Hinson Ford Cider & Mead decades in the making," Fauquier Times, Sep 19, 2019, https://www.fauquier.com/news/hinson-ford-cider-mead-decades-in-the-making/article_f3cf9f7c-db1d-11e9-8fb8-2f7a7eb89612.html.
2. The ciders in the **Try this** section are based on my preferences. Please note that some of the recommended ciders may not be available due to product availability, lack of specific apples, or cider maker's decision.
3. Email correspondence with Diane Kearns. Fruit Hill Orchard is now incorporated in Palmyra. Learn more about the orchard here: https://www.fruithillorchard.com.
4. Black current or cassis is a woody shrub known for its berries. The traditional English way to drink "Cider and Black" is to add a shot of black currant liquor to a glass of cider. Visit to Winchester Ciderworks and interview with Stephen Schuurman on September 18, 2020, https://www.winchesterciderworks.com. As of 2024, Winchester Ciderworks is now located in 30 E. Piccadilly St. in downtown Winchester: https://www.winchesterstar.com/winchester_star/winchester-ciderworks-opening-tasting-room-restaurant-in-old-town-winchester/article_25db2c6b-bf22-5de6-893c-d896d69bbc10.html
5. Phone interview with David Glaize on March 31, 2022. Anna Merod, "Old Town Cidery opens hard cider yard in downtown Winchester," *The Winchester Star,* March 15, 2021, https://www.winchesterstar.com/winchester_star/old-town-cidery-opens-hard-cider-yard-in-downtown-winchester/article_4f5b17bf-52a5-5b2b-a1a9-0841d19c9c94.html.
6. Visit to Widow's Watch at Muse Orchard and interview with Mark Muse on June 11, 2021.
7. Visit to Old Hill Cider on November 6, 2020, https://oldhillcider.com.
8. Visit to Sage Bird Ciderworks and interview with Zach Carlson on November 6, 2020, https://www.sagebirdworks.com.
9. Visit to Ciders from Mars and interview with Nikki West on June 21, 2021. https://www.ciderfrommars.com.
10. Visit to Tumbling Creek Cider Company and interview with Jerry

Bresowar, Justen Dick, and Tom McMullen on December 22, 2021, https://www.tumblingcreekcider.com.

11. Visit to Big Fish Cider Co. and interview with Kirk Billingsley on October 24, 2020, https://www.bigfishcider.com.
12. Visit to Troddenvale at Oakley Farm and interview with Will and Cornelia Hodges on November 13, 2020, https://www.troddenvale.com.
13. Visit to Halcyon Days Cider Co. and interview with Larry Krietemeyer on November 6, 2020, https://www.halcyondayscider.com.
14. Visit to Bryant's Cidery & Brewery (the Farm) and interview with Jerry Thornton on September 25, 2020, https://www.bryantscider.com. The Capital Trail is a popular bike route that goes 51 miles along the historic Virginia State Route 5 connecting Richmond to Williamsburg.
15. As of 2020 Bold Rock is the second largest cidery in the United States. Angry Orchard in New York is the largest.
16. You could see Brian and John's vision for the current tasting room and restaurant on the original Bold Rock bottles. Multiple visits to Bold Rock Hard Cider and interview with senior brand manager Lindsay Dorrier III on September 25, 2020; https://www.boldrock.com.
17. Visit to Blue Toad Hard Cider and interview with Todd (Toad) Roth on October 30, 2020; https://www.bluetoadhardcider.com. Rachael Smith, "Former Winery to Become New Home of Blue Toad Hard Cider," *Nelson County Times,* June 24, 2015, https://newsadvance.com/nelson_county_times/news/former-winery-to-become-new-home-of-blue-toad-hard/article_64f46354–1ab1–11e5–97f9-f7a37c2805e3.html. Daniel J. Kushner, "Blue Toad Makes Cider for All Seasons," *CITY News,* July 21, 2022, https://www.roccitymag.com/life/rhapsody-in-blueblue-toad-hard-cider-3114980.
18. Visit to Albemarle CiderWorks and interview with Chuck and Charlotte Shelton on October 30, 2020. Phone interview with Anne Shelton on March 8, 2022; https://www.albemarleciderworks.com.
19. Joe Bargmann, "The Many Lives of Neve Hall: In Its Nearly 100-Year History, the New Home of Potter's Craft Cider Has Seen It All," *C-ville Weekly,* Nov. 13, 2019; https://www.c-ville.com/house-of-stories-chapel-mission-party-spot-artists-studio-family-home-the-new-Potter%E2%80%99s-craft-cider-tasting-room-has-seen-it-all-in-its-95-year-history/. Malaika Tyson, "Cidermaker Q &A; A: Potter's Craft Cider: Virginia Craft Cider," *Cider Culture,* May 18, 2021, https://www.ciderculture.com/potters-craft-cider/. Visit to Potter's

Craft Cider and interview with Tim Edmond on September 25, 2020; https://www.potterscraftcider.com.

20. Visit to Patois Cider and interview with Patrick Collins on June 2, 2021; https://www.patoiscider.com. Malolactic fermentation (MLF) is used regularly in the wine world and occasionally in the cider world to achieve a buttery rich flavored beverage. The conversion of malic acid to lactic acid can occur naturally or forced. SO_2 (sulphur dioxide) is used by many wine and cider makers to achieve bacterial stability. Some cideries like Patois do not add any SO_2.
21. Visit to Castle Hill Cider and interview with Don Whitaker (Cider Maker) and Ron Campbell (General Manager) on October 30, 2021; https://www.castlehillcider.com.
22. Multiple visits to Courthouse Creek Cider and email correspondence with Eric Cioffi; https://www.courthousecreek.com.
23. Multiple meetings with Courtney Mailey and visits to Blue Bee Cider, 2012–2023; https://www.bluebeecider.com; Nick Lattanzio, "Blue Bee Cider Has Arrived in Manchester," *Richmond Times-Dispatch,* August 5, 2020, https://richmond.com/food-drink/blue-bee-cider-has-arrived-in-manchester/article_1643e994-c25e-11e2-be15-001a4bcf6878.html.
24. Multiple visits to Buskey Cider and email correspondence with Will and Elle Correll; https://www.buskeycider.com; Karri Peifer, "New cidery, Buskey Cider, opens Saturday in Scott's Addition," *Richmond Times-Dispatch,* April 21, 2016, https://richmond.com/food-drink/restaurant-news/new-cidery-buskey-cider-opens-saturday-in-scotts-addition/article_882ff142-0806-11e6-9feb-33bd51de084d.html.
25. Visit to Coyote Hole Craft Beverages on November 2020; https://www.coyotehole.com; Alix Bryan, "Coyote Hole Ciderworks aims for early spring opening in Louisa November 3, 2016," https://www.wtvr.com/2016/11/30/coyote-hole-ciderworks-opening-in-spring-2017/.
26. Visit to Ditchley Cider Works and interview with Cathy Calhoun on July 2, 2021; https://www.ditchleyciderworks.com; Nunnery, "Ditchley Cider Works: Crafting a Future With a Nod to the Past," *The House and Home Magazine,* January 27, 2020, https://thehouseandhomemagazine.com/food-and-drink/ditchley-cider-works-crafting-a-future-with-a-nod-to-the-pas/.
27. Visit to Sly Clyde Ciderworks on October 2, 2021 and email correspondence with Doug Smith; https://www.slyclyde.com; Barrett Baker, "Sly Clyde Ciderworks in Hampton Looking to Expand," *Peninsula Chronicle,* March 16, 2022, https://peninsulachronicle

.com/2022/03/16/sly-clyde-ciderworks-in-hampton-looking-to-expand/, City of Hampton, "Smith brothers plan to make, sell hard cider in Phoebus house with deep family ties," press release, July 26, 2017, https://www.hampton.gov/CivicAlerts.aspx?AID=2639&ARC=7247; Michael Curry, "Sly Clyde's: Coastal Virginia's First Cidery," *VEER Magazine*, https://veermag.com/2018/07/sly-clydes-coastal-virginias-first-cidery/.

28. Visit to Fabbioli Cellars and meeting with Doug Fabbioli on October 23, 2020; https://www.fabbioliwines.com.

29. Visit to Henway Hard Cider and interview with Henway Hard Cider crew on June 11, 2021; https://www.henwayhardcider.com.

30. Visit to Cobbler Mountain Cider and interview with Daniel Louden on June 11, 2021; https://www.cobblermountain.com.

31. Visit to Lost Boy Cider and interview with Dave Biun on October 23, 2020; https://www.lostboycider.com.

32. Visit to Valley View Farm and interview with Kendra Cummings, farm market and events manager, on June 11, 2021; https://www.valleyviewva.com. You can read more about the rich history on Philip Carter at https://www.pcwinery.com. Heidi Baumstark, "A Day Away On Valley View Farm," *Middleburg Life*, November 2019, https://www.middleburglife.com/a-day-away-on-valley-view-farm/.

33. Visit to Mt. Defiance Cidery and Distillery and interview with Marc Chretien on July 9, 2021; https://www.mtdefiance.com.

34. Visit to Old Trade Brewery & Cidery and interview with Garrett Thayer on June 11, 2021; https://www.oldtradebrewery.com; information also comes from an article that no longer appears online: "Culpeper Welcomes a Brand New Old Trade," Culpeper Tourism and Visitor Center, February 27, 2018, https://visitculpeperva.com.

35. Visit to Cider Lab on December 29, 2021; https://www.cider-lab.com; "Sumerduck Cider House Overwhelmed with Business," *Fauquier Now*, https://www.fauquiernow.com/fauquier_news/article/fauquier-sumerduck-cider-house-overwhelmed-with-business-7-27-2020; John Hagerty, "Cider Science: Father-Son Team Wins Fans with Cider Lab," *Prince William Times*, August 30, 2020, https://www.princewilliamtimes.com/news/cider-science-father-son-team-wins-fans-with-cider-lab/article_67ae1b4a-eabc-11ea-b1b9-a71b6b3708bd.html.

36. Visit to Corcoran Vineyards and Cidery and interview with Lori Corcoran on January 15, 2022; https://www.corcorancider.com.

37. Visit to Wild Hare Cider (Leesburg location) on October 23, 2020; https://www.wildharecider.com; "Wild Hare Cider under new ownership," *Loudoun Times-Mirror,* April 12, 2018, https://www.loudountimes.com/entertainment/wild-hare-cider-under-new-ownership/article_18ad85d8-3daf-11e8-9a0d-9f7128d49d12.html?msclkid=4df84890b82411ecb9929eb482f1d583; Kara Clark Rodriguez, "Local Cidery Headed to Market Station" *Loudoun Now,* December 6, 2017, https://loudounnow.com/2017/12/06/local-cidery-headed-to-market-station/?msclkid=4df8680db82411eca8255266a8bda058.

38. Multiple visits to Stable Craft Brewing; https://www.stablecraftbrewing.com.

39. Multiple visits to Hardywood Park (both locations) and email correspondence with cofounder/president Eric McKay, Hardywood Park Craft Brewery, January 2022; https://www.hardywood.com. I volunteered to pour at Hardywood's first public event back in 2011, and I have been a fan ever since.

40. Monroe Bay Winery, https://www.monroebaywinery.com.

41. Email correspondence with Moss Vineyards on March 29, 2022, and visit on October 8, 2022; https://www.mossvineyards.net.

42. Chateau Morrissette, along with a handful of other Virginia wineries (Barren Ridge, Bluemont, Corcoran, and Peaks of Otter), also make "Apple Wine"—a wine that is pressed apple juice fermented with sugar or other fermentables and will tend to reach an ABV of 12–14 percent. This is different than cider, because cider is typically just the fermented juice of apples. According to the Alcohol and Tobacco Tax and Trade Bureau (TTB), fermented apple juice under 8.5 percent ABV is cider or "Hard Cider," and any fermented apple juice above 8.5 percent ABV is considered wine. See "Amendments to the Criteria for the Hard Cider Tax Rate," TTB Industry Circular, May 16, 2017, https://www.ttb.gov/industry-circulars/ttb-industry-circulars-17-2. According to the Virginia Cider Association, "Based on current law, Virginia hard apple cider can be up to 10 percent alcohol by volume, without chaptalizing (adding sugar to the juice). Any fermented apple juice above 10 percent alcohol must be labeled 'apple wine.' A cider can not have more than 7 percent alcohol when chaptalized." See https://www.virginiacider.org/about/.

43. Back Bay Brew House, https://www.backbaybrewingco.com.

44. Garden Grove Brewing and Urban Winery, https://www.gardengrovebrewing.com.

45. Visit to the Winery at Kindred Pointe on November 6, 2020; https://www.lifeishardcider.com.

46. Phone interview with Brad Stepp, WAR Craft Brewery on May 31, 2022; https://www.sonofabearciders.com.

47. Phone interview with Doug John, owner of Apocalypse Cidery & Winery, on May 31, 2022; https://www.apocalypseciderγandwinery.com.
48. Visit to Henley's Orchard, September 17, 2022; https://www.henleysorchard.com. Here is the description for Henley's Gold from their website: "Multiple uses, superior eating apple, great cider, keeps well. Medium to large clear yellow fruit. Flesh is crisp, fine-grained, and juicy yellow flesh. Rich, distinctive, aromatic spice flavor."
49. Zoll Vineyards, https://www.zollvineyards.com.
50. Mountain Run Winery, https://www.mountainrunwinery.com.
51. Notaviva Farm Brewery & Winery, https://www.notaviva.com.
52. Rockfish Brewing Co., https://www.rockfishbrewcompany.com.
53. Crooked Run Fermentation, https://www.crookedrunfermentation.com.
54. Loudoun Cider House, https://www.loudounciderhouse.com.

Conclusion

1. "Agritourism is a growing component of Virginia's tourism industry and agriculture is the state's largest industry, with an economic impact of $52 billion annually." Virginia Cider Association, https://www.virginiacider.org. Graves, *Virginia Beer*, 271.

Appendix A

1. "Retail Sales of the Leading Cider Brands in the United States in 2021 (in Million U.S. Dollars)," https://www.statista.com/statistics/300775/us-leading-cider-brands-based-on-dollar-sales/. Virginia Cider Association Strategic Plan, 2023, https://vaw-public-prod.s3.amazonaws.com/246e90bd2153e52c6ddc78cf4e604d36.pdf.
2. Virginia Cider Association, About Virginia Cider, https://virginiacider.org/about/.

Appendix C

1. Watson, *Cider, Hard and Sweet*, 172, 173.
2. "orchard," Merriam-Webster, https://www.merriam-webster.com.

Bibliography

Books

Ayres, Edward. "Fruit Culture in Colonial Virginia." Research Report for Colonial Williamsburg. Williamsburg, VA, 1973.

Betts, Edwin Morris, ed. *Thomas Jefferson's Farm Book.* Charlottesville, VA: 1953.

———, ed. *Thomas Jefferson's Garden Book,* 1766–1824. Philadelphia: 1944.

Beverley, Robert. *The History and Present State of Virginia.* Edited by Louis B. Wright. Chapel Hill: University of North Carolina Press, 1947.

Brennan, Andy. *Uncultivated: Wild Apples, Real Cider, and the Complicated Art of Making a Living.* Hartford, VT: Chelsea Green, 2020.

Browning, Frank. *Apples: The Story of the Fruit of Temptation.* New York: North Point Press, 1998.

Burford, Tom. *Apples of North America: Exceptional Varieties for Gardeners, Growers, and Cooks.* Portland, OR: Timber Press, 2013.

Byrd, William, Richmond Croom Beatty, and William J. Mulloy. *William Byrd's Natural History of Virginia: Or, The Newly Discovered Eden.* Richmond, VA: Dietz Press, 1940.

Calhoun Jr., Creighton Lee. *Old Southern Apples: A Comprehensive History and Description of Varieties for Collectors, Growers, and Fruit Enthusiasts, 2nd Edition.* Hartford, VT: Chelsea Green, 2011.

Cook, Gabe. *Ciderology: From History and Heritage to the Craft Cider Revolution.* London: Spruce, 2018.

Coxe, William. *A View of the Cultivation of Fruit Trees: And the Management of Orchards and Cider.* Philadelphia: M. Carey and Son, 1817.

Downing, Andrew Jackson. *The Fruits and Fruit Trees of America.* 9th ed. New York, 1849.

Flynt, Diane. *Wild, Tamed, Lost, Revived: The Surprising Story of Apples in the South.* Chapel Hill: University of North Carolina Press, 2023.

Graves, Lee. *Charlottesville Beer: Brewing in Jefferson's Shadow.* Charleston, SC: American Palate, 2017.

———. *Virginia Beer: A Guide from Colonial Days to Craft's Golden Age.* Charlottesville: University of Virginia Press, 2018.

Hatch, Peter J. *The Fruits and Fruit Trees of Monticello.* Charlottesville: University of Virginia Press, 1998.

———. *A Rich Spot of Earth: Thomas Jefferson's Revolutionary Garden at Monticello*. New Haven: Yale University Press, 2012.

Hedrick, Ulysses P. *A History of Horticulture in America to 1860*. New York: Oxford University Press, 1950.

Jolicoeur, Claude. *The New Cider Maker's Handbook: A Comprehensive Guide for Craft Producers*. Hartford, VT: Chelsea Green, 2013.

Jost, Scott. *Shenandoah Valley Apples*. Chicago: Columbia College Chicago Press, 2014.

Kenrick, William. *The New American Orchardist: Or, An Account Of The Valuable Varieties Of Fruit, Of All Climates, Adapted To Cultivation In The United States*. Boston: Russel, Odiorne, and Metcalf, 1835.

Kern, Susan. *The Jeffersons at Shadwell*. New Haven: Yale University Press, 2010.

Kingsbury, Susan Myra, ed. *The Records of the Virginia Company of London*, vol. 3, *Miscellaneous Records*. Washington, DC: United States Government Printing Office, 1933.

Meacham, Sarah Hand. *Every Home a Distillery: Alcohol, Gender, and Technology in the Colonial Chesapeake*. Baltimore: Johns Hopkins University Press, 2009.

Moss, Robert. *Southern Spirits: Four Hundred Years of Drinking in the American South, with Recipes*. Berkeley, CA: Ten Speed Press, 2016.

Nichols, Lew and Annie Proulx. *Cider: Making, Using & Enjoying Sweet & Hard Cider, 3rd Edition*. North Adams, MA: Storey, 2003.

Pliny the Elder. *Natural History*. Translated by A. C. Andrews, D. E. Eichholz, W. H. S. Jones, and H. Rackham. Cambridge, MA: Harvard University Press, 1938.

Pucci, Dan, and Craig Cavallo. *American Cider: A Modern Guide to a Historic Beverage*. New York: Ballantine Books, 2021.

Rorabaugh, W. J. *The Alcoholic Republic, an American Tradition*. New York: Oxford University Press, 1979.

Smith, Andrew F. *Drinking History: Fifteen Turning Points in the Making of American Beverages*. New York: Columbia University Press, 2013.

Thompson, Mary V. *"The Only Unavoidable Subject of Regret": George Washington, Slavery, and the Enslaved Community at Mount Vernon*. Charlottesville: University of Virginia Press, 2019.

Watson, Ben. *Cider, Hard and Sweet: History, Traditions, and Making Your Own*. Woodstock, VT: Countryman Press, 1999.

Williams, Jason. *Cider Revival: Dispatches from the Orchard*. New York: Harry N. Abrams, 2019.

Other Sources

Cornille, Amandine, Pierre Gladieux, Marinus J. M. Smulders, et al. "New Insight into the History of Domesticated Apple: Secondary Contribution of the European Wild Apple to the Genome of Cultivated Varieties". *PLOS Genetics* 8, no. 5 (2012):https://doi.org/10.1371/journal.pgen.1002703.

Hayes, Darlene. "George and Ursula Granger: The Erasure of Enslaved Black Cidermakers." *Cider Culture,* February 11, 2022. https://www.ciderculture.com/erasure-of-enslaved-black-cidermakers/.

Massachusetts Historical Society's Thomas Jefferson Papers. "Farm Book, [manuscript], 1774–1824." https://www.masshist.org/thomasjeffersonpapers/farm/.

———. "Garden Book, [manuscript], 1766–1824." https://www.masshist.org/thomasjeffersonpapers/garden/.

Meacham, Sarah. "'They Will Be Adjudged by Their Drink, What Kinde of Housewives They Are': Gender, Technology, and Household Cidering in England and the Chesapeake, 1690 to 1760." *Virginia Magazine of History and Biography* 111, no. 2 (2003): 117–50.

North Carolina Historic Sites. "Southern Heritage Apple Orchard at Horne Creek Farm." https://historicsites.nc.gov/all-sites/horne-creek-farm/southern-heritage-apple-orchard.

Schröpfer, Susan, Janne Lempe, Ofere Francis Emeriewen, and Henryk Flachowsky. "Recent Developments and Strategies for the Application of Agrobacterium-Mediated Transformation of Apple Malus × domestica Borkh." *Front Plant Sci.* 13 (2022). doi: 10.3389/fpls.2022.928292.

Thomas Jefferson's Monticello. "George Granger, Sr." https://www.monticello.org/slavery/landscape-of-slavery-mulberry-row-at-monticello/meet-people/george-granger-sr/.

———. "Monticello's South Orchard." https://www.monticello.org/house-gardens/farms-gardens/fruit-gardens/monticello-s-south-orchard/.

Vintage Virginia Apples/Albemarle CiderWorks. https://www.albemarleciderworks.com.

Index

Italicized page numbers refer to illustrations.